LISTENING
TO TEACH

LISTENING
TO TEACH

Beyond Didactic Pedagogy

Edited by

Leonard J. Waks

SUNY
PRESS

Published by State University of New York Press, Albany

For information, contact State University of New York Press, Albany, NY
www.sunypress.edu

Production, Ryan Morris
Marketing, Michael Campochiaro

Library of Congress Cataloging-in-Publication Data

Listening to teach : beyond didactic pedagogy / edited by Leonard J. Waks.
    pages cm
  Includes bibliographical references and index.
  ISBN 978-1-4384-5831-1 (hc : alk. paper)—1-4384-5832-8 (pb : alk. paper)
  ISBN 978-1-4384-5833-5 (e-book)
  1. Effective teaching.   2. Teacher-student relationships.   3. Listening.   4. Classroom environment.   5. Communication in education.   I. Waks, Leonard J. (Leonard Joseph)

  LB1025.3.L565 2015
  371.102—dc23   2014045588

10 9 8 7 6 5 4 3 2 1

Contents

Introduction   1
    Leonard J. Waks

PART I: Listening in Established Pedagogies

1. A Reggio Emilia-Inspired Pedagogy of Listening   15
    Winifred Hunsburger

2. Paulo Freire's Critical Pedagogy: The Centrality of
    Teacher Listening   25
    Suzanne Rice

3. Listening in Experiential Learning   39
    Leonard J. Waks

4. Philosophy for Children and Listening Education:
    An Ear for Thinking   53
    Megan J. Laverty

5. Listening in Interpretive Discussion   69
    Elizabeth Meadows

6. Can Listening Be Taught?   85
    Sophie Haroutunian-Gordon

7. Listening for Discussion: The Conference Method or
    Harkness Pedagogy   97
    David I. Backer

PART II: Listening in New and Emerging Pedagogies

8. Listening in the Pedagogy of Discomfort: A Framework for
Socially Just Listening   113
   Ashley Taylor

9. Listening in Human Rights Education: Learning from
Life Stories of Survivors of Atrocities   137
   Bronwen E. Low and Emmanuelle Sonntag

10. Listening in a Pedagogy of Trust   149
    Katherine Schultz

11. Promoting Listening by Augmenting Uncertainty   167
    Stanton Wortham and Alexandra Michel

12. Listening and Teaching in Online Contexts   183
    Nicholas Burbules

Contributors   195

Index   199

Introduction

Leonard J. Waks

Did you ever sit in a classroom while a teacher talked her way through a lesson and you felt so tired you had to place your head on your desk? Can you remember looking up to see half your fellow students horsing around or falling asleep? Can you remember listening to a teacher lecturing to your class and wondering "what does this lesson have to do with *me*?"

Or let's turn this around. Maybe you already are a teacher. You've had a course to teach with pre-set learning objectives, a curriculum guide, a text-book and a final exam. Your job was to "cover" the material and prepare your students for the test. So you found *yourself* talking your way through lessons, drilling on important facts to be learned and memorized, or cognitive routines to be mastered. You've looked up and half of *your* students were horsing around or falling asleep, or looking up at you with their eyes asking "what has this lesson got to do with *me*?" And you have thought "something is wrong with this picture; something has to change."

If you've had these experiences and they've troubled you, you are not alone.

When didactic methods—those based on teacher talk and passive student listening—dominate instruction, students and teachers suffer from boredom, exhaustion, and alienation. Critics have condemned these methods for more than 150 years as "cram school" and "test prep." The educational visionary Paulo Freire (2000) calls didactic pedagogy the "banking" method—teachers make deposits of knowledge for students to store in their memory vaults— and he says it causes "narrative sickness" for both teachers and learners. Yet didactic pedagogy continues to dominate schooling even today. There has to be a better way.

The Problem with Didactic Methods—
Teacher Talk and Passive Listening

More than 100 years ago—which is a long time ago but also long *after* didactic methods had already been soundly denounced by educational critics and professors in teacher education programs—the eminent American philosopher and educator John Dewey identified didactic pedagogy as *the* foremost problem in education. In *School and Society*, Dewey (1899) tells an amusing tale:

> Some few years ago I was looking about the school supply stores in the city, trying to find desks and chairs which seemed thoroughly suitable from all points of view—artistic, hygienic, and educational—to the needs of the children. We had a great deal of difficulty in finding what we needed, and finally one dealer, more intelligent than the rest, made this remark: "I am afraid we have not what you want. You want something at which the children may work; these are all for listening."[1]

Dewey uses this anecdote to introduce "listening" as a term of art that extends beyond listening in the ordinary sense to include other forms of passive information reception in didactic teaching.

> The attitude of listening means, comparatively speaking, passivity, absorption; that there are certain ready-made materials which are there, which have been prepared by the school superintendent, the board, the teacher, and of which the child is to take in as much as possible in the least possible time. (*SS*, mw.1.22)

Dewey notes that most reading in schools, e.g., reading from textbooks and basal readers, is also a kind of listening: students listen in their minds' ears, so to speak, to reading contents that are predetermined by some external authority without regard to students' present interests and purposes, and in contexts where they have no opportunities to respond. He says:

> If everything is on a "listening" basis, you can have uniformity of material and method. The ear, and the book which reflects the ear, constitute the medium which is alike for all. There is next to no opportunity for adjustment to varying capacities and demands. (*SS*, mw.1.22)

School reading and teacher talk convey ready-made, secondhand materials, which even when heard remain unassimilated, not understood: just so many words standing "on a dead level, hostile to the selective arrangements characteristic of thinking . . . existing as verbal symbols to be mechanically manipulated" (Dewey, "Contributions to A Cyclopedia of Education," *Collected Works* mw.7.268).

Such materials, he says, "inevitably (have) a disintegrating intellectual influence" (Dewey, *How We Think, Collected Works* mw.6.326). Simply put, didactic methods cannot support thinking and learning. Thinking and learning are individual acts—of gathering materials, selecting from them and then organizing the elements selected, along with other resources, in creative ways, to serve individual or group purposes. In didactic instruction the materials are already all selected and organized without regard to learners' unique purposes, and without use of their specific capabilities.

We have to wonder why didactic methods continue to dominate instruction. And the answer is not hard to find. Despite their drawbacks, these methods are, surprisingly, quite well adapted to both the classroom situation and the larger society.

Classrooms are crowded with young people brimming with energy that must be controlled and directed. Intuitively, it may appear that without top-down control youthful creative energies in pursuit of emerging purposes would erupt in chaotic, boisterous, and noisy activity that would bring learning to a halt. In response, didactic pedagogy positions teachers in the front of the room where they can observe, direct, and control students and keep a lid on their energies. The historians Larry Cuban and David Tyack (1995) identify a complex arrangement of didactic methods, preset objectives, text books, and exams as forming a "grammar" of teaching. Like the rules of grammar in a language that allow us to put nouns, verbs, and adjectives together efficiently to form meaningful sentences, this grammar of teaching allows teachers to put together activities—lectures, text readings, work sheets, quizzes, and exams—into a workable and efficient pattern that is well-adapted to crowded classrooms.

In short, didactic pedagogy persists because it works—not so much to help learners learn how to think but to prevent chaos so teachers can "cope."

Shifting to the social context, Robert Dreeben (1968) added that didactic methods also work to prepare young people for life in society. Most of the roles in advanced industrial societies, he noted, don't demand thinking or creative intelligence. Workers in industrial factories or corporate offices perform repetitive tasks under close supervision. Creative thinking is counterproductive on the job. It is more likely to be crushed than rewarded. Citizens in these societies, moreover, are not expected or encouraged to take an active interest in political governance; other than voting every four years they are encouraged to leave governing to political leaders. The rules and habits that young people pick up from learning in classrooms structured by the standard grammar of teaching—passive listening, following rules, subjecting themselves to author-ity—actually prepare them well for life in existing society.

Nonetheless, as long as didactic pedagogy has been around, many educa-tors have detested it and explored alternatives—pedagogies that can liberate the energies and intelligence of teachers and students while still keeping chaos at bay—pedagogies that can reduce the stress of teaching and make learning exciting and personally meaningful for students—pedagogies that can prepare learners for creative intelligence and democratic social life. Some of their most important findings are documented in this book.

These discoveries are more important today than ever before. The indus-trial period has long ended and we are living in a post-industrial knowledge and information society. Routine and repetitive jobs—the ones demanding passive obedience and routine—no longer exist. All young people who hope to succeed must acquire intellectual and practical capabilities that can be put to use in novel ways to solve poorly structured, unpredicted problems. So today there is an especially pressing need to get beyond didactic methods that are "hostile to thinking." Nonetheless the recent efforts at school reform, with their preset "world class" learning objectives, "twenty-first-century skills" and "high stakes" tests have only dug us deeper and deeper into the didactic education trap.

Listening to Teach

The problem is not simply that teachers merely talk too much, or that learners listen passively; it lies in the didactic communication pattern—where teachers talk to "cover the material" and "convey the information," and learners listen merely to "bank" it until their exams. In just about any conceivable pedagogy, teachers will do some talking and learners some listening for information. But the alternative pedagogies explored in this book establish patterns of speaking and listening more conducive of thinking and learning. They propose meth-ods that guide teachers in constructing discussions and other "learning by doing" activities with rich built-in occasions for communication and action. This allows teachers to limit their talk so that they can pay more attention to students, observing their activities, documenting their observations, and build-ing upon them in subsequent lessons and learning activities. They can move beyond preset, uniform materials and objectives, learn about their students' interests, and adjust instruction to their "varying capacities and demands." They can teach through listening—hence the phrase "pedagogy of listening" in the Reggio Emilia project approach described by Winnie Hunsburger in chapter 1.

Listening in Observation, Discussion, and Facilitation

Listening to teach can take a number of quite different forms. In the Reggio Emilia approach, teacher listening takes place before, during, and after lessons. Teachers observe learners on the playgrounds, and even in their neighborhoods. Even before they begin with their lesson planning, they listen in when their young learners talk with one another, taking notes and forming hypotheses about their interests and the kinds of lessons that will help them grow. They share their observations with colleagues and even with their classes, listening for feedback and revising their hypotheses. This kind of listening—close observation and documentation of student speech and the formation of hypotheses about workable lessons—is also prescribed in Paolo Freire's approach to critical pedagogy with adults in *Pedagogy of the Oppressed*, and in John Dewey's classic works *Sources of a Science of Education* and *Experience and Education*.

A quite different emphasis is found in discussion-based pedagogies such as the Interpretive Discussion approach described in this volume by Elizabeth Meadows and Sophie Haroutunian-Gordon, and the Harkness Conference Method described by David Backer. In the former, teachers listen closely to learners in the course of lessons organized around texts to negotiate vital questions to be discussed. Then the teachers listen carefully to the contributions of each learner to the collaborative interpretation of the assigned text, and feed them back into the group for further elaboration or critical response by other learners as they move toward a consensus interpretation. In the Harkness method teachers may assist learners in getting the discussion moving, but then remove themselves from the center of attention and contribute primarily by their close listening as the students discuss subject matters on their own.

Still other methods of listening to teach are explored in the two chapters by Taylor, and Low and Sonntag on the Pedagogy of Discomfort. Here teachers place challenging, discomforting material into play in order to stimulate responses from learners. These materials press against learner expectations and may reveal learner perspectives that play unwittingly into patterns of social injustice. In a sense, the learner statements themselves become subject matters to be studied. The challenge for teachers is to sensitively listen to learners as they express these perspectives so that they can be teased out, clarified, and placed on the table for discussion and reconsideration.

Still another approach is revealed in Waks's description of listening in experimental learning. Waks delineates no fewer than 11 distinct points within typical experiential learning episodes where teacher listening plays a key role in advancing the learning goals of the experiential activities. At each point, from the initial orientation to the experiential activity to the final debriefing, a distinct type of teacher listening is needed. Waks goes on to suggest that this careful delineation of moments of listening within structured lessons can serve as a model for classroom teachers.

Types of Listening

What then is listening itself? Listening is something we do as active creatures bringing our energies and learning histories into each situation as we act with purpose—to achieve our ends. Acts of listening already involve "trying to get." We need to distinguish between different types of listening, because we listen in different ways in relation to different purposes. We listen to obtain information, to interpret texts, to learn how to do things, to sustain and improve our human relationships, to enjoy and appreciate, and to critically evaluate. No doubt many other ends require specific types of listening as well, but these are among the most important types. Listening in relation to each of these goals is something different, requiring different action steps and operations, and requiring specific skills.[2] Let's consider each briefly.

In *informative listening*, the aim is to obtain and understand information. To attain this goal through listening, we may take notes, make audio recordings, ask questions, ask speakers to talk more slowly or repeat or clarify what they have said, or internally rehearse speakers utterances *sub voce*. Informative listening can be improved by acquiring background knowledge, specialized vocabularies, skills of focus and concentration, note-taking, question-asking, and use of memory and organizational aids. Its success is measured by how accurately we can repeat and how well we understand. This is the primary kind of listening demanded of learners in didactic pedagogy.

A closely related kind of listening is interpretive. In *interpretive listening* the messages we confront are difficult, ambiguous, complex, or challenging. They may be vague and require clarification. They may contain multiple possible meanings that listeners need to disambiguate, or multiple levels of meaning that listeners have to disentangle and relate to one another in one complex whole. Literary, religious, and legal texts often require interpretation in these ways. Interpretive listening is the primary mode for both teachers and students in Interpretive Discussion pedagogy as discussed by Elizabeth Meadows and Sophie Haroutunian-Gordon later in this book.

In *practical* listening the aim is to learn how to do something, to learn to do it better, or to understand procedures and practices. To attain this goal through listening, we may imitate the action sequences of those instructing us in practica or real action situations by "following the leader." While acting we listen attentively for feedback and correction. Practical listening can be improved through attitudes of docility, willingness to trust and submit to guidance and emulate others, development of attentiveness and care, and repetition of lessons through drill and practice routines. Its success is measured by how well we perform. If, after instruction, the learner cannot perform the task or follow the procedure, he or she may be told "you didn't listen."

In *relational* listening we listen to sustain or improve our relationships. To attain this goal through listening we attend to both utterances and emotional resonances without critical judgment. Often our listening involves a quieting of our own minds and a silencing of our own speech. We listen for clues about the other's situation and hopes, and for things we can do to assist. In *contemplative* listening in certain religious traditions listeners attend to the voice of God, and seek to deepen their relationship to Him, so this is akin to relational listening.[3] In *therapeutic* listening, another subcategory of relational listening which also may contain elements of practical listening, the aim is to assist a speaker experiencing problems of living through establishment of a trusting relationship.

Relational listening is improved through close attention, empathy, and the suspension of ingrained habits of speaking. Like informational listening, relational listening may require asking questions or entering into discussion. But the best strategy is often silent apophatic listening—taking in the other and his or her utterances and silences and allowing them to fill the listener's psyche. Relational listening can be improved through lessons and workshops in active listening, through interpersonal feedback, meditation, and therapy. Its success is measured in the sustenance or improvement of relationship bonds. Relational listening is important in all effective teaching, since learners will draw upon deeper resources and allow themselves to be more vulnerable in their expressions, if they feel supported and cared for by their teachers. Good relational listeners bring out the best in all of us.

In *appreciative* listening, we listen to appreciate or enjoy. While we listen appreciatively primarily to literature (drama, poetry, and fiction—via electronic media or in live readings) and music, we also listen appreciatively to other people—listening just to enjoy them and their company. In this way, appreciative listening can be an important adjunct of relational listening, though the end is distinct. As with relational listening, appreciative listening requires us to quiet our mind and still our unrelated action schema. While critical attitudes have their proper place in listening to music or poetry, that place is not to be found in appreciation; when we engage in an interior critical dialogue with an object of our listening, e.g., a musical performance, we are not listening *appreciatively*. Like relational listening, appreciative listening is important in all forms of teaching, as appreciation of the unique value of learners and their creative expressions, however naïve, brings forth hidden powers of supportive response.

In *critical* listening the aim is to come to a sound evaluation—of an utterance or argument or action or person or work of art or other object. Critical listening depends upon a background of norms or standards of soundness. Critical listening generally depends on analysis of objects into their component parts. For example, evaluation of oral arguments depends on analysis into their component terms, premises, inference procedures, and conclusions. Critical listening to a musical performance depends on analysis into movements and segments, and of their pace, intonation, and other standards. In interpretive discussion, listening to the statements of participants as they attempt to arrive at a sound interpretation of a text is a kind of critical listening in that, in Haroutunian-Gordon's words, listeners "reason—and draw inferences about what is heard" in relation to questions they are trying to resolve. Critical listening is improved through training in evaluative arts such as logic and rhetoric, and in critical discourses related to objects under evaluation such as literature, art, and music. Critical listening is essential in teaching, as we can only assist learners in attaining high standards if we can note errors and shortcomings. A critical attitude, however, can be a detriment if it conveys uncaring or even hostile feelings. Criticism of student acts and works in teaching is only useful when contained within the bounds of a respectful and caring relationship with learners.

We can now return to Dewey's discussion of the "listening attitude." Didactic teaching is based on teachers' conveyance of information for passive informational listening. Meanwhile, teachers' listening is tightly circumscribed to critical listening in the narrowest sense—listening for the right (or wrong) answer, the correctly (or incorrectly) solved problem—when they are not listening to trouble brewing at the back of the room. In pedagogies that emphasize teacher listening, that listening spans all of the above categories—listening to observe and hypothesize about, and to interpret, learners' interests and capabilities, to build relationships with them and care about them, to appreciate and value them, and to form creative practical ideas—about lessons and activities that will engage their learners as individuals and as a group and help them grow. And learner listening will move from passive absorption to active intellectual and practical engagement involving all types of listening.

Listening and Social Justice

Many of the teaching practices described in this book are motivated by ideals of social justice. In the classical world, city-states were dominated by male citizens who had reached puberty—hence the *public*. Most of the residents of these societies were females, aliens, or slaves. Male citizens didn't concern themselves with justice—fair distribution of goods, opportunities and privileges—for these "others." In the Christian era, however, our conception of justice has been extended to all humans, each of whom we conceive as possessing a dignity and unique value.

In the wake of the industrial revolution, with its noxious urban environments and crushing burdens on workers and their families, philosophers and religious thinkers began to reconceive justice in *social* terms, as demanding at least minimal *material* conditions for living for all—adequate food and shelter, clean air and water, health care and old age benefits—as well as social and political rights. The demand for social justice has also come to include the right to be *recognized*, to be accorded dignity, to be heard, to participate fully in community life. Recognition is considered a necessary element of justice, whether as an independent right or as a necessary condition for the social and political realization of basic economic rights.

The concept of social justice was initially shaped by nineteenth-century Roman Catholic teachings, and continues to draw upon two central tenets of Catholic social thought, the inherent dignity of each individual human being, and the preferential option for the poor and vulnerable. Together, these teachings enjoin all of us consciously to work toward the participation of all people in social and cultural life, and above all, those who are most disadvantaged and have the greatest barriers to social and cultural participation. Social justice in this sense is now widely recognized as a value by all of the world's major religions, and as an important social goal by socialist, liberal, and centrist political parties throughout the world. It is embodied in the United Nations Declaration of Rights.

In education, young people live in small classroom and school communities and acquire there the habits that will shape their lives in the broader local, national, and global communities. Justice as an educational ideal demands more than the fair distribution of pedagogical, curricular, and technological resources, safe and clean buildings, and school lunch. It also demands individual recognition and respect, the space to speak and be heard, and for one's concerns to be considered in school practices. In this sense, didactic teaching is unjust. It proceeds without consideration of learners' needs and concerns. It does not bring out the voices of the young, or bring their contributions into play in the design and implementation of lessons or activities. Those least likely to be heard, the poor, the alien, the shy, the psychologically and mentally disadvantaged, are often neglected or "left behind."

In listening to teach, the voices of all young learners, and especially of those least likely to raise their voices forcefully and clearly, are given pride of place. The chapters of this book make this clear. The pedagogy of listening of Reggio Emilia, described below by Winnie Hunsburger, developed as a response to the needs of traumatized poor children in post-war Italy—it is a method for listening to the 'thousand voices" of children and building lessons on the basis of what children express. The critical pedagogy of Paulo Freire, described by Suzanne Rice, is a parallel response to the poor peasants of Latin America and shows how spaces for their voices can be created so they can "name the world" in their own terms rather than the hegemonic terms of the dominant classes. The conference method of Phillips-Exeter Academy described by David Backer was dedicated to removing the barriers to participation of shy young men. The pedagogy of trust developed by Katherine Schultz breaks down barriers built into hierarchical cultures so that those undergoing teacher training can express their concerns instead of being cowered by their superiors. In the pedagogy of discomfort as detailed by Ashley Taylor, and in somewhat different terms by Bronwen Low and Emmanuelle Sonntag, spaces are opened for voicing uncomfortable experiences and truths, so that all learners can reconsider assumptions and attitudes which sustain injustice and impede the growth and participation of all.

What This Book is about and How to Use It

This book details a dozen pedagogies featuring the active listening of teachers and learners. Each chapter accounts for a specific pedagogy, offering a brief explanation of the background against which it developed, the problems it aims to resolve, the educators who have pioneered it, and its treatment of listening. The chapters conclude with ideas and suggestions drawn from these pedagogies that may be useful to classroom teachers in familiar schools and classrooms. They include sidebars with memorable quotations from the pedagogy's founders, and a brief bibliography of useful readings.

While this book contains a lot of information about alternative pedagogies, it is not intended to serve merely as an inert textbook *about* active listening or active teaching methods. You cannot become a better teacher merely by learning *about* teaching strategies, or a better listener by learning *about* listening. You have to translate them into tools for your own use. As you read these chapters and the suggested readings, you can think actively about how they apply in your own teaching and learning situations. It may help to keep your observations, reflections, and notes in a journal; conduct thought experiments; and design sample lesson plans. It will help even more to talk about these teaching methods with other teachers and even with thoughtful students. The best approach is to form a personal learning network where you can try out your ideas, document lessons in videos for critical discussion, and work toward online video demonstration lessons that can help fellow teachers all around the world.

It is one thing to learn *about* creative ideas, and another thing entirely to see living proof that these ideas can work in classrooms. Don't hide your work under a bushel basket. If we hope to move beyond the boredom and alienation of didactic teaching, to recover from "narrative sickness" and liberate the energies and thinking potential of our students, and to breathe new life into our democratic societies, all of us will have to contribute. Take a few risks. Try some new methods. Share your successes with colleagues. Let's get started!

Notes

1. *The School and Society* hereinafter identified as *SS*, John Dewey, *Collected Works*, mw1. 21.
2. My treatment of these distinctions owes much to John Kline (2002).
3. Following theological usage, I refer to this kind of quiet listening as *apophatic*, from *apo* (away from) and *phasis* (speech). See (2010).

References

Dewey, J. (1967–). *The collected works of John Dewey, 1882–1953* (Jo Ann Boydston, ed.). Carbondale: Southern Illinois University Press.

Dreeben, R. (1968). *On what is learned in school*, Reading, MA: Addison-Wesley, esp. chapter 5.

Freire, P. (2000). *Pedagogy of the oppressed.* New York: Continuum.

Kline, J. (2002). *Listening effectively: Achieving high standards in communication.* Englewood Cliffs, NJ: Prentice Hall.

Tyack D., & Cuban, L. (1995). *Tinkering toward utopia: a century of public school reform.* Cambridge: Harvard University Press.

Waks, L. (2010). "Two types of interpersonal listening." *Teachers College Record* (112. 11) (2010): 2743–2762.

Part I

Listening in Established Pedagogies

1
_____

A Reggio Emilia-Inspired Pedagogy of Listening

Winifred Hunsburger

The Bishop Strachan School, Toronto, Canada

Introduction

This chapter investigates and critiques the pedagogy of listening embedded in the philosophy of the Reggio Emilia schools for early childhood education, in Northern Italy. It examines the philosophical and political underpinnings of this pedagogy and explores the multiple meanings and purposes of listening in Reggio Emilia philosophy and how they inform emergent curriculum, collaboration among teachers and children, and the practices of observation, documentation, and interpretation. The paper considers the implications for general classroom practice and the difficulties associated with enacting this listening pedagogy.

Reggio Philosophy

In order to understand the central role of listening in Reggio schools some historical background is helpful. These unique schools arose literally out of the rubble of World War II, in northern Italy. Six days after the close of the war, parents in the town of Villa Cella set out to build a school for their youngest children that would lead them away from the horrors and destruction of war toward a new, more humane understanding of the world. The school was built from bricks salvaged by the women of the village and financed by the sale of an abandoned tank, some trucks, and a few horses left behind by the retreating Germans. It was parents who invited teachers to collaborate with them both to build the school and imagine a new pedagogical foundation for it. Together, parents, teachers, and community members began the journey toward a new approach that has come to understand children, teachers, and parents as co-protagonists in the educational project (Malaguzzi, 1998, p. 58). Today, educators from around the world flock to the municipal schools in Reggio Emilia to see this philosophy in action and many are experimenting with a Reggio-inspired approach in early childhood, primary, and even junior-level classrooms.

Founding teacher Loris Malaguzzi explained that this approach to education sprang from a simple but ultimately liberating understanding: "things about children and for children are only learned from children" (Malaguzzi, 1998, p. 51). At the same time, children are understood as competent and powerful learners, capable of forming relations with the world. These notions have given rise to a complex, social constructivist philosophy of education that understands children as ever involved in efforts to make meaning of their world.

> "Things about children and for children are only learned from children."
>
> — Loris Malaguzzi

If, as educators, we accept and understand children as competent, capable learners and believe that things about and for them are best learned from them, then listening to children becomes essential. How we listen will not only influence what we learn from them, but also holds the potential to help children understand themselves as competent and capable. When an adult is fully attentive and present, and listens from a place of curiosity, respect, and openness, children are more likely to understand that the adult believes that they have something interesting and important to say and recognize their own power as meaning-makers (Edwards, 1998). According to Reggio proponent and theorist, Carlina Rinaldi, such deep listening is the very premise for learning for children and adults alike (Rinaldi, 2006). But how is such a listening stance accomplished and what implications does it in turn hold for curriculum, teaching, and learning? What does a pedagogy of listening look like in a Reggio-inspired classroom? To develop this picture, it is necessary to delve a little deeper into Reggio philosophy.

Any attempt to summarize the complex philosophy of Reggio will undoubtedly fall short. To examine this philosophy more fully, please refer to the suggested reading list at the end of this chapter. However, to explore the Reggio pedagogy of listening, we will examine three principles of the Reggio approach: emergent curriculum, the Hundred Languages, and the image of the teacher.

Emergent Curriculum

Reggio philosophy holds that education must align with the natural development of children. As children are engaged in making meaning of their world, curriculum must emerge from this meaning-making: their interests, ponderings, questions, and theories.

Curriculum in Reggio Emilia-inspired programs arises, then, from the interests and "business" of children. Teachers identify areas for investigation by attending closely to the conversations and actions of children and responses to their environment. This is not simply listening for ideas but listening to follow or enter into children's thinking and knowledge construction. Teachers listen for questions and answers, ponderings, and theories. They listen for the meaning children make of their world. As they do so teachers consider both how these interests might lead to rich investigations and how the children can be stimulated to develop and improve their ideas. This can lead to long-term "projects" involving young children in extensive exploration, problem solving and creative thinking.

Projects arising from children's interests are frequently unanticipated. At first glance, children's interests may seem unrelated to typical, prescribed curriculum expectations. For example, in a study of teachers working with a Reggio-inspired approach, a grade 1 teacher described how her students' fascination with strings of Mardi Gras beads brought by a child to class developed into a rich, mathematical, and sociocultural investigation of the purposes, meaning, and creation of jewelry (Hunsburger, 2008).

As children are engaged in making meaning of their world, curriculum must emerge from this meaning-making: their interests, ponderings, questions, and theories.

The teacher explained that she was initially resistant to the children's apparent interest in the Mardi Gras beads. How could a study of such seemingly trivial objects lead to a project of any depth? But as the children continued to drape them over their structures in the block center, trade for them in the "grocery store," and adorn each other with them she heard their powerful interest. When the children began to sneak jewelry into class from their collections at home and started to make paper bracelets for each other, she put aside her own fears that this might just be a shallow study of adornment and considered how she might challenge their interests and build on their fascination.

Inviting a parent who makes jewelry to visit the class and demonstrate how she created a piece soon led the students into an investigation of mathematical concepts of symmetry and patterning. Students began asking questions about different materials that jewelry could be made from and why people in different countries wore different types of jewelry. By putting aside her own preconceptions and listening deeply to discover the underlying interests of the children, the teacher worked with them to investigate jewelry from many perspectives and together they learned the utility of symmetry and patterning, the differences between jewelry made with organic versus inorganic materials, and discovered that jewelry could have purposes beyond simple adornment.

The Hundred Languages

"Hundred Languages" is meant to convey the notion that children's means of symbolically representing their understanding can and should be numerous.

Reggio philosophy holds that children develop and represent their understanding of the world through multiple modes, referred to as "the Hundred Languages." Drawing, painting, sculpting, dramatic play, indeed any form symbolic expression are understood to be as valuable and important as written and spoken language for communicating *and* developing ideas. "Hundred Languages" is meant to convey the notion that children's means of symbolically representing their understanding can and should be numerous. In Reggio-inspired classrooms teachers frequently ask children to show their ideas and theories by drawing pictures, creating three-dimensional sculptures, paintings, dramatic play, or musical pieces, and by writing or telling stories.

A senior kindergarten class, for example, was engaged in a project about birds (Hunsburger, 2006). To stimulate their questions and provoke their thinking, the teacher brought an incubator to school to hatch duck eggs. The students were intrigued by the incubator. Classroom discussions about what the children thought was happening in the incubator and how eggs hatch, however, did not seem to be fruitful. Wanting to know more about the children's understandings about the egg-hatching process, she offered them another "language" to share and develop their ideas. She asked the students to work with a small group of friends to draw their theories.

Each group's drawing was different. In one drawing the children had provided play things such as balls and swings for the hatchlings. In another drawing the children had drawn a kind of cosmic egg-hatching machine in which some eggs hatched and the hatchlings proceeded to a penned space of green grass and trees while other eggs turned black and were shunted off to a dark box. In some drawings the children had seemingly divided their paper into distinct sections where each child worked on her own ideas, and where in other drawings children had apparently drawn onto each other's work.

By offering another language and listening intently to it, the teacher was able to hear how some of the children held very anthropomorphic views of the hatchlings (offering play things), while others saw the egg-hatching process as a part of life and death. She could also hear how some children were able to share and build on their ideas with others, while some were developing their own ideas in isolation.

Listening in a Reggio context means being able to hear all languages, to understand all the meanings embedded in a range of representative modes.

The Image of the Teacher

In Reggio philosophy, the role of the teacher is not that of applying methods and strategies she has learned. Instead she is seen as "an author, together with others, of the pathways that will lead to the building of knowledge" (Cagliari, 2004, p. 2). The image of the teacher in Reggio is one of researcher and co-constructor of knowledge with the children. Teachers observe, document, reflect on, and interpret children's conversations, questions, representations, and work. Teachers meet together to discuss their documentation and investigate possible meanings in children's work in order to respond and challenge children to improve their growing knowledge. These practices are critical tools in the process of learning for children and teachers alike.

The teacher builds her own knowledge as she learns to understand the ways in which children build theirs. The teacher becomes, in effect, a researcher of children and a researcher of her own practice.

Essential to the role of teacher as researcher are the related practices of observation, documentation, and interpretation. These practices put listening at the heart of what a teacher does or as Cagliari explains, it is through these three practices that a pedagogy of listening is carried out (Cagliari, 2004).

Essential to the role of teacher as researcher are the related practices of observation, documentation, and interpretation. These practices put listening at the heart of what a teacher does.

Observation is not an isolated or periodic process, but a continuous one. Teachers observe children in all their contexts—in spontaneous play as well as in constructed learning situations. And while teachers may come to observation with a specific question or object in mind—to watch for social interactions, to listen for theory building, to note problem solving—they maintain an open receptivity to the situation at hand. The teacher does not passively stand outside of the experience under consideration but takes part as a participant observer.

Also important to observation are the tools the teacher uses. The perspective of the teacher when making observational notes will differ from that when she observes through the lens of a camera taking photos or videos and will have an impact on how and what she hears.

Documentation is the practice of capturing and sharing observations and is clearly dependent on the ways in which the teacher listened in the moment of observation. Documentation allows the teacher to come to the observation a second (or third) time and "re-listen" to the observation. It allows her to hear the observation again and focus more succinctly and finely. In addition, documentation may become a part of the project for the children, too. Documentation allows children to revisit their ideas, reexamine them, and reformulate their theories. Documentation assists them in understanding their own processes of knowledge creation.

Interpretation arises from the teacher's careful and ongoing attention to her observations and documentation. It also arises from her discussions with colleagues. Interpretation is never understood as a final process, but as an ongoing and provisional one.

In the bird project mentioned earlier, the teacher is engaged in precisely these practices. She studies the drawings of the children as they are creating them and again after the drawings are complete. She notes her observations and questions and discusses these with a colleague as they observe the children's work together. She arrives at provisional interpretations that guide her as she continues to construct the project with the children. Her research is carried out through an iterative process of observation, documentation, and interpretation. And it is through this process that she makes her listening apparent and part of her knowledge construction with the children.

Implications and Challenges for Classroom Practice

The pedagogy of listening embedded in Reggio philosophy has profound implications for classroom practice. In 1945, when parents invited teachers to join with them in creating a renewed, re-imagined approach to education for young children, parents effectively recast the role of the teacher from that of expert and authority to one of collaborator. In so doing, they initiated a shift in the perspective and quality of teacher listening to one that is equitable and reciprocal. Coupled with an understanding of the child as a capable, competent learner and the notion that things about the child and for the child are best learned from the child, this shift has re-conceptualized teacher listening as open, curious and sensitive and essential to the educational project.

Listening values and validates children's ideas and ways of knowing. It provides the basis and means for uncovering a curriculum rooted and emerging from children's interests, theories, and work. Listening encompasses attending to all means of expression, hearing the "hundred languages." Listening allows the teacher to enter into children's active learning and forms the basis for understanding how children learn and how classroom projects evolve. It is made visible through the practices of observation, documentation, and interpretation. Listening is iterative and ongoing.

As inspiring as this notion of listening may seem, it can be exceptionally difficult to enact. Typically and traditionally, teachers have listened to children to assess how children are learning predetermined, prescribed concepts and skills. Given the prevalence and requirement to meet state-mandated curriculums, this listening stance is completely understandable and necessary and, of course, highly ingrained in teaching practice. And while this stance continues to have value in many situations, if it becomes the predominant mode of listening it can easily preclude uncovering how and why children learn what they do. Moving to an open stance that hears and considers all that children say, listening for much more than "right answers" is enormously challenging.

Listening encompasses attending to all means of expression, hearing the "hundred languages." Listening allows the teacher to enter into children's active learning and forms the basis for understanding how children learn.

"Listening is an active verb, which involves giving an interpretation, giving meaning to the message, and valuing those who are listened to by others."

—Carlina Rinaldi (2012, p. 235)

Furthermore, many of us who come to teaching do so because we believe we know something and believe we have something to say to others about what we know. We want others to hold the understanding that we do. To put this aside so that we may listen intently and interpretively to the ideas and knowledge of children, to hear how they are constructing their own knowledge, calls into question our very reasons for teaching.

Education has also tended toward defining specific endpoints in learning, for example, by the end of grade 5 students will understand that all matter is made up of small, moving particles. Such expectations-driven curriculum provides satisfying checkpoints to measure children's learning against, which help us as teachers know "where we are" and what the children have "achieved." To switch instead to listening to uncover the ideas and theories of children, to hear them for what they are and to consider them as provisional understandings with the potential for improvement and revision, rather than right or wrong answers, may throw a teacher into shaky and unknown territory. How are we to know when we have arrived?

To ask teachers to make their listening visible through observation, documentation, and interpretation is to ask them to be vulnerable, to put their own emerging, provisional understandings out there for examination by others. In a profession that has traditionally been practiced behind a closed door between a teacher and her students such practices are not only unfamiliar but possibly unwelcome. Teachers may easily misconstrue this practice as evaluative and judgmental.

Ultimately, the challenges to enacting the pedagogy of listening embedded in a Reggio-inspired philosophy of education are well worth taking on. Open, curious, sensitive listening rooted in reciprocity and equity has the potential to help teachers and children understand what it means to learn. Adults are perhaps best able to develop this pedagogy of listening, when they reflect on the nature of the children to whom they listen. Like the early educators of Reggio Emilia, when they come to understand children as capable, competent learners and recognize that they have much to learn from them, adults find the key to this empowering pedagogy.

Suggested Reading

Edwards, C., Gandini, L., & Forman, G. (Eds.). (2012). *The hundred languages of children: The Reggio Emilia experience in transformation.* Santa Barbara, CA: Praeger.

Gandini, L., Hill, L., Cadwell, L., & Schwall, C. (2005). *In the spirit of the studio: Learning from the atelier of Reggio Emilia.* New York, NY: Teachers College Press.

Rinaldi, C. (2006). *In dialogue with Reggio Emilia: Listening, researching and learning.* New York, NY: Routledge.

Rinaldi, C. (2012). The pedagogy of listening. In C. Edwards, L. Gandini, & G. Forman (Eds.), *The hundred languages of children: The Reggio Emilia experience in transformation.* Santa Barbara, CA: Praeger.

References

Cagliari, P. (2004). The role of observation, interpretation and documentation in understanding children's learning processes. *Innovations in early educations: The international Reggio Exchange,* 11(4): 1–5.

Edwards, C. (1998). Partner, nurturer and guide: The role of the teacher. In C. Edwards, L. Gandini, & G. Forman (Eds.), *The hundred languages of children: The Reggio Emilia approach to early childhood education* (pp. 179–198). Norwood, NJ: Ablex Publishing.

Hunsburger, W. (2008). *Inquiry learning: A narrative inquiry into the experiences of three teachers* (Unpublished doctoral thesis). OISE/University of Toronto, Toronto, ON.

Malaguzzi, L. (1998). History, ideas, and basic philosophy. An interview with Lella Gandini. In C. Edwards, L. Gandini, & G. Forman (Eds.), *The hundred languages of children: The Reggio Emilia approach to early childhood education* (pp. 41–89). Norwood, NJ: Ablex Publishing.

Rinaldi, C. (2006). *In dialogue with Reggio Emilia: Listening, researching and learning.* New York, NY: Routledge.

2

Paulo Freire's Critical Pedagogy

The Centrality of Teacher Listening

Suzanne Rice

University of Kansas

Introduction

Today, there are many varieties of "critical pedagogy," and despite their differences, all are indebted to Paulo Freire. Freire's hugely influential *Pedagogy of the Oppressed* (1970, 1993) appeared in English over three decades ago, and with the passage of time, once-clear connections between the book and the social, political, and economic context in which it was written have become increasingly murky. This chapter begins with a brief introduction to Freire and to the circumstances in which he developed his pedagogical theory and practice. This sets the stage for subsequent sections discussing (1) the centrality of listening in dialogue, and (2) applications of Freire's pedagogy in educational settings today.

The Context in which Critical Pedagogy Developed

Freire was born into a middle-class family in Recife, Brazil. But during the later 1920s and 1930s as Brazil, along with much of the rest of the world, suffered the effects of the Great Depression, he fell into poverty and, as a result, had serious problems at school. Even though Freire's circumstances eventually improved and he entered university to study law and philosophy, it appears that his earlier experiences left their mark on his worldview and moral commitments. Freire was employed as a lawyer for only a short time before beginning his work in education, teaching Portuguese in secondary schools from 1941 to 1947. From the beginning, Freire focused his practical and intellectual efforts most closely on the education of those living at the margins of society, the poor and oppressed. In 1959 Freire was awarded a doctorate in education from the University of Recife and served as the first Director of the Department of Cultural Extension at that institution from 1961 to 1964. During that time, Freire gained international recognition for his work in adult education, particularly literacy training, and in 1963 was named president of the National Commission on Popular Culture (Gadotti, and Torres, n.d.). One reason for this recognition is that in 1962 Freire was able to document the effectiveness of his approach to adult literacy when 300 farmworkers were taught to read and write in just 45 days. With evidence of such success, the Brazilian government approved thousands of "cultural circles"—small, informal educational communities across the country. The military coup of 1964 curtailed these efforts and landed Freire in jail for over two months.

In 1964 Freire was exiled following the coup, and he spent the next five years in Chile working at the Chilean Institute for Land Reform and writing *Pedagogy of the Oppressed*. Freire then held a 10-month appointment at Harvard University, following which he became Director of Education at the World Council of Churches in Geneva. After 15 years in exile, Freire returned to Brazil where he held positions in several educational organizations: Adult Education Supervisor for Worker Party (1980–1986); Minister of Education for the city of Sao Paulo (1988–1991); and professor of education at Catholic University of Sao Paulo until his death May 2, 1997 (Fishman & McCarthy, 2007, p. 43).

It would be difficult to overstate Freire's influence on education, practically and theoretically. Freire's pedagogy is credited with significantly expanding adult literacy in Brazil, Chile, and Cuba. Classroom teachers in every subject area and in many parts of the world have adopted his pedagogy. A Google search of "Paulo Freire" retrieves over 7 million pages. His academic writings have been translated into 18 languages, and he has received honorary doctorates from more than 20 universities worldwide. Put bluntly: Freire has sparked the imagination of countless teachers and scholars seeking to participate in education on behalf of justice, freedom, and equality.

The context where Freire first practiced the pedagogy he developed was one in which a great many adults were illiterate and suffered extreme poverty and degradation, and a few enjoyed extreme wealth and privilege. These extremes are reflected in the "oppressed/oppressor" dichotomy that appears throughout Freire's seminal work, *Pedagogy of the Oppressed* (1970, 1993). But oppression is not always so apparent. In Freire's words, "Any situation in which 'A' objectively exploits 'B' or hinders his or her pursuit of self-affirmation as a responsible person is one of oppression" (1970, 1993, p. 37). The aim of critical pedagogy is to transform the consciousness of the oppressed, enabling them to participate in the transformation of oppressive situations, situations that take many particular forms; typically these have social, political, and economic dimensions.

Oppression in Brazil in the 1940s was very different from oppression in the United States at that time, not to mention in our own time. However, critical pedagogy was conceptualized in a way that invites observers to imagine how it might inform, or be adapted to, the particular needs of specific contexts. Indeed, one of the defining characteristics of this pedagogy is that it defies standardization. "Oppression," even when conceptualized in largely economic-class terms as Freire once

> *"Any situation in which 'A' objectively exploits 'B' or hinders his or her pursuit of self-affirmation as a responsible person is one of oppression."*
> —*Paulo Freire*

did, manifests very differently in different circumstances. Once oppression is conceptualized more broadly to include dynamics of race, gender, age, sexual orientation, etc., and the various interactions between these and other factors, the need for multiple approaches to pedagogy may become apparent.

Further, Freire's pedagogy seeks to enable students to participate in the transformation of their oppressive situation, and this entails students coming to see themselves as capable of such a task. If teachers were to prescribe a program of study based solely on the teachers' understandings, this would undermine students' growth toward greater self-efficacy. It is helpful to remember that Freire's is a pedagogy *of* the oppressed, not for the oppressed. As Freire explains:

> The pedagogy of the oppressed, which is the pedagogy of people engaged in the fight for their own liberation, has its roots here. And those who recognize, or begin to recognize, themselves as oppressed must be among the developers of this pedagogy. No pedagogy which is truly liberating can remain distant from the oppressed by treating them as unfortunates and by presenting for their emulation models from among the oppressors. (1970, 1993, pp. 35–36)

Today, critical pedagogy is more closely associated with "dialogue" than anything else, and from the very start of Freire's educational practice, dialogue was a central feature. But Freire also sought to teach adults the more prosaic elements of reading and writing. The genius of his approach was that it engaged teachers and students in dialogue in a manner that addressed both the political and more technical sides of literacy.

Freire initially pursued these twin aims in his literacy instruction through the use of "codifications"—visual representations of key aspects of students' experience. In areas where fishing plays a central role in people's lives, a codification might include a fishing boat, nets, and men rowing on the water. In the course of dialogue about codifications, encouraged by teachers and fellow learners, students begin to trust their own ability to interpret and *name* their experiences (in contrast to having an "expert" teacher do the naming) and are helped by teachers to attach symbols, written words, to these names. Learning to read the world and the word occurred simultaneously in the context of dialogue between teachers and increasingly confident students.

> As an event calling forth the critical reflection of both learners and educators, the literacy process must relate *speaking the word* to *transforming reality*, and to man's role in this transformation. Perceiving the significance of that relationship is indispensable for those learning to read and write if we are really committed to liberation. Such a perception will lead the learners to recognize a much greater rate than that of being literate. They will ultimately recognize that, as men, they have the right to have a voice. (1985, p. 51)

Participants in literacy circles were at the same time teachers *and* students, for while students gained from teachers' literacy expertise, teachers gained from the expertise students have acquired in the course of their lives. Students were enabled to interpret and understand their experiences in a new light and teachers were enabled to think anew about the content of their instruction. The corollary to students' and teachers' mental work is real-life change, transformation.

Listening in Dialogue

The centrality of listening—particularly teachers' listening—in Freire's conception of critical pedagogy becomes clearer in light of his criticisms of traditional education. Freire begins his classic critique of such education with this observation: "A careful analysis of the teacher-student relationship at any level . . . reveals its fundamentally narrative character. This relationship involves a narrating subject (the teacher) and patient, listening objects (the students)" (1970, p. 52). Traditional education, Freire says, suffers from "narration sickness," meaning that teachers do all the talking while students do all the listening. Freire sometimes refers to this as the banking approach to education. The good traditional teacher is one who is able to deposit the most content in students' minds, and the good student is the person who accepts such deposits meekly, unquestioningly. Education of this sort not only mirrors oppressive relations in society at large, but also helps to reproduce these oppressive relations by tamping down students' potential for critical consciousness and social transformation.

Critical pedagogy, as conceived and practiced by Freire, is animated above all else by a spirit of mutuality and non-domination. This spirit is evoked by Freire's term for liberatory pedagogical relations: "teacher-student with students-teachers" (1970, 1993, p. 61). No longer behaving as narrating bankers, Freirean teachers are co-investigators and partners *with* students. In an important sense, critical pedagogy is not so much a conventional method of instruction as it is a moral relation among people. This relation is fundamentally *dialogical*, rather than narrative.

Stated briefly, in Freirean terms dialogue is an encounter in which persons, mediated by the world, name and re-name the world and thereby transform it (1970, 1993, p. 69). Recent examples of this sort of dialogue can be found in schools where students and teachers (and other adults) have re-named certain kinds of verbal taunts, unflattering online postings, and gossip; what were once called examples of harmless teasing then became "bullying," and so named, susceptible to various sanctions and remedies. The world is transformed in light of the many dialogues about bullying and responses to the phenomenon.

Freire observes: "Dialogue cannot occur between those who want to name the world and those who do not wish that naming—between those who deny others the right to speak their word and those whose right to speak has been denied them" (1970, 1993, p. 69). The "right to speak" has force to the extent that there are others who will listen to what has been said. There can be no dialogue without listening and this makes listening a central and indispensable part of critical pedagogy. One cannot listen if one legislates the terms of speech. Thus, listening is not only hearing the words said; it implies a willingness to suspend one's own categories of interpretation and listen not only to words, but to worlds in conflict with your own—to make space for multiple realities and to acknowledge the realities of the speaker. If a student calls her experience an instance of "bullying," then it *is* bullying for her, and that

> "Dialogue cannot occur between those who want to name the world and those who do not wish that naming—between those who deny others the right to speak their word and those whose right to speak has been denied them."
>
> —Paulo Freire

is what needs to be heard. It is not enough to acknowledge that her world is different, but to acknowledge her alternative world as, at least as a starting point for conversation, a valid one.

In the example at hand, it was only in virtue of the facts that teachers listened to and understood students' experiences that they were able to take steps to curtail—what the students insisted was not innocent teasing—but *bullying*. Listening is not a matter of simply registering the words another utters: "Listening is an activity that obviously goes beyond mere hearing. To listen . . . is a permanent attitude on the part of the subject who is listening, of being open to the word of the other, to the gesture of the other, to the differences of the other" (2001, p. 107).

> "Listening is an activity that obviously goes beyond mere hearing. To listen . . . is a permanent attitude on the part of the subject who is listening, of being open to the word of the other, to the gesture of the other, to the differences of the other."
>
> —Paulo Freire (2001, 107)

While it goes without saying that both the facilitator and the learners in critical pedagogy engage in critical listening to messages from the world, in this passage, Freire highlights the centrality of what Waks in the Introduction to this volume calls "relational listening," one hallmark of which is trying to hear another's utterances as the other wishes them to be heard. While critical pedagogy encompasses all types of listening to one degree or another, relational listening it at its heart: there cannot be a critical pedagogy as envisioned by Freire in the absence of relational listening.

The "listening attitude" to which Freire refers is aided by a group of virtues—love, humility, faith, trust, and hope—which animate dialogue as a whole. While these are distinct character traits, they work together in a constellation where they support, and when necessary, modify, one another. These virtues speak to an attitude that, while receptive to the other, is not naive or self-effacing. There are several additional qualities that Freire sees as being especially important to listening, in particular open-mindedness, respect for differences, and humility:

> If the structure of my thinking is the only correct one, accepting no criticism, I cannot listen to anyone who thinks or elaborates ideas differently from me. Neither can I hear the person who speaks or writes outside the norms of the accepted standard language. And how is it possible, then, to be open to ways of being, thinking, and

evaluating that we consider the exotic eccentricities of other cultures? We can see that respecting differences and, obviously, those who are different from us always requires of us a large dose of humility that would alert us to the risks of overvaluing our identity, which could, on the one hand, turn into a form of arrogance and, on the other, promote the devaluation of other human beings. (1993, p. 107)

It is said that in American society, "the squeaky wheel gets the oil." Many of us feel uncomfortable with silence and rush in with words to fill perceived conversational voids. Freire reminds, however, that silence plays an essential role in communication; listening and silence are close allies in dialogue.

[S]ilence in the context of communication is fundamental. On the one hand, it affords me space while listening to the verbal communication of another person and allows me to enter into the internal rhythm of the speaker's thought and experience that rhythm as language. On the other hand, silence makes it possible for the speaker who is really committed to the experience of communication rather than to the single transmission of information to hear the question, the doubt, the creativity of the person who is listening. Without this, communication withers. (1998, p. 104)

Silence can be an outward manifestation of disinterest or disengagement. But by calling silence a "discipline" this is clearly not what Freire has in mind (1998, p. 105). "Silence as discipline" implies thoughtfulness, self-awareness, and self-control; disciplined silence requires effort. In the course of a dialogue, for the one who is silent (for some period of time) silence allows for deep concentration on the other's utterances, their posture, facial expressions, and gestures. In silence, the listener is better able to do the mental work necessary to understand the other (even if every understanding is also a sort of misunderstanding).

"In the process of speaking and listening, the discipline of silence, which needs to be developed with serious intent by subjects who speak and listen, is a sine qua non of dialogical communication."

(1998, 105)

In the process of speaking and listening, the discipline of silence, which needs to be developed with serious intent by subjects who speak and listen, is a *sine qua non* of dialogical communication. The person who knows how to listen demonstrates this, in an obvious fashion, by being able to control the urge to speak (which is a right), as well as his or her personal preference (something worthy of respect). (1998, p. 105)

We might add to Freire's observation, and this is certainly implicit in much of what Freire writes, that for the one who is *speaking*, the silence of his partner can be a sign of respect and encouragement to go on. Being "talked over" by an undisciplined, over-eager partner can bring dialogue to an end when, having been verbally trampled, a speaker shuts down. Especially in communicative situations where one party has been historically discouraged from speaking, the disciplined silence of a communicative partner may be needed if dialogue is to proceed.

Thus far, listening has been treated largely as a receptive phenomenon. By listening carefully, we are better able to take in and more fully comprehend what others are saying. But listening *is* a part of dialogue, and in dialogue there is communicative give-and-take, speaking and listening. It is the failure to listen attentively that often leads to the frustrating experience of partners in dialogue "speaking past" one another. Conversely, listening with care improves participants' vocal contributions to dialogue as well. As expressed by Freire:

[I[t is in knowing how to listen well that I better prepare myself to speak or to situate myself vis-à-vis the ideas being discussed as a subject capable of presence, of listening "connectedly" and without prejudices to what the other is saying. In their turn, good listeners speak engagedly and passionately about their own ideas and conditions precisely because they are able to listen. (2001, p. 107)

Listening-as-it-relates-to-speaking has special significance in pedagogy. By listening well, a teacher can speak with students (in the context of dialogue) in ways that are more likely to support the development of the students' *critical consciousness*, a defining aspect of critical pedagogy. What Freire found in working with oppressed adults is that many believed their current situation to be inevitable and in a sense, natural. These were people who were caught in a web of social, political, economic, and other forces that were only vaguely perceived, if they were perceived at all. The result, Freire saw, was that the oppressed were more led through their lives than they were *living* their lives.

Critical consciousness develops in dialogue as students encounter problems or questions posed by a teacher. These problems and questions must be sensitive to students' current perceptions, affirming students while challenging those perceptions that reinforce oppressive social relations. As Freire explains:

> In problem-posing education, people develop their power to perceive critically the way they exist in the world with which and in which they find themselves; they come to see the world not as a static reality, but as a reality in process, in transformation. Although the dialectical relations of women and men with the world exist independently of how these relations are perceived (or whether or not they are perceived at all), it is also true that the form of action they adopt is to a large extent a function of how they perceive themselves in the world. Hence the teacher-students and the students-teachers reflect simultaneously on themselves and the world without dichotomizing this reflection from action, and thus establish an authentic form of thought and action. (1970, p. 64)

For example, in the case of bullying, when a student says she is "picked on" because she is stupid (a common, self-blaming interpretation), a teacher may acknowledge the students' misery while posing questions that enable the child to see alternative explanations—and eventually possible solutions—for her experience. Depending on the situation, it is likely that power relations hinging on such factors as gender, age, and race will come to light in such conversations. It is only through careful listening that a teacher is able to hear echoes of students' consciousness and ask questions that respond appropriately. Together, the teacher and student are then able to act on the new perception.

Educational Listening Today

This chapter began with an overview of the context in which Freire's pedagogy developed. In light of this context, it is understandable why Freire described traditional teacher-students relations in starkly dichotomous terms; these terms were chosen to reflect the oppressor/oppressed relations existing in society at large, which were mirrored and reproduced in educational institutions. While there are large numbers of poor, victimized, and otherwise disadvantaged students in a great many of the "developed" countries, and certainly in the United States, in most of these contexts, there is not as clear a line dividing the oppressed from their oppressors as that which existed in Freire's Brazil. Indeed, while the gulf between rich and poor is growing in much of the post-industrial world, there is room to question whether relations between "haves and have-nots" are *oppressive* in the way or to the extent described by Freire. In any event, teachers as a group are not in service to a clearly identifiable "oppressor" class; and in fact a fair number of teachers suffer the same forms of disadvantage (such as those stemming from sexism and racism) as do their students.

Despite certain dissimilarities between Freire's time and place and our own, we find (in the United States at least) that high-stakes testing has breathed new life into once seemingly moribund top-down, "traditional" approaches to teaching. In a great many K-12 schools, and in some colleges and universities, teachers are expected to deliver preset curricula and to engage students in whatever activities efficiently get that curricula inside students' minds. The "traditional" classroom of the 1950s and 1960s that Freire described as a place where, "The teacher talks and the students listen, meekly," (1970, 1993, p. 54) today exists in many schools across America. There are schools where students talk among themselves and with their teacher as they work at tables or pairs of desks, but especially in the upper elementary grades and in middle and high schools the typical classroom arrangement is one where students sit in individual desks facing toward the front of the room where the teacher stands and delivers instruction. (Now there are even schools where student silence is enforced by rules banning all speech in certain contexts, such as the hallways and even the lunchroom.) Such arrangements are not favored by many teachers; they have been imposed from above. Nevertheless, the work of teaching—teachers' preferences and ideals aside—is often arranged along "traditional," teacher-centered lines.

To the extent that it improves test scores, the "banking education" Freire criticized is now held up as "best practice" in school districts across the United States. And as long as the testing regime remains intact, it is highly unlikely that listening, in the deep and profound sense intended by Freire, will be integral to formal classroom instruction in many schools.

In light of the circumstances in which they work today, what might Freire's account of listening offer contemporary teachers? Even in situations where teachers have very little flexibility in terms of how they use classroom time, it is helpful to remember that a great deal of teachers' most significant interaction with students occurs not during whole class instruction, but in less formal contexts—at recess, after school, during study hall, and in quiet moments here and there when traditional teacher and student roles are relaxed. Such spaces provide openings for dialogue—and even brief dialogical encounters can have profound meaning for teachers and students alike. In some cases, such encounters are transformative, if not singly, then when multiplied in conversations between students and teachers and other adults in different contexts. The case of bullying, discussed previously, provides one example.

In schools where testing is not so pervasive and teachers have more control over their classroom lives, it will be easier to incorporate Freirean pedagogy. Freire developed his pedagogy while teaching adults to read and write so his ideas find a reasonably good fit in contemporary language arts classes. This pedagogy is also especially amenable to social studies and its constituent subjects, such as a history, sociology, and anthropology, but there are no obvious barriers to taking a Freirean approach to teaching math and the sciences. Indeed there are examples of adapting critical pedagogy to subjects in both these academic areas (Frankenstein, 1983, pp. 315–339; Santos 2009, pp. 361–382).

Regardless of the subject taught, a teacher interested in adopting Freire's ideas begins much as he did, by identifying key themes in students' experience and representing these graphically. These representations—codifications to use Freire's term—serve as a focal point for dialogue, during which the teacher guides the students (mainly by posing questions for their mutual consideration) to ever more critically astute insights. These insights will typically have political as well as academic aspects. For example, in my city, because it has become so polluted, the Kansas River is now thought to be unsafe for many recreational and other purposes. (The river also provides drinking water for a quarter of the state and is home to fish as well as other wildlife.) The Kansas River figures prominently in the lives of many Lawrence youths and could be represented in an array of different codifications, each representing a different concern, recreation, fish and other animals, safe drinking water, and so on. As a spur to dialogue, a teacher may ask questions about how the river became so polluted and why pollution matters to students. Depending on participants' interests and insights, the dialogue might turn toward the role of big agriculture, fertilizer use, global warming, or, perhaps, the need for a safe and convenient place to swim. In the course of such a dialogue, which would span several days or weeks, students would likely learn about local history, biology, and chemistry—and the Environmental Protection Agency, the interests served by big agricultural corporations, and state and federal clean water regulations. Students might very well decide to take some action to help clean up the river, perhaps writing legislators, picking up trash, or taking pictures to share in a public awareness campaign. It is likely that a Freirean teacher would listen closely in order to gain insights into students' abilities to discern connections between their immediate concerns, the social, economic, and political conditions at the root of these concerns, and students' perceptions of their own power to challenge these conditions. Her or his dialogical interactions with students would reflect the insights gained, with an eye toward ever deepening students' critical consciousness and sense of self-efficacy.

Schools and classrooms are not the only places where education occurs, and not only holders of official teaching certificates and licenses engage with others in teaching activities that might be modeled along Freirean lines. Those working in social welfare, child development, public health, aging services, and other such organizations often have an educational component to their work. Most people who come in contact with a social services agency are vulnerable, whether because of disability, joblessness or low income, illness, age, or some other contingency to which we are vulnerable. In many cases, the people drawn to such agencies are on the suffering end of social, political, economic and other inequalities.

Certainly, much of the work of those connected with the social and health services must of necessity focus on the most immediate needs of their clients. Nevertheless, social workers, health care practitioners, and others do have opportunities, particular to their area of service, to engage in dialogue that is animated by a "listening attitude"—open to clients' experiences and oriented toward developing problem solving strategies. Taking these opportunities can benefit both clients and social service workers; clients can help educate social service workers about their experiences and the conditions in which they are enmeshed, and social service workers can educate clients about accessing resources. Together, partners from both groups can use their mutually constructed knowledge to respond not only to the current manifestation of whatever problem brought them together, but also to its roots; from a Freirean perspective, the aim is not merely to "fix" people with problems, but to transform situations that give rise to or exacerbates the problems.

Critical pedagogy is now practiced in many contexts other than the Brazilian *favelas* most familiar to Freire, and has been adapted accordingly. There are, literally, infinite possible manifestations of critical pedagogy, but understanding listening in relation to critical pedagogy must begin with an understanding of and willingness to grapple with unequal power relations. "Listening" like all other phenomena connected with teaching and learning, will support or undermine existing power relations, and before ever entering the educational situation the critical educator has committed herself or himself to the latter. The constant across all these possible manifestations is the dialogical character, and hence the centrality of listening, in critical pedagogy. Listening in a manner consistent with critical pedagogy helps teachers and other educators create communicative relations *with* students. Indeed, the teacher who is truly open to students will listen in a way that undermines aspects of her own authority and that provides opportunities for seeing, feeling, and knowing differently in light of students' contributions. In a Freirian practice, both students and teachers are vulnerable and primed for educational growth through listening.

Suggested Reading

Freire's Publications

Freire, P. (1973, 1994). *Pedagogy of the oppressed* (Rev. ed.). New York, NY: Continuum.

Freire, P. (1978). *Pedagogy in process: Letters to Guinea-Bissau.* New York, NY: Seabury Press.

Freire, P. (1985). *The politics of education: Culture, power and liberation.* South Hadley, MA: Bergin and Garvey.

Freire, P. (1993). *Education for critical consciousness.* New York, NY: Continuum.

Freire, P. (1993). *Pedagogy of the city.* New York, NY: Continuum.

Freire, P. (1995). *Pedagogy of hope: Reviving pedagogy of the oppressed.* New York, NY: Continuum.

Freire, P. (1996). *Letters to Christina: Reflections on my life and work.* New York, NY: Routledge.

Freire, P. (1997). *Pedagogy of the heart.* New York, NY: Continuum.

Freire, P., & Horton, M. (1990). *We make the road by walking: conversations on education and social change.* Philadelphia, PA: Temple University Press.

Coauthored Works

Castells, M., Flecha, R., Freire, P., Giroux, H. A., Macedo, D., & Willis, P. (1999). *Critical education in the new information age.* Lanham, MD: Rowman and Littlefield.

Escobar, M., Fernandez, A. L., Freire, P., & Guervara-Niebla, G. (1994). *Paulo Freire on higher education.* Albany, NY: State University of New York Press.

Faundez, A., & Freire, P. (1992). *Learning to question: A pedagogy of liberation.* New York, NY: Continuum.

Freire, P. (Ed.), with Fraser, J., Macedo, D., McKinnon, T., & Stokes, W. (1997). *Mentoring the mentor: A critical dialogue with Paulo Freire.* New York, NY: Peter Lang Publishing.

Shor, I., & Freire, P. (1987). *A pedagogy for liberation: dialogues on transforming education.* Westport, CT: Bergin & Garvey.

Further Readings

Darder, A., Torres, R. D., & Baltodano, M. (2002). *The critical pedagogy reader.* New York, NY: Routledge/Falmer.

Giroux, H. A. (2011). *On critical pedagogy.* New York, NY: Continuum Books.

Shor, I. (1980). *Critical teaching and everyday life.* Boston, MA: South End.
Shor, I. (Ed.). (1987). *Freire for the classroom: A sourcebook for liberatory teaching.* Portsmouth, NH: Boynton/Cook.
Weiler, K. (1991). Freire and a feminist pedagogy of difference. *Harvard Educational Review,* 61(4), 449–474.

References

Fishman, S. M., & McCarthy, L. (2007). Paulo Freire's politics and pedagogy. In D. T. Hansen (Ed.), *Ethical visions of education* (pp. 35–45). New York, NY: Teachers College Press.
Frankenstein, M. (1983). Critical mathematics education: An application of Paulo Freire's epistemology. *Journal of Education,* 165(4), 315–339.
Freire, P. (1970, 1993). *Pedagogy of the oppressed.* New York, NY: Continuum.
Freire, P. (1985). *The politics of education: culture, power, and liberation.* Westport, CT: Bergin & Garvey.
Freire, P. (2001). *Pedagogy of freedom.* New York, NY: Rowman and Littlefield.
Gadotti, M., & Torres, C. A. (n. d.) Paolo Freire: A Homage. Available online at http://chora.virtualave.net/freire.html
Gerhardt, H. (2003). Paulo Freire (1921–1997). *Prospects: The Quarterly Review of Comparative Education,* 23(3/4), 439–458.
Santos, W. L. P. D. (2009). Scientific literacy: A Freirean perspective as a radical view of humanistic science education. *Science Education,* 93, 361–382.

3

Listening in Experiential Learning

Leonard J. Waks

Temple University

Introduction

Our active powers depend upon our absorption of the world. Receptivity enables us to grow in depth and active capability, and listening is the name for this receptivity when we are receptive to other people. It should hardly surprise us, then, that many educational thinkers have sought to ground educational practice in experience, and have made listening a central element in experience.

The appeal to experience is often a cry of protest against the lifeless conventional didactic pedagogy of textbooks, teacher talk, and tests. That pedagogy nullifies experience. Instead of leading learners into challenging worlds where their own ends are at stake, learners in conventional school situations are served up, in textbooks and lectures, a pre-digested world in which nothing is at stake for them and where there is no scope for expressing their funded experience in action. Experiential educators are motivated by the insight of John Dewey that conventional education leaves out the most important educational component, the "essence—vital experience seeking opportunity for effective exercise."[1]

In this chapter I describe two widely adopted models of experiential education, and then explore the kinds of communication situations that arise and the opportunities for listening—the spaces in which interventions can foster improved listening so as to promote growth in inner depth and action power. I indicate how various types of listening can become more explicit and effective components in experiential learning, and suggest some ways that teachers in conventional school settings can draw upon insights from experiential education to promote improved classroom listening.

What is Experiential Education?

Experiential education (EE) involves learning through direct experience with situations of living. EE is a tree with many branches, including outdoor and adventure education; workplace learning; nature study, study-abroad programs, and service learning. The common feature is that learners are placed in challenging, indeterminate "real-world" situations. They have to make sense of these worlds, act in them in ways that go beyond their already-developed habits, and be receptive to the feedback provided by the world and other people. In this way they "learn by doing" or "learn from experience"—phrases that have the same meaning.

> *"There is nothing so practical as a good theory."*
>
> *—Kolb 1984, p. 9*

Models of Experiential Education

While John Dewey's *Experience and Education* is a core text for experiential education, most practical efforts in experiential education follow one of the two most frequently cited component sequence models, those developed by David Kolb (1984) and Laura Joplin (1981).

The two models differ considerably in their emphases. Kolb builds up his model from a fully developed theory of learning, and emphasizes the full flowering of experience in explicit cognitive knowledge. His model, as a result, has been widely adopted by educators using experiential education in school and college subject matter teaching and learning.

Joplin, by contrast, explicitly abjures theoretical foundations, and emphasizes the tacit and emotional aspects of learning. Her model has, not surprisingly, appealed more to those facilitating informal learning, e.g., in outdoor adventure and in leadership education. In this section we review these models and consider criticisms and refinements. In the next section we will draw from this discussion to locate places in the experiential learning sequence where listening plays an essential role, the kinds of listening appropriate to them, and how this listening can be fostered.

David Kolb's Model of Learning Styles and Experiential Learning

Kolb's primary aim as a researcher has been to understand how learners make sense of "concrete experiences." Like Dewey, who Kolb considers "without doubt the most influential educational theorist of the twentieth century," and whose work Kolb states "best articulates the guiding principles for programs in experiential learning," Kolb conceives experiences in terms of individuals "trying and undergoing," and in the process learning to make sense of their worlds.

For Kolb, sense-making requires two main phases—an initial "taking in" phase where meanings in experience are grasped, followed by a second stage where these meanings are transformed into knowledge and personalized by individual learners (Kolb, 1984, p. 5). In the grasping stage they may choose either to emphasize learning from concrete experience (C) or from abstract conceptualizing (A). In the transformational stage they choose either to emphasize reflection (R) or active experimentation (E).[2]

Kolb insists that all four strategies play important roles in learning, and his model of experimental learning assigns each strategy a place in an idealized learning sequence.

The Kolb Experiential Learning Model

(1) Concrete Experience and Action (C) → (2) Observation and Reflection (R) → (3) Abstraction, Generalization and Knowledge Construction (A) → (4) Experimental Testing of Knowledge through Supplementary Action (E).

The Kolb learning design *begins* with action in a carefully constructed situation, followed by observation of and reflection on its consequences. These phases are followed by attempts to abstract from the situation and construct general knowledge, and finally by actions which test the generalizations.

For example, in outdoor education, learners may (C) rappel down a mountain using ropes, observe (R) their reactions, generalize and abstract (A) from their experiences to what they and others may experience in similar challenges (perhaps also reading about the theory of outdoor education), and then experimentally test (E) their generalizations by assisting other learners and confirming or disconfirming their knowledge formulations.

> *"In the process of learning, one moves in varying degrees from action to observation, from specific involvement to general analytic detachment."*
> —*Kolb 1984, p. 31*

In teacher education, learners may prepare and teach (A) a lesson in a micro-teaching environment, make observations and reflect (R) on their experiences, generalize and abstract (A) from these observations to hypothesize about how they may succeed in a real classroom situation (perhaps through readings in lesson preparation), and then experimentally test (E) their new approaches to lesson preparation and teaching.

Kolb's model is regarded as "classic" and "foundational" in experiential education (Miettenen, 2000), as "detailed, useful, and widely accepted" among experiential educators (Pickwirth et al., 2000). The model has been enthusiastically taken up by educators in literally dozens of fields. It has provided practitioners with a sorely-needed resource: a design for structured action learning backed by theory and research.

Critiques of Kolb's Theory of Learning Styles

Nonetheless, critics have alleged that Kolb's model has severe defects. The model is said to have a cognitive bias, because it makes knowledge construction and explicit experimental testing of constructed knowledge—stages (3) and (4)—necessary components of experience in experiential education. This cognitive requirement narrows the field of experiential education unduly, as individuals frequently learn from experience *without* constructing general knowledge; they can be deeply affected and positively changed by learning tacit lessons from experience itself.

The model has been said to have an individualist bias; it conceives of learning as something taking place in individuals' minds as they confront experience as isolable "rational" and "autonomous" agents, not as members of language and practice communities (Miettenen, 2000). It thus neglects the importance of the learner's associations in society and the learning group.

The model, therefore, neglects the social bases for *learning*. Feminist educators have emphasized that effective learning takes place through connections within the learning group, that learners are not isolated individuals. Girls and women, furthermore, *prefer* connected learning styles and learn more in group settings where they work together, feel together, and share their observations and reflections (Belenky et al., 1986).

Kolb and Listening

When we turn to listening in experiential education, these biases undercut Kolb's approach. As the model focuses on individual learning, it obscures the role of communication among learners and between learners and facilitators in the learning situation.

In an experiential training program for physiotherapists, for example, Moore (2011) found Kolb's model unhelpful. The therapists-in-training went through the specified treatment procedures (C) and then, as directed by Kolb's model, *they*, as isolated individuals, reflected (R) on the outcomes, without attending to feedback from clients. The therapist trainees were not mandated in the training module shaped by Kolb's model to listen to the clients, much less to modify their treatment objectives based on personal information shared by the clients. By theorizing learning as something taking place in individual minds, and designing interventions for individual learning intended to build up general knowledge in individual learners, Kolb's model obscures the roles of listening in experiential education.

Laura Joplin's Model of Experiential Education

Laura Joplin, born in 1949, became an environmental educator, led and studied Outward Bound type outdoor programs as part of her doctoral work in education, and later developed her model of experiential education in a widely cited and much reprinted paper "On Defining Experiential Education." Joplin retired from her career in education shortly thereafter to manage the legacy of her sister Janis Joplin (email, April 26, 2013).

Like Kolb, Joplin's work was influenced by John Dewey. Unlike Kolb, however, Joplin did not build her model upon a psychological theory of learning, nor does her model indicate phases that individual learners actually move through. Indeed, she explicitly rejects both theoretical "foundations" and the development of experience into overt cognitive knowledge and understanding, the keystones of David Kolb's approach. Rather, her aim is prescriptive: to guide teachers and workshop facilitators in developing experiential episodes to enable learners as a group to form deeper tacit and emotional connections to the realities they are learning *about*. Like Kolb, she understands "experience" in terms of "trying and undergoing," but she takes these notions quite a bit more seriously than most experiential educators, emphasizing the place of challenge, struggle, risk and potential failure in experience.

Joplin explicitly rejects both theoretical "foundations" and the development of experience into overt cognitive knowledge and understanding, the keystones of David Kolb's approach.

Joplin's model of experiential learning offers a clearer window than Kolb's into the topic of listening. Her model is a five stage "hurricane spiral"—the final stage of each cycle in the spiral serves also as the first stage in the next cycle. The model involves extensive give and take among learners and between teacher—facilitators and learners.

The Joplin Experiential Education Model

(1) Focus → *(2) action* → *(3) support* → *(4) feedback* → *(5) debriefing.*

In the focus phase (1), the facilitator defines the material to be learned and the challenge to be encountered. The material may be determined through some process of dialogue between teachers and learners; Joplin urges teachers and facilitators to engage in these open dialogues to minimize power inequalities in the group. The focus activities of the facilitator may include short presentations or mini-lectures, assigned pre-readings, and or an introduction to the physical spaces in which activities will take place and any equipment to be used. For example, in a spelunking experience, learners are first introduced to the cave and the headlamps and their operation.

In the action phase (2), learners face the specific challenge and struggle to achieve aims. The learning situation involves stress and the possibility of failure. In many instances in experiential education learners will be unfamiliar with similar situations, lacking necessary knowledge and skills for effective behavior. This will be true in the spelunking example: many of the learners will be exploring a cave for the first time, experience fears of the dark, etc.

In the support stage (3), facilitators and fellow learners support individuals in moving through the experience and successfully achieving their aims. Support may include assurances of safety or provision of helpful resources. In the cave example, the facilitator or fellow explorers can assist with the equipment or assure learners who feel panicked.

In the feedback stage (4), the facilitator provides feedback to learners on how they have handled the challenge. This feedback is likely to be accepted and taken to heart if the power relations in the setting have been minimized. Feedback is specific to each individual learner and shaped so that each learner will have a better chance of understanding the personal significance of the episode. Feedback may best be given in private meetings between the facilitator and learners. Additional challenges exist when the feedback is delivered in a public setting.

In the debriefing phase (5), which takes place in the public group setting, the subject materials and learning objectives are reviewed, and learning outcomes are expressed and assessed. The teacher as facilitator is responsible for seeing to it that the meanings in the experience do not remain unrealized. The debriefing may include exchanges, discussions, projects, essays, presentations, or other events.

Joplin's model, like Kolb's, also focuses on special, facilitator-constructed episodes in settings removed from everyday life. It is thus open to a criticism, also leveled against Kolb, that this disconnection from the everyday life activities of learners leads to a problem of experiential continuity. Dewey's use of everyday settings like gardens, kitchens, and lunchrooms, and his emphasis on the continuity between learning areas and the surrounding homes, factories, and commercial areas of cities, assured that in learning by doing the students were acquiring meanings continuous with those brought from prior experiences that they then could carry forth into their subsequent lives. This transfer is more problematic when learning situations are separated, e.g., in outdoor adventure camps, caves, or awareness-training workshops. One critic has even argued that the problem of transfer is cooked right into the very notion of "concrete experience" as used by all experiential educators, and that this discontinuity weakens the educational value of experiential learning (Ord, 2009).

One possible response to this critique is that the "concrete experiences" isolated from everyday living are useful metaphors for living. For example, a group feeling its way in a dark and unfamiliar cave is somewhat like a work group in an organization groping "in the dark" after a setback has undermined its business model. The "live creatures" in the cave bring previously formed habits of emotional response and communication; thus the lessons learned in the cave experience can be reflected upon, abstracted, carried forward in, and become continuous with, their subsequent lives, e g., in business organizations.

Narrative and Continuity

The problem of continuity can also be addressed directly within Joplin-style experiential education. Kathy Cassidy (2001) argues, echoing Dewey, that for the experiential episodes to be educative, learners must be continuous with life—that is, must connect to personally and emotionally meaningful concepts and ideas that stem from their own life histories in their own life contexts. Their particular aims, the problems and challenges they frame, and their learning outcomes may all be distinct and unpredicted. But their life histories provide a frame within which concrete, facilitator-designed experiential education episodes fit as links between previous and subsequent experiences.

Cassidy follows up this insight by introducing a *narrative* dimension to Joplin's model. Life stories of the learners play a major role from the beginning—the focus stage—right through the end—the debriefing stage. Narrative for Cassidy restores the continuity—the organic connection between experience and education—that Dewey demands. It also helps in locating the specific sites for listening within experimental education episodes.

Initially, by sharing their stories the participants bring themselves together as a group of associated individuals—the stories get them into the same "ball park" or "on the same page." The initial focus stage thus does more than merely "introduce" the upcoming event; it situates the event as a scene in each of their connected life stories, facilitating connections between the life stories and the experiential event. In sharing their stories learners recall their previous experiences, recharge previous knowledge, and define what they see as personally relevant in anticipating the upcoming event. Similarly, the debriefing stage does more than summarize and generalize from lessons learned in the activity stage; rather it allows participants to pull various strands together from the shared information to look forward and create coherent personal meanings for subsequent life.

The connections between the group experiences and the cumulative lives of the participants will not effectively be made, Cassidy says, if the reflection phase is confined—as in Kolb's model, to intellect and cognition. The Joplin-Cassidy approach thus rejects the cognitive bias found in Kolb's model. Heartfelt sharing of emotional dimensions of the experiences undergone will hit home more forcefully than an intellectual discussions *about* the experiences. Closing experiential learning sessions with such narrative debriefings will make them continuous with life—personally significant, memorable, and transformative.

Listening in Experiential Education

The Joplin-Cassidy approach can be summarized in three basic phases that encompass all five of Joplin's stages. First is the (I) Focus or Briefing stage. The facilitator brings the participants together to introduce themselves and exchange abbreviated life stories, thereby opening lines of communication and mutual understanding. The facilitator introduces the setting, the equipment, and intended aims of the upcoming event. Participants share initial perceptions, concerns, and aims in relation to their own lives.

Second is the (II) Action stage. Participants enter the experiential setting and engage in the activity singly or in groups. They meet with significant challenges and risk failure. They communicate and provide mutual support as appropriate. The facilitator also provides information and support. In the course of the activity participants may engage in reflection-in-action, drawing on knowledge frameworks previously acquired, or withdraw momentarily from the activity proper to reflect upon it (what Kolb calls the stage of "observation and reflection").

Third is the (III) Processing stage. This can be divided into one-on-one processing with the facilitator—what Joplin calls "feedback"—and processing in the group—what Joplin calls "debriefing." Processing may (but need not) involve abstract and general reflections leading to (tentative) knowledge claims

(= knowing), and heartfelt, emotion-laden exchange of personal reactions and insights (= sharing). The relative emphasis will be determined by the broad educational aims regulating the episode, but "sharing" should generally come last. The facilitator aims to bring the various strands together into a cumulative or consummatory experience that ties up at least major loose ends and leaves participants feeling satisfied with their participation and eager to bring lessons learned into their subsequent lives.

Communication Situations in Experiential Education

The first thing to note is that there are many specific opportunities for speaking and listening in each of these three phases. We may distinguish eleven of these:

At the Focus stage, participants (1) meet one another and introduce themselves; (2) share life stories; (3) learn from the facilitator about the experiential setting and equipment; (4) share perceptions, concerns, and personal aims for the experiential learning session; and (5) recall and recharge prior memory, experience, and knowledge. The focus stage comes to an end as the associated individuals anticipate and then join in to the activity.

The Activity stage proceeds on both individual and social levels. The activity may involve individual or group tasks, but even when participants work individually, they (6) communicate with one another about the activity they are engaged in, to complete its tasks and; (7) receive multidimensional support from the facilitator and other participants. The activity phase ends with the participants working out personal or group solutions to the problems and challenges in the activity—or in some cases, failing to achieve the goals of the activity or personal goals.

In the Processing stage, learners may (8) undergo one-on-one feedback sessions with the facilitator; (9) debrief in the group through sharing of (often emotionally charged) experiences; (10) collaboratively formulate general lessons for subsequent testing related to the challenges and risks, successes, and failures in the activities; and finally, (11) guided by the facilitator, work toward personal syntheses and a "concerted consensus for (subsequent) action" that may be shared in the group, and thus bring the experience to a satisfying close.[3]

Types of Listening Experiential Learning

So what are the distinct types of listening that must be employed in these communicative situations in experiential learning, and how do they differ from passive informational listening in conventional teaching? What, in short, makes experiential learning a pedagogy of listening?

To answer this question we must refer back to the Introduction to this book, to see that listening is something we *do* as we act to achieve our aims. We need to distinguish between different types of listening, because we listen in different ways in relation to different purposes: to obtain information, to learn how to do things, to sustain and improve our human relationships, to enjoy and appreciate, or to critically evaluate. Because of its multistage and varied nature, experiential education offers rich opportunities for both engaging in and improving many types of active listening. This is, at least potentially, its greatest strength.

When participants (1) first meet facilitators and fellow participants, they listen in the *relational* mode. They open themselves to others, express interest, and welcome them to their shared worlds. As group experiences depend upon cooperative relationships among participants, this initial phase, along with other "ice-breaker" activities, lays the basis for success (or failure) in the shared activity. Facilitators can attend to fears and defensive reactions that can block learning and even threaten psychological security in the group, and make interventions that can facilitate greater openness and growth towards group cohesion.

As others (2) share their stories participants listen engage in both *relational* and *appreciative* listening, taking the others into their inner milieus while enjoying their brief accounts of life experiences. They take an interest in each other; they enjoy one another. These factors contribute to the cohesiveness of the group and its effectiveness in action. Participants also engage in informative listening, gathering information about fellow participants that might prove useful in collaborative actions.

Inevitably, in these situations participants also engage in critical listening, forming judgments about others and about the tasks we are invited to perform. At this early stage in experiential learning, critical listening may be counterproductive, stemming from irrational defenses and blocking our engagement with other participants and the tasks at hand. One of the most important listening skills is modulating or suppressing critical attitudes in situations where it is out of place—such as those calling for relational and appreciative listening. Because critical attitudes may be triggered by groundless fears and felt needs for self-protection, this skill may be both difficult and time-consuming to acquire. The feedback and debriefing contexts in experiential education, however, provide excellent opportunities for this kind of learning.

As the facilitator (3) focuses the activity by introducing participants to the setting, tasks, and equipment, listening shift to the *practical* mode. In a cave experience, for example, the facilitator may bring participants into the cave and show them how to put on their helmets, headlamps, and undersuits. She might also have them take these off and put them back on, and ask everyone to help others to put them on and take them off. In a teacher education practicum, the facilitator might explain procedures of micro-teaching and guide us through a number of mini-micro-teaching experiences. In a brain-storming session, the facilitator may explain the rules of brainstorming and then coach participants until they are acting in accordance to the rules—such as the "no critical feedback" or "piggyback" rules. Participants listen to both explanations and corrections until they can brainstorm properly on their own.

As participants focus on the activity-to-come in the focus session, they (4) recall and recharge prior experiences. In the cave experience, entering the dark humid cave may bring up past fears of suffocation or abandonment; or, as they are introduced to brainstorming, participants may recall past experiences where we were condemned for being "too critical." They listen *informationally* to *themselves*, perhaps asking themselves questions about their past experiences or making notes in a journal. They also listen *relationally* to themselves, suspending critical evaluation and allowing themselves space to remember and to feel the flow of memories and emotions to establish a better, more mature relationship with themselves.

As they move into the (II) Activity stage, participants must listen to one another to (6) coordinate their actions and complete tasks and (7) give and obtain support. Their listening will be informational, practical, and relational. They will seek information about the activity (e.g., "How far down is the end of this passageway in the cave?"), practical guidance (e.g., "How can I get my head lamp to work better?), and emotional connection ("How do you feel? I'm still scared to death").

As they complete the activity and move into (III) the Processing stage, participants will first (8) receive one-on-one feedback from the facilitator. Listening to feedback may also include informational, practical, and relational dimensions. The facilitator may provide information about their performance (e.g., "This was a pretty challenging cave" or "You scored 7 points out of a possible 10, which is about average"), practical guidance ("Since you still don't understand how to use your headlamp, let me show you again so next time you'll be ready"; or "Here's how to give feedback to someone who is frightened"), or relational bonding ("You are a wonderful learner and I'd love to have you in my workshop anytime").

In (9) the group debriefing, the listening will be relational, appreciative, and critical. First, other participants will share their experiences. Because these statements are often emotionally charged, the speakers may be taking personal risks and exposing vulnerabilities. So the listening of other participants needs to be relational, respectful, and accepting. Such highly charged statements can also be captivating and even spellbinding. As a result, they prompt appreciative listening. Many avid participants in experiential workshops become "group junkies," hungry to hear these heart-opening offerings.

The group then (10) collaborates to discover possible general lessons or insights derived from the experience. The aim in this phase is to work toward acceptable formulations so that each member listens critically to evaluate proposals offered. The group listens critically in order to discuss the proposals, enlarge upon or correct them, and seek a consensus. The group may also invite minority opinions that complete the lessons learned and conclude the group experience.

Finally, each member (11) personalizes these lessons and insights, perhaps by making notes in a workshop journal, and then charts an individual path forward from the group experience to ensuing life.

Conclusion

Experiential learning, when organized within the Joplin-Cassidy model, offers a structured approach to the design of teaching and learning episodes grounded in experience. Its "concrete experiences" are engaging and interactive, can be made continuous with everyday life, and can provide experiential depth for abstract cognitive learning.

This kind of learning provides clearly demarcated moments for many forms of active listening, with many "opportunities for adjustment to varying capacities and demands" of learners. While designed to lay out guidelines for "concrete experiences" in informal education, that model also provides a suggestive template for everyday classroom learning. In constructing lesson plans, teachers and curriculum-makers can structure classroom experiences by carefully sequencing stages with differentiated communication situations fostering different types of speaking and active listening.

Notes

1. Dewey, *Democracy and Education, Collected Works*, MW9: 78.
2. Putting these together, the result is a simple 2 x 2 matrix with the four cells each representing one of four "learning styles": the CR, CE, AR or AE styles. Kolb (1984) has investigated these styles to understand how different teaching styles interact with different learning styles so that better matches can be made between teaching and learning. See Kolb (1984) chapter 4, *Individuality in Learning and the Concept of Learning Styles*, p. 61–98. I have simplified Kolb's lettering convention for the sake of clarity.

3. The phrase "concerted consensus for action" as the aim of communication is borrowed from Dewey, *Experience and Nature* LW5: 146, where Dewey proclaims that there is no experience more satisfying.

Suggested Reading

Cassidy, K. (2001). Enhancing your experiential program with narrative theory, *Journal of Experiential Education,* 24(1), 22–26.

Dewey, J. *Experience and education, Collected Works.* Carbondale, IL: Southern Illinois University Press, LW13: 3–63 (Originally published in 1938).

Joplin, L. (1981). On defining experiential education. *Journal of Experiential Education,* 4(1), 17–20.

Kolb, D. A. (1984). *Experiential learning: Experience as the source of learning and development.* Prentice-Hall.

References

Belenky, M. F., Clinchy, B. M., Goldberger, N. R., & Tarule, J. M. (1986). *Women's ways of knowing: The development of self, voice and mind.* New York, NY: Basic Books.

Cassidy, K. (2001). Enhancing your experiential program with narrative theory. *Journal of Experiential Education* 24(1), 22–26.

Dewey, J. (1967–). *The collected works of John Dewey, 1882–1953* (Jo Ann Boydston, Ed.). Carbondale, IL: Southern Illinois University Press.

Dewey, J. *Democracy and Education,* Collected Works, MW 9.

Dewey, J. *Experience and Education,* Collected Works, LW 13: 3–63.

Dewey, J. "Qualitative thought," Collected Works, LW5:244–63.

Dewey, J. The reflex arc concept in psychology, EW 5:97–110.

Jarvis, P. (1987). *Adult Learning in the Social Context.* London: Croom Helm.

Joplin, L. (1981). On defining experiential education. *Journal of Experiential Education,* 4(1), 17–20.

Kolb, D. A. (1984). *Experiential Learning: experience as the source of learning and development.* Englewood Cliffs, NJ: Prentice-Hall.

Miettenen, R. (2000). The concept of experiential learning and John Dewey's theory of reflective thought and action. *The Journal of Lifelong Learning,* 19(1), 54–72.

Moore, K. (2011). Professional placement educational processes: Balancing student-centred education and client-centred care during clinical education. *Journal of Cooperative Education & Internships,* 45(2), 37–48.

Ord, J. (2009). Experiential learning in youth work in the United Kingdom: A return to Dewey. *Journal of Lifelong Education,* 28(4), 493–511.

Pickworth, G. E., & Schoeman, W. J. (2000). The psychometric properties of the learning style inventory and the learning style questionnaire: Two normative measures of learning styles. *South African Journal of Psychology,* 30(2), 44–52.

4

_____

Philosophy for Children and Listening Education

An Ear for Thinking

Megan J. Laverty

Teachers College

Language exists only when it is listened to as well as spoken.

—John Dewey[1]

Introduction

No one debates anymore whether children have the requisite capacities and dispositions to engage in philosophical inquiry.[2] Thanks to the pioneering work of Matthew Lipman, Gareth Matthews, Ann Margaret Sharp, and others, we now consider children naturally philosophical and that they have a right to a philosophy education. There are those who take exception to this view but even they would accept that if children are to mature into reasonable adults then they must be given opportunities to practice reasonableness while they are still young.

Philosophy would seem an appropriate discipline for the practice of reasonableness because it is a mode of inquiry that assists individuals in making better judgments.[3] It achieves this by making the processes of reasoning—questioning, speculation, thought-experiments, argument, and logical analysis—transparent and accessible. Put differently, philosophy is a participatory activity that engages individuals in the search for wisdom. It follows, therefore, that if children learn philosophy in school, then they will internalize its logical procedures and intellectual dispositions—including the consideration of alternatives, identification of fallacious reasoning, and willingness to self-correct—and become steadily wiser. In the words of A. C. Grayling "[p]hilosophy thus provides both for individual development and enrichment, and a bright set of apt intellectual tools for meeting the world's challenges" (Grayling, 2008, n.p.).

There are increasingly many approaches to pre-college philosophy but as I have experienced it, teaching philosophy to children involves a classroom of small individuals sitting around in a circle, looking back and forth at one another and earnestly listening to what each has to say. I hear them contesting concepts of "friendship" or "fairness" for example, asking for reasons, reiterating what has been said in the interests of clarification, offering experiences from their own lives to serve as examples or counter-examples, and proposing hypothetical solutions to problems posed. I see the thinking on their faces, the bodily expression of delight and surprise on hearing another's idea, the quiet wondering, the laughter, the sometimes authoritative and, sometimes playful, ways in which they express themselves, straightening and twisting their bodies. And I witness them gauging the development of their own intellectual community according to criteria which they, themselves, have agreed upon: determining who spoke and listened carefully, whether they practiced good thinking, and whether they advanced their understanding of a key idea or concept.

> Philosophy would seem an appropriate discipline for the practice of reasonableness because it is a mode of inquiry that assists individuals in making better judgments.

My focus in this chapter is on an approach to pre-college philosophy known as Philosophy for Children (P4C). I argue that P4C educates students' listening; it develops an ear for thinking by disciplining how students listen and more specifically what it is they listen *for*. My thesis is that P4C not only improves students' listening, it develops a full repertoire of listening dispositions. To quote the Italian philosopher of listening, Gemma Corradi Fiumara, their listening becomes "both accepting and critical, trusting and diffident, irrepressible and yet consoling" (1995, p. 90) There is ample anecdotal evidence to support the claims that P4C students learn to listen well and feel genuinely listened to by their peers. Students are frequently quoted as saying things like "[P4C] gives you a chance to talk without everyone laughing and all that" and in P4C we "all feel more relaxed and it's just easier to listen when you're relaxed" (Haynes, 2002, p. 54). However, little research has been done on the listening dispositions that P4C cultivates. Individuals exercise selectivity in their listening. P4C refines this selectivity by making the listening more generous, critical, aesthetic, and profound.

In the first section of this chapter I will offer a brief introduction to the history, curriculum, and pedagogy of P4C. The subsequent four sections provide analysis of the different listening dispositions that P4C cultivates. The first is what I call hermeneutical listening because it begins in receptivity and focuses exclusively on interpretation; students take seriously, and want to understand, the meaning of what their peers say. The second is what I call philosophical listening because it focuses on the logical status of what is said; students keenly listen for examples, counter-examples, reasons, implications, and assumptions. The third is what I call appreciative listening because it focuses on the aesthetic dimensions of the conversation; students become attuned to the symphonic arrangements of their different voices, the rhythmic contrast between sound and silence and the ebb and flow of enthusiasm and intensity. The fourth listening disposition I call existential because it reflects the recognition that we are each claimed by life's essential mysteriousness and its most compelling, but unanswerable, questions.

I illustrate the first three listening dispositions using excerpts taken from a transcript of a mature P4C middle school class (I have changed the names of the participants to protect their anonymity). I had no contact with participants and so cannot claim to know that they were listening in the ways that I describe. I am not primarily concerned with what actually happened. To this end, I acknowledge that there are many other, equally plausible, interpretations of these shorts transcripts. The issue, from my perspective, is not whether my analysis is empirically accurate, in the sense of its being factually correct, but whether it is intelligible. Put differently, I am interested in the possibility that these individuals listened hermeneutically, philosophically, appreciatively (and existentially). If these four listening dispositions bear witness to our shared P4C experience, then they open avenues for practicing it in more meaningful ways. They deepen our sense of the value of P4C, particularly as it is so resistant to the many of hallmarks of formal education: hierarchy, assessment, standardization, subject matter, product, testing, and so on.[4] Perhaps the ultimate value of P4C is not that it educates reasonableness—although it certainly has been shown to do this—but that it invites us to live more fully by listening and waiting. It encourages us to become more intelligently attuned to a world that endlessly escapes our ability to grasp it, celebrating a reality that simply cannot be exhausted by any understanding of it.

> "Listening is both accepting and critical, trusting and diffident, irrepressible and yet consoling."
>
> —Gemma Corradi Fiumara

I wish to conclude this section with one final qualification. While it is true that I distinguish four listening dispositions, I do not view them as incompatible with one another, nor do I see them as occurring in isolation or sequentially. In some cases they merge into one another as in the example of when in trying to make sense of what a peer is saying, a student will look for clues in facial expression. There are no rules for how to balance and harmonize the four learning dispositions. It is impossible for a P4C student to know at what points she will need to rely on aesthetic listening more than hermeneutic listening, and vice versa. The individual learns through experience and begins to rely on his or her own judgment and the judgment of others. There is no test of the success. If Corradi Fiumara is right that genuine listening is "an attitude that occupies no space but which in a paradoxical sense creates ever new spaces in the very 'place' in which it is carried out," then I think it is fair to say that P4C creates the conditions for genuine listening (Corradi Fiumara, 1995, p. 19). In the concluding section of the chapter, I address the moral significance of P4C.

Philosophy for Children (P4C)

In 1970 Matthew Lipman wrote a philosophical novel for young adolescents called *Harry Stottlemeier's Discovery*. In it, a group of school-age characters discover the principles of philosophical inquiry by reasoning cooperatively about questions of beauty, justice, truth, and education. Without making it explicit, Lipman has the characters draw from the Western philosophical tradition in order to demonstrate its abiding practical relevance. I wish to highlight just two noteworthy features of the philosophical novel. First, it appeals to the reader's full range of sensibilities including emotional, psycho-social, and aesthetic and, in so doing, reveals and engages the existential conditions of philosophical inquiry. Second, the characters in the philosophical novel represent different styles of thinking—scientific, intuitive, synthetic, and logical—that are shown to be equally valuable when engaged in philosophical inquiry.

When Lipman piloted *Harry Stottlemeier's Discovery* he found that it improved students' reasoning. Interested in writing more philosophical novels for children and accompanying resource manuals for teachers, Lipman established the Institute for the Advancement of Philosophy for Children (IAPC) at Montclair State University (MSU) in 1974. He was soon joined by Professor Ann Margaret Sharp and together they developed a comprehensive K-12 philosophy curriculum.

The pedagogical foundation of P4C is whole-class, inquiry-based conversation, otherwise known as a community of philosophical inquiry (CPI). Students are encouraged to be quite deliberate about how they conduct their whole-class, inquiry-based conversation or CPI. This is because how the students speak and listen to one another, the quality of their communication, *matters*; the CPI is not a means to an end, like the comprehension and recall of subject matter, writing assignments, or state tests. In CPI, speaking and listening are valued in their own right. For this reason, foundational procedures or rules for participation are considered vitally important. P4C students establish these procedures early on in the school year and modify them as the CPI matures and the students have internalized the procedures. Generally speaking, P4C students agree to sit in a circle facing one another; raise their hands or use a talking stick; take turns reading the text; pose questions about the text that are recorded in a central place; discuss the questions in an order and manner that most if not all of the participants judge appropriate; and conclude with a self-evaluation. The self-evaluation reflects that the CPI is a normative ideal as much as it is a set of pedagogical practices, that is, to participate in CPI is to be committed to its ongoing improvement.

In a P4C class, the philosophical novel is read by teacher and/or students as a stimulus for their own philosophical inquiry and dialogue
. Topics are wide-ranging and may run over a few weeks. They include fairness, friendship, knowledge, reality, thinking, life and death, freedom, identity, and the concept of mind. The teacher's role is to facilitate the students' dialogue by appearing philosophically weak and by being pedagogically strong. In other words, the role of the P4C teacher is not to introduce and explain philosophical theories. Instead, it is to model philosophical inquiry by (a) asking philosophical questions, seeking to define concepts, giving, and evaluating reasons and so on; (b) being inclusive and respectful of all students, using encouragement and patience with some and directing skepticism and criticism at others; and (c) engaging in the dialogue with the view to having it genuinely contribute or his or her understanding of the concepts and questions under consideration. The P4C teacher models philosophical inquiry in the hope of distributing responsibility for its logical, social, and normative procedures; students are to take responsibility for these procedures as they learn to inquire together and on their own.

In P4C, students are encouraged to identify, name, and make various "thinking moves." They ask questions of *clarification*, offer *examples* and *counter-examples*, evaluate *reasons*, and make *inferences*. Some critics of P4C find the discussion overly scripted and somewhat contrived. It is worthwhile noting, however, that P4C students develop logical literacy at the same time as they seek "answers" to existential questions—about love, death, beauty, and justice—that ultimately resist logical resolution (I return to this point toward the end of the chapter).

P4C has many educational aims, one of which is intelligent self-correction. Intelligent self-correction indicates that students have been listening rather than appearing to listen; it is a natural outcome of their involvement in the conversation. Reasonable self-correction is not a sign of intellectual weakness or lack of character in P4C. Instead, it shows communicative and intellectual leadership. If a P4C student can change his or her mind and explain his or her reasons for doing so, then he or she has heard contrary points of view; successfully evaluated the different viewpoints; and been able to exercise a degree of control over his or her own thinking.

This brings me to the four modes of listening that P4C educates for: hermeneutical, philosophical, appreciative, and existential. I will address each of them in turn.

Hermeneutical Listening

P4C is inherently dialogical: the philosophy for children texts represent characters in dialogue with one another; students formulate philosophical questions in response to these texts; and they formulate their ideas in response to one another. Because P4C is dialogical it begins in receptivity. Students address and are addressed by their peers. They listen to one another because they aspire to understand and be understood. There is a spirit of warm hospitality that characterizes P4C. Individual perspectives are welcomed (as is evidenced in the example of appreciative listening). Also, "while it *is* hospitality to new themes, facts, ideas, questions, it is not the kind of hospitality that would be indicated by hanging out a sign: 'Come right in; there is nobody at home.' It includes an active desire to listen; to give heed to facts from whatever source they come; to give full attention to alternative possibilities; to recognize the possibility of error even in the beliefs that are dearest to us."

The background or horizon for this listening is their engagement with fundamental philosophical questions: What does it mean to be a true friend? What should our relationships to animals be? Am I my body? Is it possible not to think? Do animals think? Clearly these questions provoke a range of responses. If P4C students are to cultivate mutual understanding, then they must exercise hermeneutical listening; P4C students must listen carefully to what others say and they must continually check with the speaker to make sure that their interpretation is correct. For this reason, you will frequently hear P4C students say: "Are you trying to say . . . ," "I didn't think that that's what she meant, by um . . . I thought that she meant . . . ," and "Um, I think what you're saying is. . . ." In actuality, much of the time in CPI is dedicated to clarifying what others say because logical/procedural priority is given to questions of clarification.

Hermeneutical listening is reflected in the following two examples, both of which typify P4C interactions. In the first example, Chloe claims that, like Joseph, she believes that to be human is to think. She illustrates the claim by explaining that trying not think is itself an occasion of thinking. Mark, the teacher, checks that he has heard her correctly by reformulating her claim: it's impossible not to think. She agrees and elaborates on her earlier explanation. The teacher refines his reformulation: impossible to stop thinking, i.e., we are already underway. The transcript is as follows:

> *Chloe*: I agree with Joseph and I think you have to think all the time because when you're trying not to think you're thinking about not thinking. [Laughter]
>
> *Mark*: So you're saying it's impossible to not think?
>
> *Chloe*: Yeah because, um, whenever I am trying not to think, something in my mind, in the back of my mind, like, maybe, is telling me to doodle or come up with something. But I think it is impossible to stop thinking.
>
> *Mark*: Impossible to stop thinking?

The second example is subtly different. It begins with the teacher offering a reflection on how complicated the conversation is becoming. He suspects that the students had difficulty understanding the last comment. Rather than calling attention to the student who made the comment, Mark invites the students to reflect on the conversation: Are they following? Are they finding it complicated? At what point did they begin to find it complicated? Cally responds to the invitation by offering a correction: the student did not say what she had said. The teacher invites her to say more by suggesting that she begin with the similarities between what she said and what the other student said. He knows that for Cally to do this, she must reformulate what she heard the other student say. When Cally is not forthcoming, Mark explains what the student had said.

Mark: Ok, this, this is getting, this is getting complicated.

Cally: That's not really what I was saying.

Mark: But it's related, right?

Cally: Yeah.

Mark: He's saying the bad person thinks that his thinking is right. Because he doesn't . . .

> To do philosophy with children is to honor their dignity by honoring their reflective capacities no matter how seemingly inchoate.

One of the reasons P4C students are motivated to listen so attentively to the meaning of what others say is because they know that it forms the basis of the possible philosophical moves they can elect to make. For example, once a student has established that another student is making a generalization then it becomes appropriate for that student to offer an illustration that supports and maybe even complicates the other student's generalization.

It is worthwhile noting that hermeneutical listening involves the heart as much as it does the mind. In P4C students must listen carefully to what others are saying if they are to understand what they are thinking. However, as participants in an ongoing inquiry and in the shared life of a classroom, P4C students also wish to understand one another as people. This involves oftentimes, attending to the histories, relationships, and feelings that animate and lie behind the words. To highlight this important aspect of hermeneutical listening, Matthew Lipman features in one of the philosophical novels, a character named Brian who does not speak. The main character, Pixie, speculates endlessly about why Brian does not talk and yet she also becomes astute at reading him emotionally.

Philosophical Listening

In P4C, students come to see themselves as making moves in a shared philosophical inquiry. For this reason, they listen for the kinds of philosophical moves that others are making. They learn to detect when they are being asked to engage in a thought experiment and when a counter-example challenges a generalization. Their movement toward philosophical listening is reflected in their questions and how they formulate their responses to questions from others. For example, having listened for quite some time to the discussion on thinking, a student says: "Oh I just wanted to say, I had a question. Are we saying that there are different kinds of thinking or is everything just bunched up in one group?" In newly formed CPI, the conversation is dominated by opinion and anecdote, but as the CPI matures student responses become more philosophically diverse and appropriate.

In the first example, the students have introduced the distinction between right and wrong thinking when the teacher asks them for criteria. Instead of proposing criteria Susanne introduces an example of wrong thinking—in part because she is unsure. The teacher clarifies that Susanne is offering an example from which they may be able to derive criteria.

Mark: How could we judge between wrong and right thinking? Susanne.

Susanne: Um, well I think what Laurie saying is um, like if you, I don't know if this is really right but, if you're like thinking of a math problem and it's wrong . . .

Mark: A math problem?

Susanne: . . . um, yeah I'm just going to a math problem . . .

Mark: That's a good example.

Susanne: . . . um, I think if you're thinking wrong, like, ok like Katie saying 2 + 2 = 5. That was wrong. Are you thinking, like it's wrong?

What you notice about this interchange, is the effort involved in Susanne's struggle to entertain, and really make sense of, the distinction between right and wrong thinking. Clearly, she does not want to adjudicate on the distinction before first having understood it. Yet, she is finding the understanding elusive. She is genuinely groping to find an example of wrong thinking that everyone would accept. She knows that "five" is a definitely incorrect answer to the question "What is 2 + 2?" She assumes that to answer incorrectly is to have calculated incorrectly. Her hypothesis is that calculating incorrectly is an example of wrong thinking. She is concerned to know, however, whether the other P4C students would agree.

In the second example, Jeff rejects the distinction between right and wrong thinking by introducing a further distinction. He distinguishes between

Megan J. Laverty

the process of thinking and the subject matter of thought. The argument is not clear, in part because Jess shifts from talking about "right" and "wrong" to talking about "good" and "bad." The teacher acknowledges Jeff's intellectual contribution by referring to the distinction as "fancy." He qualifies his praise by suggesting that true potential of the distinction relies on further work. Given that Jeff is returning to an earlier topic, it is a question for the community whether to pursue this work. The transcript is as follows:

> *Jeff:* Um, this is from wrong thinking, there is no such thing as wrong thinking because thinking is something itself, but it can be wrong what you're thinking about. I mean it's like . . .
>
> *Lauren:* Yeah I guess that's . . .
>
> *Mark:* Is that the distinction you were looking for?
>
> *Lauren:* . . . Yeah, pretty much.
>
> *Mark:* So, thinking in itself is just thinking?
>
> *Jeff:* Thinking is just thinking, there is no wrong and no right, but what you're thinking about can be bad or good.
>
> *Mark:* Well that's, that's a pretty fancy distinction but I'm not sure that we should accept it right away.

As well as listening for philosophical moves in the conversation, the students' listening becomes informed by overarching philosophical questions. It is not long before they begin to respond to one another's truth claims by asking such questions as: "Who told you that?" and "How do you know that what you say is true?" These questions lead P4C students to compare and evaluate the relative trustworthiness of their different epistemic sources: Are parents more or less reliable than teachers? How reliable is the television? P4C students are also fascinated by questions of "ought" and "should."

Appreciative Listening

Appreciative listening refers to the aesthetic dimension of CPI. In P4C, students develop an appreciation for the qualitative dimensions of CPI: the improvisatory rhythms of conversation; the varying degrees of interest and intensity;

the flow of ideas; and the moments when the conversation seems discordant and the moments when it seems orchestrated. Appreciative listening develops over time as the CPI participants move toward collective ownership of the inquiry; they become less absorbed in their own perspective and more attuned to the community as a whole. Their impulse always to speak and be heard is subordinated to an emergent interest in engaging collaboratively together with questions and ideas.

Appreciative listening is discernible in how students respond to the discussion, their laughter, the pleasure or discomfort palpable in any CPI, and their sense of one another. Students begin to recognize who the cautious, creative, careful, and considerate thinkers are. Appreciative listening enables students to experiment with modifying and diversifying their patterns of behavior in light of how they contribute to, or detract from, the qualitative dimensions of CPI. Classroom teachers will frequently report that they teach P4C if only because it changes the class dynamics.

Up until now, I have been focusing on the social dimensions of appreciative listening. There is also an intellectual dimension. P4C students begin to experience a certain intellectual satisfaction in the CPI. Initially, their participation in CPI feels more like play than work. Compared with other class time, the CPI seems low stakes, informal and free. P4C students shortly discover the intense intellectual labor involved in getting clear about a philosophical question and potential ways to think about it. It is in this context a new sense of play emerges, having to do with ideas. P4C students begin to take delight in questioning, disagreeing, connecting ideas, and developing arguments.

The restlessness, playfulness, and humor of P4C students engaged in CPI do not betray a lack of seriousness on their part. Children are undeniably troubled and fascinated by the profound ambiguity and seeming inconsistency of life. Their seriousness may not be reflected in concerns about vanity, authenticity, or philosophical integrity. They are less wedded to securing an answer that they can stake their identity on. As Joanna Haynes observes: "[o]n the whole, young children seem to worry less about changing their minds than do adults. They do not appear to see as a sign of weakness the inability to hold a position" (Haynes, 2002, p. 63).

Appreciative listening is harder to illustrate than either hermeneutical or philosophical listening because it is so context-dependent. The first example includes only the teacher's response to a question from Katie.

Mark: . . . so Katie's teasing us with a mystery question. She doesn't know the answer herself. Um, Jeffery.

As with all the examples, I am not in a position to know what inspired the teacher to make this comment. Perhaps the question was so long that he stopped listening; perhaps he listened but couldn't understand the question. In either case, it is conceivable that he employed and wished to display appreciative listening. Rather than ignore the question as irrelevant or dismiss it as improperly formulated, the teacher wishes to acknowledge but not pursue the question. He does this by alluding to it as an aesthetic contribution. He indicates that he detects a teasing and mysterious note to the question and, by so doing, acknowledges a host of other reasons a person might have to say something.

The second example concerns an interchange between the teacher and two students in reference to something said by Lydia. It is clearly a case of hermeneutical listening because the teacher and William are trying to make sense of what Jeffrey means when he says that he thinks in pictures: the teacher requests an example and William asks a clarifying question. It is also a case of philosophical listening. Jeffrey makes a general statement, the teacher calls for an example, Jeffrey provides one, and William asks a hypothetical question namely, "If you think in pictures, then does it follow that you don't think in words?" The transcript is as follows:

Jeffery: Um, I have something to say about something that Lydia said. "I think in pictures in motion."

Mark: Could you give us an example?

Jeffery: Like, let's say um right now, let's say I'm thinking of something like . . . yeah cars. Um, let's say, I can, I don't, I don't write it down in words, uh, blah blah blah blah blah blah blah blah. Instead I think it out of pictures, motion, like picture comics, the inside of it.

William: You don't think about "car," the word.

Jeffery: I know I think car. There's no, if, if, thinking was just words, right now I would think Julian is a word literally and chair. . . . Oh never mind.

The example also reveals appreciative listening. Jeffrey is clearly excited. It might be because he has something to say or it might be because he is speaking about how he thinks. Mark and William take Jeffrey seriously, but without feeding his excitement, by asking short and simple questions that show they have been listening. Mark and William care for Jeffrey as much as they do his claim: the teacher asks Jeffrey for an example, precisely because he knows that Jeffrey is inclined to get knotted up in his own speaking; William truly wants to understand what it is like to *be* Jeffrey and to think like him. Jeffrey's response to William is disappointing as he seems at that moment to have exhausted his resources; his intuitions about his thinking outstrip his ability to articulate them—a common phenomenon in life as much as it is in P4C. Everyone sees this as an opportune time to change topics; Jeffrey has been heard and another student may choose to build on what he has said, just as Jeffrey has chosen to return to an earlier comment by Lydia. Their conversation shows, I think, that Mark, William, and Jeffrey became absorbed in the inquiry while they remain attuned to each other and the larger context.

Existential Listening

With appreciation comes a willingness to imagine others as independent "centers of reality" (Murdoch, 1997, pp. 29 & 283).[5] A mutual recognition among the P4C students is established as they come to see themselves as claimed by life's essential mysteriousness: addressed by life's compelling and unanswerable questions, such as "Why am I here?," "What is it to be true friend?," and "How is it that I exist?" P4C returns students to the ambiguity of existence, revealing the commonality of our human condition: that we are compelled to inquire into life's existential questions as we are forced to move ahead in life without the aid of secure answers. How is this reflected in existential listening? It is difficult to say but I do think it is discernible in the comfortable silences that begin to punctuate the CPI. P4C students begin to simply dwell with the questions *and* the impossibility of solving them, inspired by the community that such inquiry creates. They find themselves increasingly engaged in an intra-personal dialogue that reverberates with untold depths.

Conclusion

In summary, to do philosophy with children is to honor their dignity by honoring their reflective capacities no matter how seemingly inchoate. It is an important ethical gesture in a cultural and historical context that represents children as having only nascent agency or as being exceptionally innocent, creative, unselfconscious, spontaneous, and free. Both conceptions serve to justify adult-child paternalism and to deny children the seriousness that we attribute to individuals with whom we consider ourselves to share a common humanity. It is against this background that giving children the opportunity to do philosophy functions as an acknowledgment that they, like adults, are endeavoring to live better, more meaningful lives; that they have the potential for wisdom, and the ability to educate our 'adult' understanding of how to live better.

Notes

1. Dewey, J. (1987). Art as Experience. In J. A. Boydston (Ed.), *John Dewey: the later works 1925–1953*, Vol. 10. Carbondale, IL: Southern Illinois University Press. (111).

2. For an example of this debate see Kitchener, R. (1990). Do children think philosophically? *Metaphilosophy,* 21(4), 416–431; and Lipman, M. (1990). Response to Professor Kitchener. *Metaphilosophy,* 21(4), 432–433.

3. I do not offer a positive argument for teaching philosophy in schools and nor do I examine and refute those who object to the teaching of philosophy in schools on the grounds that that it is a peculiarly difficult and inaccessible subject or that it inclines children toward relativism. For responses to these and other objections as well as positive arguments for the inclusion of philosophy in the school curriculum, see Hand, M., & Winstanely, C. (Eds.). (2008). *Philosophy in schools.* London: Continuum.

4. Jonathan Lear beautifully exemplifies the approach that I am adopting here, referring to it as philosophical anthropology. See Lear, J. (2006). *Radical hope: Ethics in the face of cultural devastation.* Cambridge, MA: Harvard University Press.

5. Murdoch argues that tolerance is exemplified in nineteen-century authors Jane Austen and George Eliot. They apprehend their characters' "separate mode of being which is important and interesting to themselves" (271). Murdoch may be right that a better name for tolerance is love.

Suggested Reading

Haynes, J. (2002). *Children as philosophers: Learning through inquiry and dialogue in the primary classroom.* London and New York: Routledge.
Gregory, M. (Ed.). (2006). *Philosophy for children practitioner handbook.* Montclair, NJ: Institute for the Advancement of Philosophy for Children.
Matthews, G. (1994). *Philosophy of childhood.* Cambridge, MA: Harvard University Press.

References

Corradi Fiumara, G. (1995). *The other side of language: A philosophy of listening.* London and New York: Routledge.

Dewey, J. (1987). Art as experience. In J. A. Boydston (Ed.), *John Dewey: the later works 1925–1953*, Vol. 10. Carbondale, IL: Southern Illinois University Press.

Grayling, A. C. (2008). Foreword. In M. Hand, & C. Winstanely (Eds.), *Philosophy in schools*. London: Continuum.

Gregory. M. (Ed.) (2006). Introduction: Philosophy for children and/as philosophical practice. *Philosophy for Children Practitioner Handbook*, pp. 85–90. Montclair, NJ: Institute for the Advancement of Philosophy for Children. Reprinted from *The International Journal for Applied Philosophy*, 18(2), 141–150.

Hand, M., & Winstanely, C. (2008). *Philosophy in schools*. London: Continuum.

Haynes, J. (2002). *Children as philosophers: Learning through inquiry and dialogue in the primary classroom*. London and New York: Routledge.

Kennedy, D. (2006). *The well of being*. New York, NY: SUNY Press.

Kitchener, R. F. (1990). Do children think philosophically? *Metaphilosophy*, 21(4), 416–431.

Laverty, M., & Gregory, M. (2009). Philosophy, education and wisdom. In A. Kenkmann (Ed.), *Teaching philosophy. Practical dialogues* (pp. 155–173). New York and London: Continuum.

Laverty, M., & Gregory, M. (2010), Philosophy, education, and the care of the self. *Thinking: the Journal of Philosophy for Children*, 19(4), Special Issue: Philosophy, Education and the Care of the Self. Guest editor with M. Gregory, 2–9.

Laverty, M. (2007). The role of dialogical philosophical inquiry in the teaching of tolerance and sympathy. *Learning Inquiry*, 1(2), Special Issue: Listening and Reflecting. Guest Editor: Leonard Waks, 125–132.

Laverty, M. (2008). A place to be philosophical: Dialogue and the epistemology of receptivity. *Bridges: An Interdisciplinary Journal of Theology, Philosophy, History and Science*, 15(1/2), Special Issue: Philosophy as Transformative Practice. Guest Editor: Ann J. Cahill, 161–180.

Lear, J. (2006). *Radical hope: ethics in the face of cultural devastation*. Cambridge, MA: Harvard University Press.

Lipman, M. (1990). Response to Professor Kitchener. *Metaphilosophy*, 21(4), 432–433.

Matthews, G. (1994). *Philosophy of childhood*. Cambridge, MA: Harvard University Press.

Murdoch, I. (1997). *Existentialists and mystics: Writings on philosophy and literature*. London and New York: Penguin Books.

Splitter, L. (2001). Listen to them think: Reflections on inquiry, philosophy and dialogue. In M. Robertson, & R. Gerber (Eds.), *Children's ways of knowing: Learning through partnerships* (pp. 112–127). Melbourne: ACER Press.

5
_____

Listening in Interpretive Discussion

Elizabeth Meadows

Roosevelt University

Introduction

In interpretive discussion, the teacher and participants listen in order to understand one another's ideas about a text. Here, "listening" happens when someone tries to understand what another person is trying to communicate.[1] This definition of listening embodies "interpretive," "relational," and "critical" listening as described in the Introduction. Listening in interpretive discussion involves building a community and working to develop each participant's capacities to reason and to communicate. The teacher listens to students carefully, questions them, and listens to their responses with the aims of helping them develop their thinking and their abilities to communicate their ideas clearly. The teacher needs to listen for students' capabilities and areas for growth in order to support students' learning. Likewise, the teacher responds to students to help them understand one another's ideas, evaluate their own and others' ideas based on evidence from the text and their lived experiences, and work to identify and resolve a question that concerns them as a group. In this way she works to cultivate a community of learning where students assist one another in developing ideas, communicating these clearly, listening to understand one another's thinking and evaluating one another's ideas in a communal inquiry.

In an interpretive discussion, facilitators and participants explore the meaning of a text that embodies ambiguity (a reading, film, or work of art), by listening to one another and by interpreting the text in order to identify and resolve a shared concern about the meaning of the text. Interpreting the text involves saying what one thinks the text means in one's own words.

Interpretive discussion differs in several ways from other frequently used forms of discussion in schools. Participants focus on questions that they have about the text and then they focus in on finding textual evidence to support their claims about possible resolutions to their questions. The students' own questions form the bases of the discussion. With the help of their teacher, the group tries to arrive at one focus of inquiry about the text that most, if not all, participants want to resolve. Then, during the interpretive discussion, the group tries to stay focused on this shared question toward the end of trying to resolve it in one or more ways that are satisfying to the group. They work together to try to resolve their shared question by discussing and listening to their interpretations of the text that pertain to their shared question.

In sum, there are three basic parts of an interpretive discussion. In the first part, students share their initial questions about the text and clarify and develop ideas about their questions through talking to the group and listening to their teacher and to other students. In the second part, which often overlaps with the first part, the teacher helps students arrive at a question about the text that they share and that they want to work together to resolve. In the third part of the interpretive discussion, the teacher and the students work together to resolve this shared question. (For a further discussion of interpretive discussion compared to other forms of discussion please see Meadows (2012).)

Students and teachers actively engage in exploring their own and one another's questions and ideas in an interpretive discussion which distinguishes it from didactic teaching. Furthermore, interpretive discussion challenges the assumption of didactic pedagogy that students are empty vessels that a teacher is responsible for filling with knowledge. In an interpretive discussion, the teacher listens to students to understand what they are trying to say about a text and to help them develop their thinking further. Therefore, this model presumes that students have sound ideas and that their responses to a text involve both their reasoning about ideas there and about their past experiences that relate to the text. The interpretive discussion process also challenges the assumption of didactic teaching that the teacher is the only source of learning. Given the group nature of interpretive discussion, as a teacher responds to individual students, other students listen to that student's ideas and thus learn from one another as well as from the teacher.

Interpretive discussion process addresses social justice in at least three ways. First, it affords a space for everyone to be heard, including those whose voices often are not heard because they come from marginalized groups. Unfortunately, in the United States and elsewhere, the ideas and perspectives of people who have been systematically undervalued and oppressed are not often given voice. Everyone can benefit from taking these ideas seriously. Second, participants work to identify common concerns about an ambiguous text and can then seek to identify other common concerns about social injustices such as poverty. Third, participants work together to resolve these shared concerns. Opportunities to practice all three of these skills are needed for people to learn to work together for the well-being of everyone, which is one definition of social justice.

> *In an interpretive discussion, facilitators and participants explore the meaning of a text that embodies ambiguity (a reading, film, or work of art), by listening to one another and by interpreting the text to identify and resolve a shared concern about its meaning.*

Background of Interpretive Discussion

Sophie Haroutunian-Gordon has been a proponent and key developer of interpretive discussion in schools. She describes interpretive discussion as "a pedagogical approach . . . which emphasizes questioning and thinking as these occur when interpreting texts" (2009, x) and adds that "[t]he Great Books Foundation uses the phrase 'Shared Inquiry' to refer to a very similar approach" to interpretive discussion (2009, p. 191). In addition, she lists the Paideia Project, St. John's College, and the North Carolina Institute for the Advancement of Teaching as places where interpretive discussion has been utilized and fostered for many years (1999, p. 191). Haroutunian-Gordon describes the background against which interpretive discussion was developed in terms of at least five interrelated problems in education in the United States today (1999, 2009). These are first, the widespread use of fact-based, multiple choice standardized testing and its effects on pedagogy and curricula; second, the often exclusive focus in business-driven educational reform on preparing students to fulfill needs of the economy; third, a common view of the student as being empty of knowledge and in need of being filled up; which is related to a fourth problem—the often predominating conception of teaching as the delivery of factual knowledge didactically to students through demonstration and lecture; and fifth, a prevailing lack of interest among students for what is often taught through this delivery model in schools.

Interpretive discussion responds to these five problems in the following ways. An overabundance of standardized testing, based in factual, multiple choice questioning, is a reality in most U.S. schools today. Haroutunian-Gordon responds in *Learning to Teach through Discussion: The Art of Turning the Soul,*

In an age when following a script has come to replace thoughtful, creative approaches to teaching and students' attention has been turned from questioning and reflecting to scoring well on multiple standardized tests, this book argues for a different focus. The claim is that life in school can be more engaging and productive for all—teachers included—if thinking, rooted in questioning is placed at the center of at least some experiences. (2009, x)

Questioning and interpreting a text in interpretive discussion can afford participants opportunities to reflect and think deeply about questions that matter to them. Doing so is compelling for both students and teachers because it can help them both want to learn and then actually learn about matters that are important to them.

Haroutunian-Gordon describes how interpretive discussion responds to a second problem in education that comes from "business and political interests" and that has greatly affected school reform since the mid-1800s: ". . . that society needs the schools to provide competent workers, people who can help to sustain its economic prosperity" (2009, pp. 1–2). Haroutunian-Gordon responds, "But surely, such a response seems limited" (2009, p. 2). She analyzes John Dewey's aims for education and concludes,

According to Dewey, then, what American society needs is an individual whose unique qualities have been developed so that they may contribute productively to the welfare of all which involves more than contributing to the economy. In addition, it means having the ability to communicate effectively with others so that institutional change is effected, social barriers are eliminated, and change is orderly. (1999, pp. 2–3)

Interpretive discussion teaches people how to communicate effectively with one another. It also helps individuals develop their "unique qualities" and thereby addresses a third problem that Haroutunian-Gordon addresses: the common view of the student as being empty of knowledge and in need of being filled up. In contrast, Haroutunian-Gordon explains in *Turning the Soul: Teaching through Conversation in the High School,*

Teaching, Plato says, is *turning the soul,* which I take to mean directing the students to objects that draw out the vision or understanding they already possess, thanks to their experience in the world. . . . Plato does not imagine the learner to be some sort of empty container into which vision or understanding must be poured. On the contrary, he assumes that the students have understanding that may be drawn out and directed. (1999, p. 6)

Plato asserts and Haroutunian-Gordon agrees that learners have developed understandings from their experiences in the world and are not empty headed. Haroutunian-Gordon describes how interpretive discussion draws on students' understanding in contrast to what she describes as a problematic way of teaching: didactically filling them with understanding and telling them how to think. She writes,

While a great many educational theorists . . . have espoused the idea that teaching is drawing out understanding from the learner, by and large, education both in America and abroad has assumed that teaching is showing or telling students what to think or do. (1999, p. 7)

In contrast, interpretive discussion involves the students in shared inquiry about a text, with the teacher drawing out their questions and ideas about it. In contrast to interpretive discussion, the problematic emphasis on didactic teaching which happens almost exclusively through lecture and demonstration can often lead to an unproductive focus on a student's lack of knowledge. For example, when studies show U.S. students falling behind students from other countries, Haroutunian-Gordon explains that people think, "How can we enjoy the 'leisure' of learning by doing when our students score far behind the Russians and Japanese on mathematics and science tests?" (1999, p. 14). She explains that the usual response to this relative gap in test scores is to fall back on teaching as demonstrating and telling. When this happens, the focus shifts to facts and what our students do not know because "[w]e assume that American students do less well because they haven't been stuffed with enough facts" (1999, p. 15). This focus on what students do not yet know often leads educators and others to overlook what students already do know. She clarifies that "[t]he plea in this book [on interpretive discussion] is that we turn our focus toward the resources that students bring naturally into the classroom. By doing so we resuscitate the hope of connecting school experiences with effective learning" (1999, p. 15). By connecting school experiences with what students already know, students' interest in learning in school can increase.

Consequently, interpretive discussion can foster students' motivations to learn ". . . when the interests and ideas students bring to the classroom have been drawn out enough so that the material the teacher demonstrates has meaning and significance . . ." (1999, p. 15). Haroutunian-Gordon refers to a fifth problem of students' lack of interest in material presented by lecture and demonstration,

> While the purpose of the discussion is not to prepare students to receive lectures, there is no question that participation in discussion may open students to ideas that might otherwise mean little to them. A well-positioned demonstration or lecture may then prove truly educative. (1999, p. 15)

Interpretive discussions begin with students' own genuine questions about texts that embody ambiguity and important learning. When teachers help students ignite and kindle their questions, students are more likely to want to find answers which can come through lectures and demonstrations. In describing these five problems in education today, Haroutunian-Gordon does not claim that interpretive discussion is a panacea that should be used in education to the exclusion of other approaches. Instead, she writes,

> The book is meant to be suggestive, to inspire readers to explore the potential of interpretive discussion in settings where they might not have imagined trying it out. Perhaps they will discover that it can improve some learning experiences in some settings at some times. (1999, p. 19)

Pedagogy of Listening in Interpretive Discussion

I focus now on how a teacher and students listen and learn to listen through the first part of the interpretive discussion wherein students share their initial questions about a text. My questions are: What helps people both learn to listen to and become interested in listening to others in the interpretive discussion process? How does the teacher become interested in listening to students? What can a teacher do to help students become interested in what other students have to say? To investigate these questions, I explore accounts of elementary students engaging in interpretive discussions and the leaders' preparations for these discussions as described by Haroutunian-Gordon in *Learning to Teach Through Discussion: The Art of Turning the Soul* (2009). My reflections on my own experiences as a leader of interpretive discussions of both elementary students and teacher candidates—coached by Haroutunian-Gordon—also informed my reflections.

The teacher in this first part of the discussion listens to students with four goals as she helps them identify, clarify, and develop their questions about the text. First, she listens to understand what their questions are about the meaning of the text. Second, she talks with and listens to students about their questions in ways that help students clarify their individual questions and their interpretations of the text. Third, she asks students if they agree or disagree with interpretations made by other students in order to help them listen to and learn from one another. Throughout all of this listening, the teacher also listens with a fourth goal. She listens to the text and to what she thinks it may mean. (Listening to an author's meaning is similar to listening to try to understand what a speaker is trying to say, the overarching kind of listening focused on in this chapter.) She attends to what the text says and develops her own interpretations of it. She also encourages students to listen to the text and say what they think it means to them.

Students also listen with four goals as they work to identify, clarify, and develop their questions about the text. First, they listen to their own questions about the text and share these with their teacher and classmates. (As above, listening to one's own ideas is similar to listening to try to understand what another speaker is trying to say.) Second, they listen to understand other group members' questions about the text. Third, they listen to the teacher as she listens to, questions, and talks with students about their questions. Students listen with the goal of understanding their classmates' questions even better as the teacher helps students clarify their individual questions and their interpretations of the text. Throughout all of these forms of listening, the students also listen with a fourth goal: each student listens to the text. Each student attends to what the text says and develops her own interpretations of it. In addition, with continued experience in interpretive discussions, students may begin to emulate some or all of the ways of listening that the teacher does with their classmates.

Haroutunian-Gordon (2009) describes an interpretive discussion of *The Giving Tree* in which teachers and students listen as described. *The Giving Tree* is a picture book about a tree who gives all that she has to a boy who repeatedly asks more from her as he grows into a man. Finally, when he has cut the tree to a stump to make a boat, she tells him that she has nothing left to give. He then sits on the stump to rest after telling her that he does not need much anymore, just a place to rest (Silverstein, 1964).

In the discussion, two teacher candidates in Haroutunian-Gordon's program at Northwestern University, Marsha and Paula (pseudonyms), read the story aloud to a group of fourth graders. They then gave students time to quickly note down any questions or thoughts about the story before the discussion began. The teachers thus invited students to think of and share their thoughts and questions about the story. A student named Tracy (pseudonym) asked a question, "I want to know why the tree kept on calling him, 'Come, boy,' and he was grown" (Haroutunian-Gordon, 2009, p. 25). Tracy listened to what puzzled her about a text, identified a question that she had about the meaning of the text, and shared this question with her teacher and with the group.

For the teacher, beginning with students' questions, and thus, with their interests, is important to maximize the learning opportunities in an interpretive discussion. Students may be more motivated to explore the text and to listen to the thoughts of other students and the teacher when their own questions are the basis for the discussion. Their interest may be less when they are presented with information to learn or questions to consider. Interestingly, it can also work well if the teacher presents her own, genuine question about a text to students to begin an interpretive discussion and invites students' comments and questions about her question. Here, participants' own questions and responses to this question still help drive the discussion. Someone's question from the group—whether from the teacher or students—is being considered. This focus on participants' own questions differs from a situation where the author of a textbook poses a question, for example, that is not necessarily personally relevant to members of the classroom. Interpretive discussion involves students' and teachers' interests in the pedagogy and curriculum—an important strength of this approach that has implication for reforming many pedagogical experiences.

For example, educational standards include literacy skills to be acquired. A teacher may have some choice about how to help students meet the standards and can, for example, engage students in reading a book on a topic that interests them. Likewise, a teacher can often include reading and writing about areas of interest to him- or herself. Including her own areas of interest can help a teacher stay more engaged in teaching.

Listening continued in the discussion of *The Giving Tree* as other students listened to Tracy's question. In an interpretive discussion, participants speak one at a time so that everyone can hear everyone else's questions and comments. The practice of taking turns speaking is used by teachers to help students in their listening to different points of view. One strength of interpretive discussion is that people learn to listen to interests that differ from their own, work to identify a shared concern or problem, and work together to resolve it. These are fundamental ways of communicating and living together that people in a democracy need to learn (Meadows, 2013). By engaging in interpretive discussions in elementary, middle, and high schools, people can learn to listen to one another; that is, they can learn to work to understand what someone else intends to communicate. Learning to listen to others can be done in ways that may help them work together with people previously unknown to them and different from themselves to identify problems that they have a common interest in and to work together to resolve these.

In the discussion of *The Giving Tree*, Marsha asked the group, "Who else wondered that?"—referring to the question that Tracy shared (Haroutunian-Gordon, 2009, p. 25). Asking students if they had the same question draws them into the conversation and can be used in other forms of teaching and learning as well. It is important for teachers to model and teach students how to disagree with others' ideas in respectful and constructive ways. The purpose of asking for and listening to all students' points of view is to foster an understanding of different points of view and questions/ideas about the text held by individual members of the group. The teacher fosters this understanding by inviting everyone to state their questions and ideas, by asking everyone to listen as each speaker shares, and by helping students understand each other's questions and ideas.

For example, before any other students respond, Marsha said, "I wondered the same thing, Tracy. Because, you know, in that picture, when it's talking about the old man, and he's all hunched over, and the tree is still calling him 'Boy,' isn't he?" (2009, pp. 25–26). Marsha listened for the meaning of Tracy's question and to her own interpretation of the text. She responded to Tracy with a question about Tracy's question and then Marsha listened to Tracy's subsequent responses. Haroutunian-Gordon's listening to Marsha in their work together as teacher and student in the teacher preparation program seems to have helped Tracy make the

Students may be more motivated to explore the text and to listen to the thoughts of other students and the teacher when their own questions are the basis for the discussion.

meaning of her question as clear as possible to herself, to other students, and to the discussion leader. Marsha seemed genuinely interested in learning more about Tracy's question and about her reasons for asking it. (Marsha may have become interested in this way in part because she experienced her teacher listening to her in preparation for this discussion, a point that will be explored later.)

Marsha's listening to Tracy may also help Tracy develop her thinking about her own question. Marsha does not ask a question specifically phrased to clarify Tracy's question (as in, "What do you mean, Tracy?" or "Could you say more about what you mean, Tracy?") Nevertheless, Tracy responds with a possible answer to her own initial question that contains in it another question and further ideas about how to answer her initial question, saying "I think she must still think he's young in some kind of way." Tracy seems to be stating that the tree continues to call the man "boy" when he is older because the tree still sees him as young. Her statement implies another question: "How could the tree see the older man as still young when he is clearly getting older and older throughout the story?" The teacher repeats what Tracy said in the form of a question, "She still thinks he's young in some kind of way?" The teacher then asks another member of the group what he thinks about what Tracy has said: "What do you think, Ethan? Do you think the tree sees the boy as being young?" Here, the teacher asks for and listens to another discussant's views on Tracy's question. Ethan responds, "No," to which Tracy responds, "I think because she said, 'Come swing on my branches.'" Here, Tracy seems to be listening to and responding to Ethan's comment with her reason, based in the text, for thinking that the tree thinks the man is still young. The tree asks the boy to swing on her branches as if he is a young boy. Tracy is listening to the text in her response: she quotes a passage that gives evidence for her idea that the tree sees the man as young (Haroutunian-Gordon, 2009, p. 26).

Right after Tracy gives evidence for her idea, Ethan says: "He's too strong" (Haroutunian-Gordon, 2009, p. 26). Ethan may be saying that the man is stronger than he was as a boy and so, he cannot swing on the tree's branches without possibly breaking them. Ethan's statement may imply that it does not make sense that the tree could be calling the man a "boy" because she sees him as young. As evidence for this, Ethan explains that the man is stronger than he was as a boy and so, he is clearly not young. In this exchange, Tracy and Ethan, with the help of their teacher, are listening to one another's differing views. That is, they are working to understand what each other is trying to say about their ideas about the text even when they disagree.

A benefit to their learning is that Tracy and Ethan may not have thought through their ideas as thoroughly as they did here if they had not been presented with views that differed from their own. For example, Tracy may not have thought through the ways in which the tree sees the older man as being young if someone had not disagreed with her in a context where mutual understanding was being fostered. Fostering respectful conversations about disagreements that students have with one another about matters that they care about is a practical way of learning that can be promoted in other forms of teaching as well. Marsha's co-teacher, Paula, asks Tracy to show her and the group where in the story the tree asks the man to swing on her branches. Tracy finds this place in the story and reads it aloud: "On line twenty-four, 'Boy, climb up my trunk and swing from my branches and be happy.'" Here, Tracy listens to, that is, she pays attention to, the text and gives evidence from it to support her interpretation that the tree calls the man a boy because she thinks he is still young enough to swing on her branches. This is an example of how paying close attention to how a participant interprets a text is a defining aspect of an interpretive discussion.

This process of paying close attention to participants' interpretations of texts can help teachers address the Common Core State Standards for English Language Arts & Literacy in History/Social Studies, Science, and Technical Subjects with their students. These standards have been adopted in most U.S. states (2010). For example, the interpretive discussion process addresses the following standards:

Standard One of the Speaking and Listening Standards K–5

First Grade: Ask and answer questions about key details in a text.
Third Grade: Ask and answer questions to demonstrate understanding of a text, referring explicitly to the text as the basis for answers.
Fifth Grade: Quote accurately from a text when explaining what the text says explicitly and when drawing inferences from the text

Standard One of the Reading Standards for Literacy in History/ Social Studies 6–12

Grades 6–8: Cite specific textual evidence to support analysis of primary and secondary sources.
Grades 11–12: Cite specific textual evidence to support analysis of primary and secondary sources, connecting insights gained from specific details to an understanding of the text as a whole.

Common Core Anchor Standard

> Delineate and evaluate the argument and specific claims in a text, including the validity of the reasoning as well as the relevance and sufficiency of the evidence.

Throughout the discussion of *The Giving Tree*, teachers and students are working to try to understand what others are trying to communicate as well as what they think the text is trying to say.

What Helps People Learn to Listen to One Another in Interpretive Discussion?

If listening happens when someone tries to understand what another person is trying to communicate, how does someone learn to listen to another person?

Furthermore, how does a teacher learn to listen to her students so that students feel that they are genuinely listened to with a teacher's full respect, support, and attention to them as individuals? In 2009, Haroutunian-Gordon published an account of how she listen to two of her students—teacher candidates—Marsha and Paula, in ways that help them learn to listen to and become interested in listening to elementary students during the interpretive discussion process. In the process of helping Marsha and Paula prepare to lead interpretive discussions, Haroutunian-Gordon tried to understand what they were trying to communicate about the questions that interested them about a text. She engaged the co-leaders in preparing what she calls a "cluster of questions" that "identifies a point of ambiguity about the meaning of the text . . . which is phrased as the basic question (BQ)—the question the leader wants most to resolve" (2009, p. 91). The cluster also includes eight follow-up questions that focus on "at least eight places in the text that seem to suggest evidence for resolution of the BQ" (2009, p. 26). The cluster questions are further interpretive questions that ask about the meaning of the text and not about the facts of the text or about the reader's evaluations or judgments about the text.

In order to test if *The Giving Tree* would sustain a rich discussion with elementary students, Haroutunian-Gordon suggested that these teacher candidates try to develop a cluster of questions about it. If they could do so, then this would mean that there were both enough ambiguity in the text and enough places to explore this ambiguity to sustain a fruitful interpretive discussion. Haroutunian-Gordon suggested that all three of them read the story twice and make note of things that were puzzling to each of them and that they had some curiosity about resolving. This is just what Marsha and Paula asked the elementary students to do at the beginning of their discussion and is a practice that a teacher could use in any form of teaching when introducing some new topic or activity. When Paula and Marsha met to discuss their questions, Haroutunian asked them, "Okay, what are you trying to figure out? I mean, do you have a sense of a basic problem emerging yet . . ." (2009, p. 92). Marsha and Paula each responded with their questions. Haroutunian-Gordon tried to understand what each co-leader was trying to communicate and which questions were of most interest to them individually and together.

When a teacher pays close attention to her own genuine questions, this can make teaching more interesting. It seems probable, and accords with my experiences as a teacher and teacher educator, that when students see that their teacher has genuine questions and wants to resolve them, this can stimulate students' learning. A teacher's interest in the material can spread to his or her students. Pursuing their own questions and areas of uncertainty is something for teachers to consider as they plan for their teaching. It is also something for administrators to consider as they evaluate teachers: not knowing everything and a strong desire to discover answers can be strengths in a teacher.

I mentioned in the last section that the experience of being listened to by their teacher may have influenced Paula and Marsha to try to understand the questions that their students were trying to express about the story. Marsha and Paula made a plan and made it explicit to students at the beginning of an interpretive discussion after they prepared with Haroutunian-Gordon. They told the students that they would invite questions, make these clear to all, then go back and ask "how they want to tackle" the four or five questions that students shared (2009, p. 26). They also told the students that the group would decide "what we want to talk about" in the interpretive discussion (2009, p. 137). They gave the elementary students the same freedom that Haroutunian-Gordon gave them to express and choose questions of concern to them in preparing for the discussion. Furthermore, the co-leaders worked to understand what the students were trying to communicate when they asked their questions.

Does this freedom to express one's genuine questions play a role in learning to listen? It could be that the experience of having someone else, and perhaps especially one's teacher, take one's questions seriously helps a person want to listen seriously to others. Also, when a teacher tries to understand her students' questions without limiting their questions, this may help students identify their genuine concerns and also become interested in those of others.

As I have explored in an earlier work (Meadows, 2007), teachers benefit when someone they respect listens to their questions and ideas. Mentorship of new teachers that involves listening carefully to their questions is supportive. Providing opportunities and time for veteran teachers to listen to one another's questions and ideas also supports their desire to teach well. The teacher educator takes interest in finding out what the teacher candidates are interested in and they do the same with their students.

How does a teacher become interested in what her students are interested in? Haroutunian-Gordon writes that Marsha's and Paula's interest in listening to the participants and understanding what they were trying to say increased over the several discussions that they led with them. She argues that "the co-leaders have studied the text and clarified a point of doubt, which increases their desire for help with textual interpretation from the participants" (2009, p. 133). She may mean that because the teacher candidates were interested in getting help with their own pressing concerns, they listened to the students closely. The teacher candidates wanted to learn more about the story and listened carefully to students because the students' ideas could help them resolve their points of doubt about the text. Haroutunian-Gordon's claim is consistent with my experiences leading interpretive discussion.

In addition, those who lead interpretive discussions also take interest in students' ideas and questions for other reasons. It is interesting to me to find out what my students think and what their questions are. This interest stems from my desire to help my students learn more and develop their capabilities to read and reason. The more familiar I am with the text, which happens when I create a cluster of questions based on my most pressing concerns, the more interesting the text is to me. This process of building a cluster of questions also helps me prepare to ask questions of my students to help them deepen their thinking individually and collectively. My questions can help my students discover and generate more ideas. Often, their interest in their own questions and ideas spreads to me and other participants

Ambiguity sparks interest in discussants. Haroutunian-Gordon writes, "A group becomes committed to resolving questions about the meaning of a text when consistency of interpretation is called into question" (2009, p. 55). She may mean that students become clearer about their most pressing questions and more interested in resolving them through encountering conflicting evidence in a text and in their own and one another's interpretations of it. Thus it is essential to choose texts that embody ambiguity—something that teachers can do in other forms of teaching and learning as well. In addition, since ambiguity is an inevitable part of life, it is important to help students learn to work through points of ambiguity productively with the help of others.

Conclusion

In interpretive discussion, "listening" happens when someone tries to understand what another person is trying to communicate. Participants and leaders of interpretive discussion actively try to understand what others are trying to communicate about a text and thus, they listen to one another and engage in a process of learning to listen to one another. Interpretive discussion challenges and provides a productive alternative to the didactic paradigm of teaching and learning.

Using aspects of interpretive discussion can help classroom teachers increase their own interest in their students' ideas and questions, which can help teachers learn to listen more closely to students. This increase of interest happens when teachers identify their own questions about readings and try to resolve these during discussions with their students. Seeking answers to one's own questions also motivates a teacher to listen well to her students' ideas and questions because she can get help resolving her own questions. Likewise, when a teacher asks students what they are interested in, students tend to be more engaged in the discussion and more apt to listen to their classmates' ideas. The importance of a learner (student and teacher) having his or her questions and ideas listened to carefully and taken seriously by a teacher shows in increased motivation for learning. For example, the teacher candidates described by Haroutunian-Gordon (1999), learned to try to understand what their elementary students were trying to communicate by having this same experience with their teacher. They became interested in listening to their students by having their questions be a source of interest to their teacher.

Interpretive discussion helps people learn how to engage in the practices of taking others' ideas seriously, working to understand what people are trying to communicate, identifying common concerns, and working to resolve these concerns together. These practices of listening are fundamental to ameliorating social injustices and working for the well-being of all. (For a further discussion of the ways that interpretive discussion can help us live democratically in a problematic world, please see Meadows 2013.)

Note

1. This definition of listening is based upon Sophie Haroutunian-Gordon's definition of listening in an interpretive discussion: "trying to grasp what another person intends to say" (Haroutunian-Gordon, 2009, p. 129). Haroutunian-Gordon further developed and made pioneering changes to other forms of teaching through discussion including the practice of Shared Inquiry as developed by the Great Books Foundation, the Paideia program developed by Mortimer Adler, and the liberal arts program at the University of Chicago developed by Robert Maynard Hutchins, and Mortimer Adler (Haroutunian-Gordon, 2009, pp. 152–153).

Suggested Reading

Haroutunian-Gordon, S. (1999). *Turning the soul: Teaching through conversation in the high school.* Chicago, IL: The University of Chicago Press.
Haroutunian-Gordon, S. (2009). *Learning to teach through discussion: The art of turning the soul.* New Haven, CT: Yale University Press.

References

Common Core State Standards (2010). Washington, DC: National Governors Association Center for Best Practices and Council of Chief State School Officers.

Haroutunian-Gordon, S. (1999). *Turning the soul: Teaching through conversation in the high school.* Chicago, IL: The University of Chicago Press.

Haroutunian-Gordon, S. (2009). *Learning to teach through discussion: The art of turning the soul.* New Haven, CT: Yale University Press.

Meadows, E. (2007). Transformative learning through open listening: A professional development experience with urban high school teachers. *Learning Inquiry* (1) 115–123.

Meadows, E. (2013). Learning to listen to differences: Democracy, Dewey, and interpretive discussion. *Journal of Curriculum Studies* (online).

Silverstein, S. (1964). *The giving tree.* New York, NY: HarperCollins Publishers.

Shared Inquiry Handbook: A basic guide for discussion leaders and participants (2007). Chicago, IL: Great Books Foundation.

6
_____

Can Listening Be Taught?*

Sophie Haroutunian-Gordon

Northwestern University

Introduction

While the topic of dialogue has fascinated philosophers and philosophers of education since the time of Plato, it is the speaking side of the topic that has received most of the attention—at least until recently (e.g., Burbules (1993), Burbules (2000), Burbules & Bruce (2001), and Haroutunian-Gordon, (1991)). Today, philosophers, as well as psychologists (e.g., Berlak (2004), Lear (2006), educators (McCaslin & Good (1996), Schultz (2003)), and people in other professions have begun to study the heretofore neglected side to dialogue, namely, listening.

In what follows, I begin by defining the term "listening." While there is more than one kind of listening, the listening that takes place in order to learn has a particular character, and I will describe what that is, with brief mention of Plato and Gadamer. As it turns out, listening so as to learn is not easy to do. Furthermore, because listening is so important in carrying out dialogue, it is important to ask: How can listening be learned, and indeed, can it be taught? The large part of the paper will address these questions by examining a dialogue that occurred in school setting. My claim is that participating in dialogue about the meaning of texts teaches people to listen.

Now, in Western philosophy, it is commonplace to think of Plato as the father of dialogic teaching, that is, teaching through conversation between people. Such teaching differs from the circumstance in which the teacher lectures to students about a topic. Plato's portrayals of Socrates in conversation with interlocutors date from the fifth century BCE, and these classic dialogues have a place in the curricula of many academic disciplines belonging to the Western tradition. The image of Socrates as teacher, engaging people of all ages and walks of life in conversation, the object of which was to learn, is no less than iconic.

From Plato and his depictions of Socrates, we learn that dialogic teaching involves listening—a particular kind of listening. Rather than passive, auditory reception of what is heard, the listeners reason about what is heard in relation to a question that they are forming or trying to resolve (Haroutunian-Gordon, 2011). Both the students and the teacher in a dialogic conversation engage in this active listening. The German philosopher, Hans-Georg Gadamer (1985, p. 266), writing nearly 2500 years after Plato, maintains that such listening opens one to a "text"[1]—to an object that provides the listener help in forming and/or answering a question of concern.

How is Listening Taught through Dialogue?

While, thanks to Plato, we have long seen questioning as necessary for learning, we now recognize, with the help of Gadamer, that listening is both central to and a precondition of that questioning. And so we ask: How do we learn to listen, and can such listening be taught?

In the remainder of the paper, I address these questions.[2] I do so by taking an empirical case of dialogic teaching—one in which there is evidence that people are learning to listen. That is, they are learning to hear what is said in relation to a question they form and work to address. The case involves a group of fourteen students and a discussion leader (myself) who are conversing about the meaning of the Nobel Lecture delivered by the American writer, Toni Morrison, on December 7, 1993, in Stockholm, Sweden.

The students and I have gathered to have what I call an "interpretive discussion," that is, discussion about the meaning of a text—in this case, a written document. In an interpretive discussion, leader and discussants try to help each other better understand the meaning of the text. They identify a question about its meaning which they—both the students and the leader—cannot answer. Then, they look at particular passages to find evidence which will help them resolve their question. The purpose of the discussion is not

> *Dialogic teaching involves listening—a particular kind of listening. Rather than passive, auditory reception of what is heard, listeners reason about what is heard in relation to a question that they are forming or trying to resolve.*

to teach students what the discussion leader believes the correct answer to be. Rather, it is to help the members of the group, including the leader, to develop a resolution that is well supported by textual evidence.

As the leader, I prepared for the discussion by developing a *cluster of questions* about the meaning of Toni Morrison's lecture. A cluster of questions consists of a *basic question*—the question about the meaning of the text that I most wish to resolve—and eight *follow-up questions*. These questions point to passages in the text that, if interpreted in at least one way, suggest an idea about the resolution of the *basic question*. All of the questions may be answered in more than one way, given the textual evidence, and so, are called *interpretive questions*. Before the discussion takes place, the students are asked to read the text and write questions that they have about its meaning.

When the leader and participants prepare as described, all come to the discussion seeking help in understanding the text. All have questions about its meaning that they cannot yet wish to answer. No one comes to the discussion as the expert or the authority, although some will have more experience and expertise than others. The assumption is that all have ideas to contribute, and they come together to hear the ideas and test their value through conversation about the text.

Because the participants may have come to different questions in preparing for the interpretive discussion, their first goal, upon meeting, is to arrive at a question about the meaning of the text that most if not all wish to address. I call this question the *shared point of doubt*. Often, it takes a group time to arrive at a *shared point of doubt*, as we will see. Once that question has been identified, the second goal of the discussion is to pursue its resolution by studying parts of the text that seem relevant to it.

Now, in the particular case before us, I was told that the discussion participants had never before engaged in an interpretive discussion. They were about to graduate from high school and so were approximately 18 years of age. Some but not all were planning to go to college. Some had struggled in school, and most came from lower socioeconomic backgrounds. Prior to the discussion, I had met the group members informally on one previous occasion. So, they did not know me, and the text was new to us all.

After learning all of the students' names,[3] I open the discussion by asking them whether they wish to begin with a question they have about the meaning of the text or whether they would like me to pose one.[4] Not surprisingly, because they do not know me and so are hesitant, they ask for my question.

In her Nobel lecture, Toni Morrison tells a story: "Once upon a time, there was an old woman. Blind. Wise. One day, she is visited by some young people who wish to disprove her clairvoyance and show her to be a fraud. One says to her, 'Is the bird I am holding living or dead?' She does not answer, and cannot see her visitors. Finally she replies, 'If it is dead, you have either found it that way or you have killed it. If it is alive, you can still kill it. Whether it is to stay alive, it is your decision. Whatever the case, it is your responsibility.' "

The young people and the old woman converse, and at the end she says, "I trust you now. I trust you with the bird that is not in your hands because you have truly caught it. Look. How lovely it is, this thing that we have done together."

The question that I pose to the students is: Does the old woman come to trust the young people because she hears them trying to learn or because she hears them speaking the truth?

The discussion proceeds and at one point, I say:

Excerpt #1

SHG (1): What does she (the old woman) mean when she says, "It's your responsibility?"

ALAN (1): I think she's saying like, you should know right from wrong.

SHG (2): So that what?

ALAN (2): You should know what you should do and like . . . if something was bad you should know not to do it, and if it's good then you should go on and do it.

SHG (3): So it's your responsibility to know right from wrong?

ALAN (3): Yeah.

SHG (4): Eban, do you agree with that? When [the old woman] says on line 34, "Whatever the case, it's your responsibility," does "It's your responsibility" mean that it's their responsibility to know right from wrong?

EBAN (1): Well . . . Like my [interpretation] of right and wrong may be different from Judy's interpretation of right and wrong. So it's my responsibility to take action for what I believe is right and wrong.

SHG (5): Okay. So you're supposed to take action for what you believe is right and wrong and it means you're supposed to do what's right and wrong or do what's right, I gather.

EBAN (2): Yes.

SHG (6): Okay. Is everybody agreed that that's what taking responsibility is? It's knowing what's right and doing what's right?

When I ask (SHG 1) what the old woman means when she says, "It's your responsibility," the discussants respond. Alan (1) says the old woman believes taking responsibility means knowing right from wrong; Eban (1, 2) says that taking responsibility means doing what you believe is right, even though someone else may disagree with your view of what is right.

Notice that Eban does not answer my question (SHG 1), "What does she (the old woman) mean when she says, 'It's your responsibility'"? Instead of studying the text to find evidence about what the old woman might mean, he draws upon personal experience and explains what he thinks it means to "take responsibility." Alan (1), although he refers to the old woman's view, does not provide textual evidence to support his claim about her view, but like Eban, seems to draw on personal experience to address my question. Neither Alan nor Eban addresses the question I have posed. Instead, they change it.

How do I respond to them? As we will see, I follow several patterns repeatedly—patterns that interpretive discussion leaders typically follow. First, I ask discussants to clarify what they mean. For example, at SHG (2), I ask for clarification of Alan's meaning by saying, "So that?" Here, I want him to say more so that I can get a clearer understanding of what he intended to say at Alan (1).

Second, I repeat back what I understand a speaker to mean.[5] At SHG (3) I say, "So it's your responsibility to know right from wrong?" thereby repeating to Alan what I understand him to be saying. Likewise, at SHG (5), I repeat what I hear Eban saying: "So you're supposed to take action for what you believe is right and wrong and it means you're supposed to do what's right and wrong or do what's right, I gather." In both cases, I offer the discussants the opportunity to correct my understanding of that they have said.

Third, I repeat questions that I have posed previously, for example, at SHG (1) and (4), I ask what the old woman means when she says, "It's your responsibility." Repetition of an unresolved question helps to keep it in focus and allows discussants target their remarks.

Fourth, I repeat ideas I hear and ask others if they agree with the positions. For example, at SHG (4), I repeat the question posed at SHG (1) and ask Eban if he agrees with Alan's response, "It's their responsibility to know right from wrong." I then ask the other group members whether they agree with the ideas that I have heard Alan and Eban express: "Is everybody agreed that that's what taking responsibility is? It's knowing what's right and doing what's right?" (SHG 6).

The purpose of following all of these patterns is the same: I hope to better understand what the participants wish say and to help them and the others in the group do likewise. However, despite good intensions, my listening is not perfect. For example, Eban (1) says, "Like my [interpretation] of right and wrong may be different from Judy's interpretation of right and wrong. So it's my responsibility to take action for what I believe is right and wrong." Here he may mean: "What I believe is right may be different from what Judy believes is right, so taking responsibility is doing what I believe is right." Yet, in an attempt to repeat what Eban has said and ask others if they agree, I ask the group whether taking responsibility means "knowing what's right and doing what's right" SHG (6). My question ignores the relativism in Eban's claim—the idea that each may have a different notion of the morally correct or appropriate thing to do.

Furthermore, at SHG (3), having asked Alan for clarification, I repeat back the idea that he offered at Alan (1)—that responsibility is knowing right from wrong—without adding the clarification that he offered at Alan (2)—responsibility is knowing that you should do what is good. Interestingly enough, Eban, in expressing his position, may have heard Alan's idea, for he says: "So it's my responsibility to take action for what I believe is right and wrong," Eban (1), which seems to mean: If I am responsible, I do what I believe to be the right thing to do.

Now, one might ask: Why, if the first goal of an interpretive discussion is to come to a shared point of doubt about the meaning of the text, do I not shift the focus back to the query I posed at SHG (1)—"What does she (the old woman) mean when she says, 'It's your responsibility' "? After all, that is an interpretive question and addressing it would re-focus the discussion on Toni Morrison's text.

However, because these students were unfamiliar with interpretive discussion, and because I did not know them, I had to learn what they were ready to speak about and help them do it. If the question that concerned them was not an interpretive question, I felt that I needed to follow patterns that would help them express that point of doubt nevertheless.

In the next excerpts, we see the discussants initiating patterns that I had initiated previously. By so doing, the discussants help people to listen—to focus upon a question and to relate what is said to its resolution.

Excerpt #2

CARL (1): Somebody said that responsibility is doing the right thing, always doing the right thing.

SHG (7): Eban said: what you *think* is the right thing, right?

CARL (2): But I can't agree with that because being responsible to me is: you do whatever you have to do to take care whatever the situation is, whether it's negative or positive.

Here, Carl identifies the question that he is addressing. When he says, "Somebody said that responsibility is doing the right thing, always doing the right thing" (Carl 1), he returns to the issue of what it means to take responsibility, setting aside, for the moment at least, the issue of what the old woman in the text means when she says, "Whatever the case, it is your responsibility"—my original question (SHG 1). In addition to stating the question that concerns him, Carl repeats back what he has heard someone say in answer to it (Carl 1). He is therefore initiating two patterns of participation I had initiated previously, namely, posing a question of concern and repeating back what he has heard another say in response to it.

At SHG (7), I continue to follow the patterns: I repeat back the answer I heard from Eban at Eban (1), which differs slightly from what Carl has repeated back. Here, I show that I have heard the relativism is Eban's remark after all. In so doing, I offer the possibility that there may be a difference between the claim that taking responsibility means "doing the right thing" (Carl 1) and doing what "you think" is the right thing—the idea I heard Eban express at Eban (1). I ask Eban whether he made the latter statement because I want to be sure that I am remembering his position correctly. I am also underscoring the importance to hearing differences as well as similarities between positions that people express.

At (Carl 2), Carl makes clear that from his perspective, taking responsibility does not mean doing the right thing or even doing what you believe is the right thing. Rather, it is "doing what you have to do to take care of whatever the situation is, whether it is negative or positive." Perhaps he is saying: taking responsibility means doing what you think the situation calls for, whether or not you are doing something that is morally correct. In so saying, Carl points a difference between his view and another that he has heard.

Larry, the next speaker, tries to clarify Carl's position by following a pattern previously initiated by the leader.

Excerpt #3:

LARRY (1): And you're responsible for the negativity too.

SHG (8): What does it mean to be responsible for the negativity, Larry?

LARRY (2): Like you have to face the consequences and then be responsible for them, for whatever you do.

SHG (9): Okay, I see you nodding [SHG looks at Carl]. Do you think that's right?

CARL (3): Uh-huh [Yes].

SHG (10): Okay, so you've got to face the consequences.

Larry (1) repeats back part of what he has heard Carl say when he says, "And you are responsible for the negativity too." In initiating that pattern, he indicates both that he has heard this part of Carl's position and that he agrees with it. But what does Larry mean by "responsible for the negativity"? And does he mean the same thing that Carl meant when he said, "you do whatever you have to do to take care whatever the situation is, whether it's negative or positive"?

I am unclear as to whether Carl and Larry hold the same position, so I ask Larry what he means (SHG 8). Having heard Larry's answer, I turn to look at Carl and see him nodding affirmatively (SHG 9). To confirm my interpretation of his gesture, I ask Carl directly whether he agrees with Larry, and he indicates that he does.

In what follows we see more evidence that the discussants are learning to listen and by initiating useful patterns, helping others, including me, to do likewise.

Excerpt #4

(SHG 11) You said you've got to think about what's good for everybody—That was Carl's idea, right Carl?

CARL (4): [That was] somebody else . . . That was Sonya.

SHG (12): That was Sonya. I thought you said that too. Okay, so say again what you said.

CARL (5): That responsibility isn't necessarily that you have to be positive about what you're doing. You just have to take care of whatever you have to take care of, whether it be negative or positive.

At SHG (11), I try to repeat back to Carl what I have heard him say— "You've got to think about what's good for everybody." Carl (4) says that I have repeated Sonya's position, not his. Here, it is Carl, not I, who seems to hear a difference between two positions—his and Sonya's. At SHG (12), I indicate that I hear the two positions to be similar in meaning, so I ask Carl to restate his position. Carl tries to clarify his view (Carl 5). I am struggling to hear what each speaker means to say, and Carl and Larry come to the rescue:

Excerpt #5

SHG (13): Okay, so you have to take care of what you're supposed to take of. All right. And, Larry, your point was . . . that if it's negative?

LARRY (3): That if it's negative or positive you still have to be responsible for it.

SHG (14): Okay, all right.

CARL (6): Repercussions.

SHG (15): So what I hear coming out of several of these [comments] is that being responsible involves paying attention to what happens *after* you do [something] . . . Being responsible isn't just doing what you think is right . . . It's being concerned about what happens when you do what you've done.

When Carl says, "Repercussions," (Carl 6), he helps me to hear that in explaining what it means to take responsibility, he and Larry are focused upon the consequences of one's actions, whereas others (like Alan, Eban, and perhaps Sonya), have focused upon the moral justification for the action—whether one thinks that what one is about to do is morally right, or will affect everyone well. Hence, my statement at SHG (15): "So what I hear coming out of several of these [comments] is that . . . Being responsible isn't just doing what you think is right . . . It's being concerned about what happens when you do what you've done."

Here, Carl and Larry have helped me clarify what has been said in response to the question of what it means to "take responsibility." At SHG (13), I repeat back, almost verbatim, what I have heard Carl say, indicating that I am unsure about exactly what he means. I then ask Larry directly to state his point, hoping to hear its relation to Carl's, and he answers my question (Larry 3). Carl (6) repeats back the idea that he hears Larry offering—"repercussions." His doing so finally enables me to distinguish between the difference between the views that he and Larry, on the one hand, and Alan, Eban, and perhaps Sonya, on the other hand, hold. And I specify that difference at SHG (15).

Conclusion

As it turns out, these students do not talk about the meaning of Toni Morrison's text in the excerpts above. Indeed, they shift the question that I offer initially to a different one, namely: What does it mean to take responsibility? Nevertheless, the evidence suggests that if by "listening" we mean drawing inferences about the meaning of what one hears in relation to the question that one is forming or addressing, then indeed, people can learn to listen, and furthermore, listening can be taught.

We have seen the leader and discussants teach each other to listen by following and initiating patterns that focus attention on things that have been said or requesting particular kinds of utterances to be made. These patterns include: (1) asking people directly what they mean; (2) repeating back what one understands them to mean; (3) repeating questions posed previously if they have not been resolved and are still of concern; (4) repeating what has been said and asking others if they agree with it; (5) identifying similarities and differences between the positions/questions that one has heard. By following these patterns, speakers direct attention toward particular aspects of the utterances. And when the attention is so directed, questions may be posed that help a speaker to clarify his/her position and help others to grasp it.

So even though they were not illuminating the meaning of Morrison's text in the excerpts we have seen, they were teaching each other to listen. Indeed, they were doing so by following patterns that later in the discussion *did* yield interpretation of the text.

Notes

*A version of the present paper presented at Fudan University, Shanghai, China, January.

1. A text may be a written document, an artefact, set of statistical data, the remarks of another—any object that has enough ambiguity to permit its meaning to be questioned and explored.

2. The reader will find views critical of my perspective in Waks (2007), and Rud and Garrison (2007).

3. The students and I sit in a circle of chairs when having an interpretive discussion. I quickly learn their names in the following way: one student starts by stating his or her name. The student to his or her right then recites the previous student's name and follows it with his or her own. The third student recites the first two students' names in the same order and then adds his or her name to the list. The procedure is repeated until all students have repeated their names and those of the speakers before them. I am the last person to state my name, and I recite all of the discussants' names before so doing.

4. An interpretive discussion opens with the *basic question* that the leader has prepared or with a question that one of the discussants offers. In either case, the goal is the same: to come to *a shared point of doubt* about the meaning of the text and pursue its resolution.

5. I refer here to what O'Connor and Michaels (2007) call "revoicing."

Suggested Reading

Haroutunian-Gordon, S. (1991). *Turning the soul: Teaching through conversation in the high school.* Chicago, IL: University of Chicago Press.

Haroutunian-Gordon, S. (2009). *Learning to teach through discussion: The art of turning the soul.* New Haven, CT: Yale University Press.

References

Berlak, A. C. (2004). Confrontation and pedagogy: Cultural secrets, trauma, and emotion in antioppressive pedagogies. In M. Boler (Ed.), *Democratic dialogue in education: Troubling speech, disturbing silence (Counterpoints: Studies in the postmodern theory of education)* (pp. 123–144). New York, NY: Peter Lang Publishing.

Burbules, N. C. (1993). *Dialogue in teaching: Theory and practice.* New York, NY: Teachers College Press.

Burbules, N. C. (2000). The limits of dialogue as a critical pedagogy. In P. Trifonas (Ed.), *Revolutionary pedagogies: Cultural politics, education, and the discourse of theory* (pp. 251–273). New York, NY: Routledge.

Burbules, N. C., & Bruce, B. C. (2001). Theory and research on teaching as dialogue. In V. Richardson (Ed.), *Handbook of research on teaching* (4th ed., 1102–1121). Washington, DC: American Educational Research Association.

Burbules, N. C., & Rice, S. (1991). Dialogue across differences: Continuing the conversation. *Harvard Educational Review*, 61(4), 393–416.

Fiumara, G. C. (1990). *The other side of language: A philosophy of listening*. London: Routledge.

Gadamer, H. G. (1985). *Truth and method*. (Sheed and Ward, Ltd., trans.). New York, NY: The Crossroad Publishing Company. (Original work published 1960.)

Garrison, J. (1996). A Deweyan theory of democratic listening. *Educational Theory*, 46(4), 435–439.

Haroutunian-Gordon, S. (1991). *Turning the soul: Teaching through conversation in the high school*. Chicago, IL: University of Chicago Press.

Haroutunian-Gordon, S. (2009). *Learning to teach through discussion: The art of turning the soul*. New Haven, CT: Yale University Press.

Haroutunian-Gordon, S. (2011). Plato's philosophy of listening. In S. Haroutunian-Gordon, & M. Laverty (Eds.), Listening: An exploration of philosophical traditions. *Educational Theory*, special issue, forthcoming.

Haroutunian-Gordon, S., & Waks, L. (Eds.) (2011). Listening: Challenges for teachers. *Teachers College Record* special issue, 113(10). (online; forthcoming in paper).

Lear, J. (2006). *Radical hope: Ethics in the face of cultural devastation*. Cambridge, MA: Harvard University Press.

McCaslin, M. M., & Good, T. L. (1996). *Listening in classrooms*. New York, NY: HarperCollins College Publishers.

O'Connor, C., & Michaels, S. (2007). When is dialogue 'dialogic'? *Human Development*, 50(5), 275–285.

Rud, A. G., & Garrison, J. (2007). The continuum of listening. *Learning Inquiry*, 1(2), 163–168.

Schultz, K. (2003). *Listening: A framework for teaching across differences*. New York, NY: Teachers College Press.

Thompson, A. (2003). Listening and its asymmetries. *Curriculum Inquiry*, 33(1), 79–100.

Waks, L. (2007). Listening and questioning: The apophatic/cataphatic distinction revisited. *Learning Inquiry*, 1(2), 153–162.

7

Listening for Discussion

The Conference Method or Harkness Pedagogy

David I. Backer

Teachers College Columbia University

Introduction

Harkness pedagogy celebrated its 80th birthday in 2011. Though the "pedagogy" (it is variously described as a mode, method, and style of teaching) is relatively old and widely used, little has been written about it by those unaffiliated with its birthplace, Phillips-Exeter Academy. The present essay, then, has two aims. First, it aims to introduce Harkness pedagogy to academic audiences interested in pedagogies of listening and discussion. Drawing on archival documents, original manuals composed by Harkness teachers, and relevant philosophy the paper sketches the pedagogy's history and practice. Second, the paper will establish that there is a mode of listening unique to Harkness pedagogy called *listening for discussion.*

I first heard about Harkness pedagogy from a friend. He was listening to me complain about how my high school seniors would not listen to me. I was teaching Theory of Knowledge, part of the International Baccalaureate Diploma Program, at an American international school in Quito, Ecuador. My job, essentially, was to facilitate discussions with students about topics of interest. As a young ignorant gringo, only a few years older than my students and with little experience of their culture, I was teaching a class of which very few understood the point—so they did not listen.

I was going to try something new, though. I had noticed that these seniors—waiting for graduation already in October—would discuss amongst themselves. They would have fruitful and interesting discussions despite me, listening and speaking to one another in turns as I was trying to get class started. My idea was this: I would take myself out of the center of attention. I would give them a topic to talk about or a text to read and let them discuss it. If I could get out of the way, then maybe they would discuss interesting things as part of the class instead of despite the class. But I was not sure about the details or how to get started.

I ended my rant with a sigh. My friend nodded and said something very heartening. He said he had a friend at another international school who taught in the way I had described: letting students discuss. I listened intently. He said this friend had given him packets of information about the pedagogy, which were sitting in a drawer in his desk. My friend promised to drop the packets off at my classroom the next day. He did. The packet was on Harkness teaching. My friend's friend got it from the Exeter Humanities Institute (EHI), a professional development seminar at Phillips-Exeter Academy in New Hampshire devoted to student-centered discussion. I read it and put it to use. I became somewhat obsessed with it. A year later I studied the history and efficacy of Harkness teaching for my master's thesis, and two years later I attended the EHI just as I began researching the philosophy of discussion as a doctoral student.

I tell this story because "letting students discuss" defines Harkness teaching and the particular variety of listening it requires. Had I never felt the need to get out of the way I would not have approached my friend with my problem; nor would I have been ready to listen to what he had to say; nor would I have found and followed a research interest that, only very recently, has brought into focus what "getting out of the way" really means.

What it means, or what it points to at least, is a tension in teaching. The direct presence of a teacher's voice, the authority of it, can decrease the quality of the learning that occurs or even prevent learning from occurring at all. This is (nearly) a paradox,[1] as learning is stereotypically what's supposed to happen from and around teachers. The fact that a teacher's voice, his or her authority as a teacher, could prevent quality learning from occurring tragically undermines the whole enterprise; which is what happened to me in Ecuador, I believe.

Harkness teaching, or what was once called the Conference Method, is a response to this tension. After a brief history of the pedagogy, I will situate the pedagogy into the wider field of research on teaching discussion. I will then propose three general rules for practicing Harkness pedagogy, with illustrative concepts and vignettes. My concluding thought will be that there is a kind of listening peculiar to Harkness, listening for *discussion*, which permits a group to address a question in common through an equal and various sequence of turns.

History of the Pedagogy

In the mid-1920s Edward Harkness and Lewis Perry met on a train and started chatting.[2] They discovered that they were both going to the same wedding, and that they were both interested in education. The former was the son of Stephen Harkness, second only to Rockefeller in nineteenth-century oil wealth, and had decided to give away vast sums of his inherited fortune to elite educational institutions in the United States. The latter was the principal of one such institution: Phillips-Exeter Academy, perhaps the oldest and most prestigious of the New England boarding schools.

Having just received a huge gift from Exeter alumnus Colonel M. Thompson, Perry was on the lookout for more funding to build better dormitories and facilities for his school. Harkness was known for giving vast sums to universities for pedagogical and curricular improvement, most notably Harvard and Yale, where he funded the reorganization of those colleges into house systems and expanded their campuses. (He also funded the construction of Columbia University's Butler Library.) The two men developed a correspondence. In 1928, Harkness hinted that he might be interested in giving to Exeter, but wanted a thorough proposal for how the money would be used. Perry made extensive preparations for a grant proposal, including a trip to England to research the boys schools there (a suggestion from Harkness) and the formation of a committee at Exeter devoted exclusively to pedagogical proposals. Perry sent the document later that year. Harkness, much to Perry's frustration, rejected it somewhat vehemently. It was this rejection, sent from a pseudonym to protect Harkness's identity, which would form the core of what is now called Harkness teaching.

"A major challenge in discussion-based teaching is modulating the authoritative voice of the teacher."
—*EHI Handbook*

Edward Harkness would not give Exeter money unless Perry accommodated his vision of students sitting in a circle around a single table, where a teacher taught by listening and talking to them. This can be understood as a desire to replace the traditional didactic—lecture and recitation—method of teaching with a pedagogy of discussion.

Perry rushed to assuage the billionaire. Reflecting on Harkness's strongly worded letter, the principal stressed to his committees of teachers the importance of making proposals that would satisfy Harkness's adamant vision, underscoring one central requirement that Harkness would not drop: the conference method.

Perry gathered another faculty committee together to rewrite the proposal, emphasizing a section proposing to hire 25 new teachers, train them in a new method of teaching based on "conferring," and design classrooms for the purpose. In the fall of 1929, just before the infamous stock market crash that would yield the Great Depression, Harkness agreed to give Perry one of the single highest gifts ever handed to a secondary school: $5.8 million ($77,981,424 in 2013 dollars).

Perry went on to build new buildings and order special Conference Method tables (for which there remains a company that specially constructs them). Teachers began training in a new method of teaching: sitting around the tables instead of standing and leading recitations. An English teacher named Frank Cushwa, who headed a team committed to integrating the conference method in classrooms, quoted in a personal letter the words of a teacher who had adopted this new method in 1931,[3] which, to those who practice it, may still be true today:

> Sitting in a group about a table instead of in formal rows of seats has abolished almost completely the stiff duality which used to obtain between instructor and class, when, I am afraid, his elevation on a platform tended to hedge him about with too much dignity and make him somewhat unapproachable . . . and which did tend to make the student still less articulate. The very naturalness of the new arrangement, besides being more comfortable, has in good part wiped out that class-consciousness.[4] Now, there is a freedom of discussion, an eagerness to participate, that I never saw before, the value of which to both student and instructor is incalculable.

Eight decades later this conference method, on which the billionaire had so adamantly insisted, is still a "core ethos of the entire school" (Smith & Foley, 2009, pp. 477–496).

Harkness Teaching in Context

Despite its relatively long history, little research has been published about Harkness teaching by academics outside Phillip-Exeter Academy. A high school teacher has written one short article mentioning its success in his American history classroom (Mullgardt, 2008). Another high school teacher has praised the pedagogy for its potential in ESL classrooms (Sevigny, 2012). A legal scholar has written an essay speculating that Harkness could improve the law school experience (Courchesne, 2005). Beyond that, very little. One major essay does exist, but, like much of the writing about Harkness teaching, it was co-authored by Exeter employees—Lawrence Smith and Margaret Foley—and appeared only recently, in 2009. By no means exhaustive, Smith and Foley's article appears, at this writing, to be one of the only peer-reviewed texts that deals explicitly with what the conference method looks like, how to do it, and what distinguishes it from other ways of teaching. What follows will knit this account together with the wider literature on discussion.

The Conference Method and Discussion

Stripped of its history and unique locale, Harkness teaching is another name for what educators have for nearly a century identified as teaching discussion. The literature on this subject is huge. Below are a few key distinctions from that literature separating discussion-based teaching from other methods, each of which help to place Harkness in a wider research context.

Starting broadly, Harkness teaching is dialogical rather than monological. Though Burbules and Bruce warn against taking this dichotomy too seriously, it serves to locate pedagogies that emphasize "ongoing discursive involvement of participants, constituted in a relation of reciprocity and reflexivity" (Burbules & Bruce, 2001, p. 18). Discussion, along with conversation, debate, seminar, dialectic, bull session, etc., is located in this realm of teaching practices. Within this realm there are important differences between the kinds of dialogical practices just listed. James T. Dillon gives an exact account of how discussion differs from these other kinds of educational interaction, defining discussion as "group address of a question in common" (Dillon, 1994, p. 8). Discussion is not wandering talk that jumps from topic to topic (conversation); it is not competitive talk between two positions (debate); nor is it a group rant or bull session. Importantly, as Harkness himself specified in his letter to Perry, discussion is not what takes place when a teacher asks a question, listens to a student response, vocally evaluates the response, and follows up with another question (recitation). While Walton makes the observation that back-and-forth talking (dialogue) can shift in and out of these modes, Dillon is clear that each mode is distinct from the others (Walton, 1992, p. 56). Discussion, in this essay, is—following Dillon—what takes place when a group addresses a question in common. To avoid recitation, the whole group must come up with the question. Practically, this requires that the students talk with one another as much or more than they talk with the teacher during class time. In Dillon's terms, this requires an equality and variety in the sequence of turns taken during the interaction. No single participant (whether student or teacher) will speak after other participants more or less in this formulation.[5]

This last criterion indicates one last distinction which situates Harkness teaching in the discussion literature: student-centered vs. teacher-centered pedagogy. Student-centered pedagogies tend to follow models of Vygotskyian distributed cognition, Peircian community of inquiry, and/or the democratic-theoretical traditions of educational communication represented by John Dewey and later David Bridges. Each of these approaches de-center the teacher position in the classroom, differentiating discussion from Socratic dialogue, for example, where the teacher acts as a kind of gatekeeper with respect to student comments. In other words, teachers in student-centered pedagogy (as I discovered in Ecuador) permit students to interact with one another rather than compelling them to interact exclusively with or through the mediation of the teacher.

Harkness teaching is therefore a dialogical, student-centered style that prioritizes group address of a question in common in equal and various turns. This formulation accords with Smith and Foley, who write that Harkness teaching means:

> leading student-centered discussions in class, finding ways to get students to make the discoveries for themselves, to get them to draw their own conclusions, to teach them how to consider all sides of an argument, and to make up their own minds based on analysis of the material at hand. Harkness teaching tries to develop in students their own sense of responsibility for their education. The teacher is the cultivator of that sense of responsibility, rather than the fount of information and analysis. (Smith & Foley, 2009, pp. 477–496)

Cultivating this sense of responsibility and practicing Harkness/discussion-based teaching requires a particular set of behaviors. The literature on discussion is replete with tips and tricks, and Harkness teachers have their own. Below is one general idea—"modulated authority"—present in the manuals on Harkness teaching distributed at the Exeter Humanities Institute. We can extrapolate three rules for practicing Harkness pedagogy from this general concept of modulated authority, which together converge on a unique kind of listening: listening for discussion.

Near the beginning of the handbook given to teachers at the Exeter Humanities Institute, there is a section entitled "sample strategies for discussion." One of these sample strategies is "keeping quiet."

Keeping Quiet: A major challenge in discussion-based teaching is modulating the authoritative voice of the teacher. These strategies may help you combat the natural tendency the students have to listen for, and to, your voice.

- Invite students to take responsibility, to be clear when they change subjects in the flow of discussion, rather than looking to you to clarify transitions.

- When the class has gained its own dynamic and degree of familiarity, sit away from the table on occasion, or outside the circle. Say to the students that you understand how demanding your absence may be but you think they are up to the challenge.

- Tell the students that you are the scribe/recorder of the day and will make every effort to be quiet and listen to their thoughts; leave time at the end of the class to summarize those thoughts and show them the diagram you make of the class. It's refreshing sometimes to free yourself from the content and record the statistical aspects of discussion, the patterns of address and response.

- Gesture to the rest of the table when a student seems to have eye contact only for you. Occasionally say something like: "Are you talking to Camilla who just spoke? Then look at her, not me." Though students address the teacher, they are, at times, addressing the class through you. (EHI Handbook, 2001, p. 3)

Not all Harkness teachers would point to this as being an essential strategy for Harkness teaching. Many might even object to it. I exaggerate the importance of this sample strategy however because, from all those in the manual, it touches on the core principles of Harkness teaching that I have observed both as a researcher and teacher of Harkness method.

Conceptually, the pedagogy hinges on this idea of "modulating the authoritative voice of the teacher," or "modulated authority." Practically speaking, modulating authoritative voice entails shifting or changing the kind of thing a teacher is authoritative about during class. The Harkness teacher should modulate from being an authority about *content* to being an

> "When the class has gained its own dynamic and degree of familiarity, sit away from the table on occasion, or outside the circle. Say to the students that you understand how much more demanding your absence may be but that you think they are up to the challenge."
>
> —*EHI Handbook*

authority about the *process* of learning, guiding the way in which students go about learning as opposed to what it is they learn. There are a number of ways to guide the process rather than the content of learning, which Harkness teachers themselves describe later in the handbook. For example, Peter Greer, an English teacher at Exeter, does not "make eye contact with the students when they are talking."

> I scan the room to judge the engagement of other students, I look down, I flip through the text, I look into the center of the table, but I rarely look at the student who is speaking because I know that he or she is then likely to look back at me.[6]

In this case, preventing eye contact is one way to modulate teacher authority. If students do not make eye contact with the teacher, s/he will be less likely to guide the content of learning during the interaction. Similarly, when asked "When did you first think of yourself as a Harkness teacher?" Becky Moore, an English teacher, responded, "The first time I sat quietly without getting nervous while students thought and then began the conversation again in a useful and detailed way—without my prompting . . . ." Moore does not prompt the students, nor does she instill within them a "proper" way of thinking. Rather, without any reservation or "nervousness," she allows the students to talk amongst themselves. Moore elaborates in another response that "the students' ideas [in a Harkness discussion] are to structure the outcome . . . students eventually choose, steer, junk, embrace, and clarify ideas." It is the students, not the teacher, who "structure" the outcome in a Harkness discussion. While the teacher may guide the way in which students talk (who has said what to whom), the students have direct purview over their own concepts during class time.

Margaret Foley, the history teacher who co-authored the 2009 essay with Smith, writes in the handbook that "how much and when I intervene is a constant issue for debate in my mind and one that I feel pretty insecure about. . . ." By "intervention" Foley may mean both speaking about the content or process of student interaction, which would be a more radical modulation of teacher authority: complete non-intervention. Commenting on the theme of intervention, Kathy Brownback writes that she plays "a pretty significant role in a lot of discussions, less in others, but [I] try to make sure it's not to interject my own point of view, as much as to open questions or ideas that no one has yet brought up yet. . . ." Here is a less radical form of modulation: when the teacher interjects new avenues for students' thinking. Despite this "significant role" Brownback claims to play during discussion, she admits that "the less the classroom is about me either personally or as the teacher the better off we seem to do." In this case we still have modulated authority as a value or guiding ideal for the teachers' behavior. Bruce Pruitt phrases the ideal in a different way, claiming that being a Harkness teacher requires "a sense of humor . . . sensitivity to group dynamics, individual needs. Humility." Modulating authority, particularly when one already has authority, entails a humble sensitivity to individual needs. In this way, the teacher permits an equal and various sequence of turns, thereby helping a group to form and address a question.

Each teacher, in different ways, describes how to work against the students' tendency to rely on a teacher's authority for content. Thus the power of "keeping quiet." Permitting student discussion therefore means "leaving it up to them" and "letting it go," two tropes which iterate throughout the EHI manual as well as Smith and Foley's essay on Harkness teaching. Tracking, another important tactic ("being the scribe of the day") is what a teacher can do to both express and modulate her authority. "Among our various tracking devices," Smith and Foley write,

> are those to track types of comments, types of questions, types of interruptions, gender interaction, body language, number of comments, length of comments, text references, name usage, length of silences, and individual participation; it all depends on what it is that the observer or teacher wants to see.

During class, a Harkness teacher may be seen writing notes about any or all of these behaviors and referring to them every during class. Their role is to be a kind of mirror for the students, so that the group can think more clearly about where it is going and why it is going there.

Three Principles of Harkness Teaching

Reflecting on the ideas and observations above, these rules for Harkness teaching stand out:

(1) *Let it go and leave it up to them*: A Harkness teacher must relinquish some control of classroom events, allowing the group as a whole to "share in the administration"[7] of the educational outcome.

(2) *Track*: A Harkness teacher, like a sociologist of the classroom, must produce some account (or trace) of what occurred during

class. This typically takes the form of detailed notes on the kind, frequency, and quality/substance of comments, as well as other paralinguistic behaviors.

(3) *Learn through discussion*: The Harkness teacher's goal is to create discussion, which is group address of a question in common through an equal and various sequence of turns taken. The aim is for all participants to learn in this distinct way.

Listening for Discussion

There is a kind of listening unique to this pedagogy. Harkness listening, or what I will call listening for discussion, is a form of relational listening, as discussed in the introduction, since it "improves" or changes the quality of relations among a group when the teacher listens in this way. The relational change that listening for discussion creates however happens both between individual members of the discussion, like the teacher and student, and at the level of the group as a whole. Building on what has already been said, to teach Harkness one must listen for modulated authority. Smith and Foley give a complex but evocative metaphor to describe this kind of listening:

> If you have ever read about switches in computers, braved the language in a Microsoft manual, or tried to decipher a "Help" page on the Internet, you find that much of a computer's function and operation depends on a series of switches. To present this in an overly simplistic image, the information enters a computer and immediately comes to a switch. Depending on the information and the computer settings, the information goes either "left" or "right" (for lack of better terms) and then immediately comes to a new switch, and will either go "left" or "right," after which comes another switch, and will go "left" or "right," etcetera, etcetera, ad infinitum. Eventually, a nanosecond later, the computer completes processing and outputs the resulting data, or solution. The next time the computer handles information, even if the input is similar, it will probably not follow the exact path of the previous sequence. Regardless of whether the solutions are similar or different, the path that the information takes will not be the same as it was before. This same concept works when trying to imagine of the function of a Harkness teacher's brain. The teacher listens to the discussion and has to make a decision: "Do I step in here?" or "Do I let

them go and see what develops?" If the teacher does step in, he/she immediately has to decide, "Do I stop the conversation to fill in some background?" or "Do I keep the conversation going and just give them a quick reminder?" . . . the path of the discussion is invariably going to be different class to class, and teachers must accept and embrace these differences if the discoveries and understanding of the material is going to be left up to the student.

In this metaphor, the teacher's brain must follow students as they make their way through a discussion, just as information passes through a computer. This will happen in unique ways from group to group, day to day, subject to subject. Listening, for the Harkness teacher, means "listening for modulated authority." Using the rules mentioned earlier, this means listening in order to leave learning up to students. It means listening to track the ways in which they themselves learn. Finally, as Smith and Foley imply above and as the third rule states, this means listening for *discussion*, in Dillon's sense. This isn't listening for recitation of facts or opinions, listening for debate between two competing positions, or listening for conversation that wanders from topic to topic. It means listening such that the group addresses a question in common. Listening for discussion is therefore a kind of relational listening: one that creates the conditions for a group to form between teachers and students.

> "The whole time I was thinking 'when should I say something . . . shut up . . . shut up . . . don't talk.'"
>
> —Anonymous teacher in the beginning stages of learning Harkness, EHI Handbook

Rather than expressing and maintaining his or her authority, when the teacher listens to discussion, s/he modulates authority to permit an equal and various sequence in the turns taken during the interaction. "Listening for discussion" can accordingly be contrasted to listening in traditional didactic pedagogy. When students and teacher speak and listen in turn, as Aristotle writes of constitutional democracy, it will appear—though briefly—as though as they are "different persons." When a teacher modulates authority in the way that Harkness listening requires, s/he distributes the authority which the teacher accrues in such a way as to create a situation where students teach and teachers learn, recalling Freire's famous formulation of the "students/teachers and teachers/students" (Freire, 2000, n.p.) Though the teacher will remain in control of certain facets of the situation beyond the interaction, such as grading and curriculum, traditional didacticism permutes into a different relation in the moment of discussion—so long as s/he listens for it.

Conclusion

As a teacher in Ecuador, I experienced firsthand the (near) paradox mentioned at the start of this essay. The more I talked, the more I tried to engage my students in discussion, the less engaged they became. When I got out of the way and let them talk about something without my direct presence, however, they came up with insightful questions they were able to discuss amongst themselves as I listened and took notes on what they said. It wasn't perfect of course, but I could sense that the "revolution in methods" Edward Harkness prescribed roughly 80 years ago occurred there in my classroom. This revolution, described by scholars and educators for more than a century, is that of teaching discussion—of which Harkness teaching is one style or mode. This style of teaching requires a particular kind of listening—listening for discussion—that permits students to share in the administration of an educational outcome, tracks specific behaviors, and ensures that learning occurs through group address of a question in common.

Notes

1. cf. Santoro (2008). ". . . the problem of pedagogical authority is 'the pedagogical paradox.' [Gert Biesta] explains that 'child-centered pedagogy has tried to circumvent the paradox by excluding authority from education, arguing that the only road *to* freedom is *through* freedom. In its most extreme forms it has thereby eradicated pedagogy altogether.'"

2. Conversation with Edouard DeRochers, July 31 2012. Harkness's personal papers are notoriously spare and only a few records are kept in the archives at Exeter. I thank Edouard for his guidance and help in the archival work done for this piece.

3. Undated facsimile of letter signed by Cushwa from Philips-Exeter Archive, accessed July 31 2012.

4. Though he does not say it explicitly, there is a political quality to Cushwa's phrasing that should be noted: "class-consciousness" sounds like a play on the Marxist concept of class consciousness. Harkness teaching does evoke radical formulations of democracy, which I mention later in the chapter.

5. Socrates, for instance, typically follows up each comment during a dialogue. An interlocutor will speak, then Socrates will speak, then another interlocutor will speak, after which Socrates responds. This is not an equal and various sequence of turns. See Dillon, J. T. (1990, 14).

6. The following series of quotations are taken from the *EHI Handbook*, 2011.

7. cf. Aristotle's *Politics*, 1261b. The implications for social justice in Harkness teaching have yet to be expressed fully. The types of behaviors required for a Harkness

discussion at least prepare and at most enact behaviors sufficient for an Aristotelian formulation of constitutional democracy. When students are permitted to share in the educational outcome that will affect them, their process of interaction itself is democratic. Listening for discussion, on the part of the Harkness teacher, therefore, creates the conditions for this kind of democracy to emerge between students. Rather than merely talking about democracy, students enact democracy in the form of their interaction as they discuss the subject matter.

Suggested Reading

Smith, L. A., & Foley, M. (2009). Partners in a human enterprise: Harkness teaching in the history classroom. *History Teacher,* 42(4), 477–496.

References

Biesta, G. (1997). Revolutions that as yet have no model: Performance pedagogy and its audience. *Philosophy of Education,* 198–200.

Burbules, N. C., & Bruce, B. C. (2001). Theory and research on teaching as dialogue. In V. Richardson (Ed.), *Handbook of research on teaching.* 4th ed. (pp. 1102–121). Washington, DC: American Educational Research Association. *Google Scholar.* Web. May 2012.

Courchesne, C. G. (2005). A suggestion of a fundamental nature: Imagining a legal education of solely electives taught as discussions [Electronic version]. *Rutgers Law Record,* 29, 21–64.

Dillon, J. T. (1990). *The practice of questioning.* Taylor & Francis. Print. International Ser. on Communication Skills.

Dillon, J. T. (1994). *Using discussion in classrooms.* Open UP.

Freire, P. (2000). *The pedagogy of the oppressed.* Continuum.

Gomez, D. S. (2008). Women's proper place and student-centered pedagogy. *Studies in Philosophy of Education,* 27, 313–33.

Mullgardt, B. (2008). Introducing and using the discussion (aka Harkness) table. *Independent Teacher: The eJournal for Independent School Educators,* 6(1). Retrieved from http://www.independentteacher.org/vol6/6.1-5-Harkness-Table.html.

Sevigny, P. (2012). Extreme discussion circles: Preparing ESL students for "the Harkness method." *Polyglossia,* 23.

Smith, L. A., & Foley, M. (2009). Partners in a human enterprise: Harkness teaching in the history classroom. *History Teacher,* 42(4), 477–496.

Walton, D. N. (1992). *The Place of Emotion in Argument,* University Park, PA. Penn State Press.

Part II

Listening in New and Emerging Pedagogies

Listening in the Pedagogy of Discomfort

A Framework for Socially Just Listening

Ashley Taylor

Syracuse University

Introduction

The "pedagogy of discomfort" arises out of educators' concerns that classroom practices of dialogue and discussion relating to difficult issues—such as racism, sexism, heterosexism, ableism, and classism—frequently reproduce rather than disrupt students' taken-for-granted ways of seeing the world and understanding the injustices that permeate our educational institutions and practices. Consider the following story (adapted from one described by Berlak, 2005). Ms. Franklin, a white teacher in a seventh grade classroom, observes that one of her students, Sandra, is frequently angry and distracted during class, unable to answer Ms. Franklin's questions or concentrate on reading or writing exercises. As Sandra's grades begin to slip, Ms. Franklin resolves to learn from Sandra what is causing her behavior. Sandra explains that she is angry and unfocused because the girl sitting in front of her is tormenting her by swishing her long blond hair across Sandra's desk. Sandra, an African-American girl, tells the teacher that her classmate Rachel, a white girl, is doing it because Rachel is white and Sandra is black. Ms. Franklin, being familiar with the petty behaviors of seventh graders and having a strong commitment to a "work hard, be nice"[1] motto, explains to Sandra that she ought to take the higher moral ground and ignore Rachel's behaviors. She tells Sandra that there will be many people in her life whom she will find disagreeable and that it is better to learn how to tolerate them now. Separately, she takes Rachel aside and chastises her for her behavior, telling her that she ought to be more respectful and repeating her lesson about tolerance.

Ms. Franklin decides not to outwardly acknowledge Sandra's reference to race. Perhaps privately, Ms. Franklin thinks to herself that Sandra is using race as an excuse for her undisciplined behavior, or, perhaps, she is uncomfortable with Sandra's mention of race, having been raised to think that talking about race is impolite and imprudent. While for Sandra the experience of noticing—and being noticed by—racial differences is commonplace and therefore seeing race as a factor in Rachel's behavior is a reasonable response, given her experiences, Ms. Franklin sees it as inappropriate, even dangerous. The consequence of this interpretive difference is that Sandra's felt experience of racism—and perhaps that of other students—goes unrecognized within Ms. Franklin's classroom, just as "color-blind" (see Lewis, 2001) or race-ignorant messages about hard work, discipline, and attitude are made paramount. Both Sandra and Rachel therefore learn that character and attitude are more important than one's race when it comes to being a successful person, a message not consistent with the documented lived experiences of people of color (see Bonilla-Silva, 2001). Sandra's experientially informed belief that white people get away with more than black people is affirmed and she is reminded of where she fits in the racial hierarchy, even as her white peers are enabled to remain unaware of their place within this hierarchy. Sandra is effectively silenced in her experience and obliged to acquiesce to the norms of Ms. Franklin's classroom.

The "pedagogy of discomfort" arises out of educators' concerns that classroom practices of dialogue and discussion relating to difficult issues —such as racism, sexism, heterosexism, ableism, and classism—frequently reproduce rather than disrupt students' taken-for-granted ways of seeing the world. . . .

For proponents of the pedagogy of discomfort, this example illustrates how social injustices and inequalities are frequently perpetuated within classrooms and schools by the implicit assumptions that teachers and students carry with them, even when their intentions are good. This pedagogy is "an educational approach to understanding the production of norms and differences"—such as Ms. Franklin's differential expectations based on race—that occurs in and through our everyday habits and routines and that sustains our beliefs about what is natural, normal, and good (Boler & Zembylas, 2003, p. 111). It asks: What happens when one rationalizes profound racial and class oppression with arguments about equality through hard work, determination, and good intentions? How do our explanations about biology and nature serve to obscure how norms of gender or able-bodiedness are socially produced and reproduced? Why do we hold fast to our worldviews in the face of the intellectual and emotional challenges of others' testimonies about their experiences? This pedagogy aims to equip teachers and students with the tools to critically examine their emotional responses to difficult discussions—like Ms. Franklin's frustration and discomfort in response to Sandra's complaint—and to understand that listening involves active responsiveness to rather than passive receptivity of others' testimonies about their experiences. It therefore looks at listening as a political and ethical act that has the potential to disrupt unjust social patterns when teachers and students engage in combined critical analysis and emotional self-awareness. As such, listening in the pedagogy of discomfort directly challenges didactic listening both in its emphasis on listening as a political and ethical act, and in its de-centering of teacher authority and its repositioning of the teacher as learner. Here, listening involves students' challenging of their own preconceived assumptions, expectations and emotional responses to others' differences, a discomfiting process to be sure.

In this chapter, I provide an overview of the pedagogy of discomfort as an approach to classroom listening practice that is aimed at preparing teachers and students to situate themselves within and to tackle systemic social injustices. Because this pedagogy emerges as a critical response to existing classroom dialogue and listening practices, I begin by describing its central claims and then move to a discussion of the problems and tensions to which it responds. I utilize examples of educational listening to challenging testimony to illustrate a listening practice that Megan Boler (1999) calls "witnessing," which replaces passive listening within this pedagogy. A first example illustrates the problem of empathetic identification in listening responses to difference. A second example demonstrates the use of the pedagogy of discomfort to provoke students' development of a critical and emotional responsiveness to difference and testimonial ambiguity. These examples demonstrate a form of listening that recognizes how each of us participates in perpetuating received and dominant value frameworks and norms. In this sense, I describe listening in ways consistent with both relational and critical listening, in following Waks's definitions in the Introduction to this volume, but I also work to critique and transform how both of these categories of listening are conceptualized. In sum, this chapter explores why some listening practices fail to challenge ingrained social patterns and why the view of listening advised by the pedagogy of discomfort is, by contrast, responsive and responsible to social justice.

The Pedagogy of Discomfort

Boler first introduced the pedagogy of discomfort in her *Feeling Power: Emotions and Education* (1999) where she described how critical inquiry into social injustice is frequently stifled by students' resistant and uncomfortable emotional reactions and responses. Boler argues that these "emotional stances" (2004, p. 121) of fear, anxiety, and anger are often defenses against the potential identity and worldview-shattering experiences of confronting one's place in hierarchies of oppression.

The pedagogy of discomfort, rather than shying away from these emotional stances, engages them as critical tools in students' examination of their emotional and cognitive investments in their beliefs about oppression and inequality. Students learn to question their place within social hierarchy, to ask who benefits from such institutions of power, and to—perhaps painfully—disrupt their rigid patterns of thinking about race, gender, sexuality, class, ability, etc., patterns that perpetuate injustice and prevent understanding across differences (Boler, 1999, p. 157). It demands, furthermore, that students and teachers emerge from their comfort zones and question dominant social narratives—of presumed equality, hard work, good intentions, among others—that are in many ways built into their identities and that color their emotional responses (see Boler & Zembylas, 2003). For teachers especially, this requires the recognition of the non-neutrality of educational processes. That is, educators are forced to confront their own investments in "the stubborn myth that education can be fully objective, neutral, apolitical" (Boler & Zembylas, 2003, p. 114); in other words, the myth that educational practices and institutions are value neutral or divested of political agendas. Importantly, the pedagogy of discomfort argues for students' and teachers' development of a critical consciousness that refuses norms and dominant categories of judgment (Boler & Zembylas, 2003, p. 127).

> *"I see education as a means to challenge rigid patterns of thinking that perpetuate injustice and instead encourage flexible analytic skills, which include the ability to self-reflectively evaluate the complex relations of power and emotion."*
>
> *—Boler, 1999, p. 157*

Boler and Zembylas (2003) describe the pedagogy of discomfort as follows:

As its name suggests, this pedagogy emphasizes the need for both the educator and students to move outside their comfort zones. By comfort zone we mean the inscribed cultural and emotional terrains that we occupy less by choice and more by virtue of hegemony: "Hegemony refers to the maintenance of domination not by sheer exercise of force but primarily through consensual social practices, social forms, and social structures produced in specific sites such as the church, the state, the school, the mass media, the political system, and the family" (McLaren, 1998, p. 182). The comfort zone reflects emotional investments that by and large remain unexamined because they have been woven into the everyday fabric of what is considered common sense. (p. 111)

It is helpful to consider the pedagogy of discomfort as consisting in the following three claims:

1. We enact and reproduce dominant values through our everyday habits and routines that go unexamined and appear commonplace.

Each of us internalizes, enacts and sustains—through our daily habits and routines—the dominant norms and values of our particular social, political, and historical context. Boler calls these "inscribed habits of emotional inattention:" unconscious habits and practices framed by dominant myths and cultural narratives that rationalize inequality and oppression (Boler, 2004, p. 122). We assume, for example, that individual hard work and good intentions are solely responsible for our success and we ignore or dismiss evidence of the systematic benefits that dominant individuals receive or the institutionalized disadvantages weighted upon the marginalized (see Bonilla-Silva, 2001). Consider Ms. Franklin's belief that hard work and discipline can trump adversity, as evidenced in her message to Sandra that she ought to "buck up" and ignore Rachel's behavior. Or, we believe that our fear of difference is a natural rather than a socially trained response, and this belief ignores the way that we daily notice and categorize others who we perceive as different from us (see Moya & Markus, 2010; Baron & Banaji, 2006). These beliefs and assumptions display "a tendency to abdicate responsibility for how differences are produced and perpetuated by individual beliefs and through psycho-social relations" (Boler & Zembylas, 2003, p. 114).

> "The failure to recognize and honor troubling feelings in our classrooms sustains cultural secrets. It permits students to remain comfortable by reading stories of oppression and injustice as exaggerations and exceptions, and narratives of justice as the rule."
>
> —Berlak, 2005, p. 142

The everyday-ness and invisibility of these unexamined habits and practices—such as the way we recognize and conform to particular gendered norms
of beauty and bodily appearance by waxing, dieting, covering up grey, undergoing cosmetic surgery—make it difficult for us to see the way that we all, no
matter what our social position, participate in producing values and norms and,
however unintentionally, in perpetuating dominant social patterns. Importantly,
everyone participates in this cultural reproduction of dominant values; that is,
it is not only members of the dominant group who must grapple with these
processes of power as we have *all* internalized them, if perhaps differently
(Boler, 2004, p. 121).

**2. The cognitive and emotional aspects of learning are crucially
intertwined and students can be taught to combine "passionate response
with critical analysis" in a way that privileges neither their cognitive nor
their emotional response to difficult knowledge (Boler, 1999, p. 117).**

At the heart of this pedagogy is the role of emotions in education, both as natural elements of the learning process and as culturally and politically invested
tools—and impediments—to learning about and across difference. Emotions
"reflect our complex identities situated within social hierarchies, 'embody' and
'act out' relations of power" (Boler, 1999, p. 4). The view that emotions reflect
and perpetuate ideological forces is informed by critical work in feminist theory
that demystifies and politicizes the space of emotions and lived experience,
and looks at the intersections of emotions, theory, and social power (see Scott,
1990; also Narayan, 1998; Ellsworth, 1989; for an in-depth discussion of
feminist theory and emotions in education, see Boler, 1999). The pedagogy of
discomfort contends, then, that the cognitive and emotional aspects of learning
are fundamentally interconnected, each playing an important role in the labor
of learning across difference. For example, students learn to recognize the fear
that colors their perception of disability, or that obstructs their ability to re-
imagine their beliefs about sex and gender. Responsible engagement in learning
about difficult issues involves students' critical examination of the emotional
impediments to their changing the way they view social relations, to their
situating themselves within the relations of power that perpetuate injustice,
and to their recognition of their own role in shaping how others' narratives
and experiences are made intelligible within the social world. Thus, emotions
act as windows into our ideological commitments and invisible habits, offering us a starting point from which to become "witnesses" to social injustice
(Berlak, 2005).

3. Students must learn to negotiate ambiguity, non-resolution and discomfort in learning, and especially in learning about difference and social relations of power, something that requires deep emotional and intellectual risk as it demands enormous self-discovery and self-analysis (Boler, 1999, p. 195).

Sophie Haroutunian-Gordon's (2003) work on listening tells us that opening oneself up to challenging perspectives involves both puzzlement and agitation, and the potentially destabilizing experience of questioning one's deeply held beliefs about the world. The discomfort that is this pedagogy's namesake is precisely this discomfort with challenging one's own

> *"The call to listen is a radical call."*
>
> *—Thompson, 2003, p. 89*

intellectual and emotional investments that shape ideas about normalcy and that sustain intelligible and unintelligible social forms. The pedagogy of discomfort aims to promote students' acceptance, perhaps even embrace, of ambiguity in learning about or across difference, and their resistance to the desire for closure or resolution. This view is supported by Deborah Britzman's (1998) pedagogical theory, which explores the enormous educative potential of non-resolution in learning: ". . . to act as if education is or even should be a site of continuity and a movement toward resolution shuts out consideration of how discontinuity, difference, and learning might be conditions of passionate subjectivity" (Britzman, 1998, p. 28). In inciting students to confront and challenge their ingrained worldviews and perceptions of social relations, the pedagogy of discomfort aims to disrupt the easy reliance on reductive categories and tidy constructions of difference and in doing so invite students and their teachers to remain in the potential anxiety of this lack of closure and, indeed, the discomfort that accompanies it. Ultimately, "An ethical aim of a pedagogy of discomfort is willingly to inhabit a more ambiguous and flexible sense of self" (Boler, 1999, p. 176). For Ms. Franklin, for example, this might mean confronting the tension that exists between her belief in race neutrality and Sandra's expressed experience of racism.

Listening Within the Pedagogy of Discomfort

Listening emerges out of these three claims in the pedagogy of discomfort. Accordingly, listening is a political and ethical act that takes place from within unjust social structures, and that can produce *and* resist social injustice. While many scholars of listening have emphasized particular virtues, skills, and dispositions that enable good listening practice and which individuals develop within educational contexts (see, for example, Burbules & Rice, 1991), the focus of this pedagogy is somewhat different. The pedagogy of discomfort is focused on making visible the structural impediments to listening across difference that persist even in the presence of virtuous or skilled listening. It therefore emphasizes the conditions under which socially just listening can take place, notably in the presence of a recognition of the role of social power, of ingrained distrust, and, frequently, of historical lack of understanding or engagement. Developing this critical consciousness towards systemic inequality and oppression, then, means acknowledging that even the virtuous listener—the one who exercises respect for difference, a willingness to listen, an inclination to admit errors, even a willingness to assess one's biases—might fail to recognize his or her own place within hierarchies of social power that condition what testimony is or is not regarded as intelligible, as making sense (for further discussion, see Narayan, 1998 and Medina, 2011).

Thus, the pedagogy of discomfort proposes a view of listening that challenges students to learn how their emotional investments inform their listening responses; how, for example, one's fear of talking about race complicates one's ability to see students' experiences of racism as reasonable, or how one's discomfort with disabled bodies colors one's response to disabled people's testimony about their lived experience, perhaps even in spite of one's best efforts at practicing the virtues of good listening. Boler (1999) distinguishes between empathetic listening or "spectating" that sustains cultural practices of exclusion and critically engaged listening or "witnessing" that interrogates power relations and disrupts these practices. An examination of emotional responses supports the development of this latter form of listening because it offers students an opportunity to explore how social practices, symbols and discourses define our interior realms and how our emotional responses enact and sustain social and cultural meanings (Boler, 1999, p. 142). It is this understanding that responsiveness to emotions can be at once compassionate understanding *and* critical analysis—that emotions can be analyzed and critiqued—that lays the groundwork for the ultimate view of listening as a political act. By critically analyzing their place within social structures and the way these appear to them, students can come to recognize how listening—in both its emotional and cognitive aspects—has political and ethical implications.

This pedagogy reconceives of classrooms not as safe-zones for academic learning but as sites of social justice education wherein difficult knowledge—of ableism, racism, sexism, homophobia, and heterosexism—is confronted, discussed, and challenged. Further, it holds that classrooms are never safe to begin with, but are rather spaces wherein social power is produced and repro-duced. Finally, it begins from the position that engaging in learning across and amongst differences is in itself part of an ideological *ideal* that, absent critical reflection, can sustain oppressive social norms and practices. This ideal is structured around the belief—and perhaps the hope—that we can develop a complete understanding of others. Audrey Thompson (2010) describes class-room listening in a way that exposes this ideal:

> Face-to-face ideals, ideals of personal integrity and intimate understanding, assume that there is a whole to be grasped and a positionality that could allow us to grasp it. Positing the whole-ness we hope to discover, such ideals make it impossible for us to hear and value ourselves and one another as fragmentary, broken, sometimes trustworthy, sometimes not (sometimes both at once), and as right now in the middle of *that* relationship. It is not pos-sible to restore what never was. It is not simply that the grounds for intimacy, trust, and understanding are broken and dangerous, although I think that is true. It is that, even in what we imagine to be equal or innocent or exceptional relationships, we are standing on imaginary ground. (p. 4)

Thompson's passage emphasizes the partial or "fragmentary" nature of classroom listening across difference; that is, the sense in which understanding across differences is always partial or incomplete because of our individual com-plexity and the normal perils of communication. Further, in Boler's account we see that "[t]he listener plays a tremendous role in the production of truth" (1999, p. 168) as the listener participates in shaping the meaning of the nar-rative and the discursive meanings to which we all have access in shaping our stories about our own experiences.

In order to examine the social justice implications of classroom listening we must shift the focus from what is understood or what can be understood between individuals within listening, to a focus on how students "hear" through their beliefs, desires, values and commitments and how, as listeners, they attend to these interpretive filters. Certainly, attending to these interpretive filters—like Ms. Franklin's interpretation of Sandra's complaint as inappropriate—can pave the way for later understanding. Still, in describing this potential shift, the pedagogy of discomfort departs from frameworks that emphasize empa-thy as moral response and in doing so permits an examination of how such frameworks and empathetic listening practices often sustain the status quo of socially unjust educative practices and interpersonal exchange.

The Role of Emotions in Listening:
The Problems of Passive Empathy

The pedagogy of discomfort regards empathy as preventing, rather than promoting such socially just and socially responsive listening. Empathy, whether manifest as compassion or pity, does not require that the listener take responsibility for another's suffering. Empathy excuses the listener from examining how her own assumptions, beliefs, and values contribute to the conditions of the other's misfortune; it excuses her from what Boler calls "self-reflective participation" or an awareness of oneself as firmly placed within relations of power (1999, p. 166). Boler points out that calls for teaching empathy and instilling conditions of empathy in children as a way to remedy social problems are ubiquitous in the contemporary academic and political world (1999, p. 156). Empathy is celebrated as bridging difference and forming relationships through the bonds of understanding. However, the multiple and differing meanings of "empathy" complicate an easy understanding of its role in moral education. To clarify its meaning, Susan Verducci (1998) distinguishes between versions of empathy as projective and versions of empathy as receptive: projective empathy involves "stepping into another's shoes," knowing them as if from within; while receptive empathy, by contrast, imagines or envisions that the listener or empathizer receives the other's subjective state, understanding them as they would want to be understood (pp. 335–342). Both kinds impart problems for socially responsible listening from the perspective of the pedagogy of discomfort.

> "Listening is fraught with emotional landmines."
>
> —Boler, 1999, p. 179

Consider a view of empathetic listening according to which empathy involves putting oneself in the other's shoes. According to this view, one puts aside one's own interests and one's evaluative judgments in attending to what is being said by another. Leonard Waks (2010) describes this sort of listening through an example of a classroom reading lesson. Waks stipulates that a teacher—Ms. Green—has two modes of listening available to her: an evaluative form of listening that is aimed at categorizing students into reading performance categories and an empathetic one, which involves "bracketing" the self and one's critical or evaluating goals and is aimed at "a readiness to learn and to know not motivated by any focused particular interest or end . . . an attitude of 'being with' the other" (p. 2747). Waks's description of "bracketing the self" means that ". . . the inner milieu becomes an ever-expanding empty space that can receive (accept) the other" (2010, p. 2754). This sort of empathetic listening avoids categorization and judgment.

At first sight such a mode of listening appears to conform to the listening practice advised by the pedagogy of discomfort. Indeed, we know that educational categorization and classification frequently invite stigma and can deleteriously affect students' academic performance (Ferri, 2006; Hehir, 2002; Minow, 1990; Taylor, 2006). Where students are concerned, furthermore, with the strictly rationalist assessment of their narratives, they may not feel comfortable sharing them. As a different form of interpersonal listening, then, empathetic listening might enable students to relax and feel safe from the judgment that often characterizes evaluative listening (Waks, 2010, p. 2756). However, this mode of empathetic listening does not appear to acknowledge the necessity of one's own critical evaluation of one's beliefs, nor of the recognition that all listening is shaped and informed by our emotional investments.[2] The notion that one can suspend one's beliefs appears problematic from the standpoint of the pedagogy of discomfort because it falsely assumes that we can step outside of ourselves or create such a space of radical receptivity of the other. Recall Boler's emphasis on teaching students to combine compassionate response with critical analysis (1999, p. 142). Accordingly, we should not aim to cultivate such empathy in students—teaching them to eschew a cognitive response—but rather to cultivate their abilities to recognize the intertwining of intellectual and affective components in their listening responses. Further, the sort of "in the other's shoes" empathetic listening described in Waks (2010) confronts the critique that it involves projection; that is, it involves the projection of one's own feelings, beliefs and experiences onto the person with whom one attempts to identify. In so doing, the projective empathizer "transforms the human other into an object" by deflecting the other's actual mental state (Verducci, 1998, pp. 336–337). According to these critiques, projective empathy is either morally dangerous or unsuccessful. In either case, it fails to challenge—even to encounter—the problems at the core of listening across difference, namely the mechanisms of social power the perpetuate inequalities and injustices.

Similar problems arise when we view empathy as receptive rather than projective. What might it mean to assert that one receives the other in empathetic identification, rather than imagining oneself "in their shoes?" At first, the ideal of receptivity appears to imply that the listener displaces him- or herself in the act of listening to another's story, or to imagining his or her experience. However, Thompson writes that this move of displacing oneself by receiving the other's beliefs,

> again preserves the self while temporarily removing it from a position in which it could do harm. The ascetic denial of self in the face of the other, the moral leap of faith, means that we humble ourselves before the other, wash the feet of the other, accept the other (for a

moment) as taking the place of oneself. Yet one does not, finally, displace oneself . . . When push comes to shove, though, many of us will protect our particular agentic privileges by reverting to the judgment we can rely on—our own. (2010, p. 6)

According to Thompson, then, this receptivity that is wholly for the other is imagined; at best, this receptivity is partial (2010, p. 7). Her "listening at an angle" is a call to listen in a way that attends to the possibility that we will listen inadequately and in doing so hear things that we might never have expected (Thompson, 2010, p. 7). That is, we listen in a way that is accountable but not divested of the self. As in Thompson, Verducci's analysis does not require that receptive empathy involve one's displacement or erasure. Rather, it requires a "dynamic conversation" (1998, p. 431) and the recognition of *partial* identification. Says Verducci (2000), "This epistemological stance on empathy requires affective resonance, cognitive understanding and cognitive distance. At the same time, the empathizer grasps the other's emotional and situational reality; she recognizes the distance between herself and the other" (p. 78).

It is not simply, then, that these forms of empathy fail as means of learning across difference, but rather that these projects of empathetic identification fail to disrupt social oppression. Boler (1999) argues that while empathy is celebrated as bridging differences and forming relationships through the bonds of—even *partial*—understanding, rarely do we ask *who* benefits from empathy, nor do we question the root of this notion, that we can step into another's shoes and know their experience, or, indeed, receive them in all their complexity. This notion, she says, obscures our recognition of our own implication in "the social forces that create the climate of obstacles that the other must confront" (1999, p. 159). In fact, by attempting this sort of encounter with the other, we permit ourselves to be excused from acknowledging our own role in shaping their experience. For Boler, then, the promotion of empathetic listening, even as receptivity, lacks a critical evaluation of our own role in perpetuating others' social exclusions or the norms that enable those exclusions.

> "I now believe that if a major purpose of teaching is the promotion of students' abilities to receive information that is dissonant, not just congruent, with what they have learned before, then confrontation with its attendant trauma is necessary."
>
> —Berlak, 2005, p. 141

Listening in Action

Important research in educational theory and social justice education, as well as feminist pedagogy and critical race pedagogy has explored how those in positions of societal dominance and privilege often deny, dismiss, or rationalize away testimonies of social oppression in order to affirm their deeply held beliefs and worldviews. There now exists a significant body of research documenting denials of racism and racial privilege among white students when presented with the experiences of racism by people of color (see Case and Hemmings, 2005; Hytten & Warren, 2003; McIntyre, 1997) as well as denials by men of women's experiences of sexism, misogyny, and inequality (Frye, 1983; Narayan, 1998). What this research shows is that the deeply held and frequently invisible beliefs of dominant group students about presumed natural differences in hard work and achievement, and family values and commitment, among other things, shape the way that students listen to these narratives of the lived experience of oppression. In the ensuing examples, I explore how such dismissals arise within discussions of disability experience and narratives of gender ambiguity, respectively.

The Problem of Empathy: Listening to Disability Experience

The following example shows how empathetic projection can mask or erase nondominant narratives or accounts of disability experience that transgress dominant expectations and assumptions. Scholars of disability studies have documented the prevailing social regard of people with disabilities as objects of pity and sufferers of biological deficiency and abnormality and have pointed to social processes and practices as responsible for sustaining such a reductive view of disability as necessarily bad and undesirable (see, for example, Garland-Thomson, 2006; Linton, 1998; Shapiro, 1993). Dominant social norms of bodily functioning, physical form and beauty, and ingrained ideas about competency and productivity support these prevailing beliefs in the manifest inferiority of people with disabilities.

This "ideology of ability" is "the preference for ablebodiedness, which appears as a conceptual horizon beyond which it is difficult to think" (Siebers, 2009, p. 5). Such powerful ideological processes shape how students engage with disability and, often, impede their ability to be challenged by narratives that contradict these beliefs.

Not infrequently, students in K-12 or university classrooms are introduced to the concept of disability through simulation exercises, in which students identifying as (or identified as) able-bodied are invited to "experience" the lives of students labeled with physical disabilities—riding around in a wheelchair, putting on a blindfold, etc. These activities are meant to permit the able-bodied person's empathetic identification with the disabled person's lived experience. However, "By eliciting either pity or sentimentality, simulations reinforce the subject/object relations and distant regard for an 'unfortunate inferior'" (Ferri, 2006, p. 294). Simulation practices, instead of facilitating this putting of oneself in the shoes of the other rather reaffirm precisely how socially distant the other appears to be. Beth Ferri (2006) calls such practices "[a] particularly troubling way to keep one's distance" (p. 293). Rather than facilitating students' imagining the world otherwise, they are simply imagining *themselves* and applying their own able-bodied experiences to the simulation of disability. Here we see empathetic identification—and the emotions attached to it—perform the very act of distancing they are meant to interrupt.

In their study of able-bodied individuals' assessment of the quality of life decisions of people with disabilities, Catriona Mackenzie and Jackie Leach Scully (2007) describe the role of imagination in moral engagement to illustrate how empathy becomes problematic. They argue that such imaginative engagement fails because it involves a projection of one's own thoughts, feelings, and attitudes, experienced through one's own embodiment:

> Imagining oneself differently situated, or even imagining oneself in the other's shoes, is not morally engaging with the other; rather, it is projecting one's own perspective onto the other. When the other person is very different from ourselves, the danger of this kind of projection is that we simply project onto the other our beliefs and attitudes, fears and hopes, and desires and aversions. (Mackenzie & Scully, 2007, p. 345)

This sort of disconnect is supported by studies that show significant differences in how individuals with disabilities rate their own quality of life compared to assessments of their lives provided by individuals identifying as able-bodied (Mackenzie & Scully, 2007, pp. 344–345).

As a response, disability studies scholars often advocate the use of narrative testimony (or counter-narratives) of disabled people themselves—through memoir, interviews, personal narrative poetry, song, comedy, etc.—as a more appropriate—and, indeed, accurate—means of engaging with disability (see Ferri, 2008; Smith & Sparkes, 2008; Ware, 2008). Through this exposure to accounts of the lived experience of disability, students are encouraged to develop a more nuanced view of disability as a complex experience of cultural identity, embodiment, and relationship with the world. Nevertheless, the pedagogy of discomfort reminds us that all students arrive in the classroom with preconceived and usually unexamined ideas about ability, normalcy, and quality of life that shape their view of disability and people with disabilities. Further, these students are understood to enact and perpetuate dominant values and norms through their everyday habits. When they confront the testimony of lived experience of disability, students' listening abilities are colored by these background conditions. Thus, even the perhaps well-intentioned efforts to imaginatively and empathetically engage with another's assessment of their own quality of life can, in the absence of a critical examination of their own vested beliefs, lead to a preservation and assertion of the able-bodied observer's feelings about their own embodiment and their possibly prejudicial attitudes— including fear—towards disablement.

The Discomfort of Ambiguity: The Case of Gender

This second example shows how the pedagogy of discomfort can provoke students' development of a critical and emotional responsiveness to difference and to testimonial ambiguity. Here I use the example of nondominant or non-conforming gender identity because it offers a conceptual arena that provokes tremendous discomfort and conceptual challenge to students. I contend that through the pedagogical tools of the pedagogy of discomfort, students can develop listening responses to personal narrative about nonconforming gender identity that resist the conceptual closure of gender binaries.

Educational processes and practices, as reflections of broader cultural and social patterns, rely on oversimplified and reductive understandings of difference and offer little opportunity for students to explore contradiction and ambiguity in identity, a reality readily apparent in the unquestioned binarized sex/gender system (Boler & Zembylas, 2003). With respect to sex and gender, "[a]mbiguity is feared; it is a source of discomfort to those forced to live in a culture defined by simple binary oppositions" (Boler & Zembylas, 2003, p. 122). Feminist theorists have long argued that gender is a social process and an organizing concept, rather than a simple reflection of one's biological sex (Butler, 1994). Yet, while students are frequently able to recognize how each of us "performs" our gender through our appearance, our actions, and even our choices, the notion that gender is a transgress-able social category and one that is frequently done and undone by people who fail to conform (whether intentionally or not) to the gender binaries and attendant social expectations and norms of "man" and "woman" is met with a good deal of discomfort and confusion. Nor are students exposed to an understanding of why anyone would want to live with gender ambiguity, indeed, why this might be a positive, preferable identity. Meanwhile, those who identify as or who are perceived as gender nonconforming, gender-queer, transgender, transsexual, or intersexed continue to face enormous stigma, negative or under-representation in popular media, and frequent threats of violence in schools and elsewhere (see Bornstein, 2006; Fausto-Sterling, 2000; Meyer, 2007; For a discussion of dialogue, speech codes, and sexuality and gender harassment in schools, see Mayo, 2005).

Consider the following example. In a class discussion on gender identity, I presented students with a video clip of Jennifer Miller, a "bearded-lady" feminist performance artist and activist who discusses her experience of non-conforming gender identity and gender ambiguity. In her performances, Miller draws on old-time "freak-show" exhibits of deviant bodies put on display, using her own embodiment as a bearded lady to distort the audience's understanding of easily bifurcated gender images. After watching, a number of students expressed confusion, frustration, and a desire to understand why she would not choose to just "shave it off" (for discussion of gendered norms surrounding facial hair, see Dowl, 2005). In expressing their confusion over her display of gender ambiguity, students appeared to have difficulty listening to why one might choose not to conform to normative standards of embodiment. They called into question her identification as "woman" even as they recognized the enormous variety of ways that femininity is expressed. In many ways, the social identity of bearded *woman* simply does not fit within the dominant conceptual framework and discourse of gender and gender binaries.

That Miller's identity as a woman is called into question or disrupted by her bearded face is a product of our problematic discursive construction of gender. Many students are quick to invoke an individualistic narrative of responsibility and claim that Miller is responsible for her own oppression because she chooses not to conform. Yet absent in this narrative is an understanding of how the process of gender as a system of power enacts this oppression, and how the students, in maintaining this blame-the-victim narrative, contribute to it. Further, these students reveal themselves to be taking their gender identity as "unproblematically normal, not in need of explanation, transparently intelligible" (Scheman, 2001) and natural (see Boler, 2004, for further discussion of gender and the pedagogy of discomfort). In doing so, then, they maintain that gender is innate, mapped on easily to our biology, and that those who deviate do so unnaturally. Indeed, the success of these dominant narratives about gender is that they remain invisible to us (Boler & Zembylas, 2003, p. 117).

Naomi Scheman (2001) describes this privileging of her own gender identity in discussing her experience with ascribing unintelligibility to trans-gendered and transsexual people. She writes,

> What I learned . . . was the need to balance my own critical faculties, my intellectual autonomy, against the recognition of the systemic epistemic liabilities of privilege—in this case the privilege of being normatively, intelligibly gendered . . . Not to leave ourselves open and vulnerable to alternative understandings when our own come in part from locations of discursive privilege is to close ourselves to the possibility of learning from others. . . .

As this passage illustrates, listening to the apparently unintelligible involves witnessing what is unknown and sometimes threatening. What is crucially needed is "an openness to the possibility that one simply does not understand" (Scheman, 2001). Yet, to set aside one's seemingly intuitive drive to "make sense" of another's testimony is to threaten the very foundations upon which one makes meaning. This openness is discomfiting, even painful because it involves a disruption of our understanding of the world and our place within it. Indeed, we might squirrel to shore up resources to protect what we seem to know, and to defend our deep-seated beliefs and assumptions about the world.

How can interrogation of their own assumptions about gender, normalcy, etc. alter students' reactions to Miller's gender ambiguity? They cannot know her experience as if stepping into her shoes, but they can ask why it matters, why they are disturbed by her difference. They can ask in what ways we are all socialized to act, speak, dress, react in certain ways as gendered subjects, and how gender—as well as race, class, ability, and sexuality—organize our world and our understanding of it. This is reflective of Boler's account of active listening or witnessing that offers a view of listening practices as combining self-critique with historical analysis and an examination of social power. Examining our emotional responses is an integral part of understanding our own vested beliefs that induce us to turn away from, ignore, or malign others who appear different or whose stories appear unintelligible. The pedagogy of discomfort helps students confront gender ambiguity while resisting the desire for closure. It demands an understanding that change can happen through resistance to participation in dominant discourses surrounding gender; that by resisting conceptual closure of gender as dichotomized, students act against dominant values and act in the service of social justice.

Conclusion: Lessons from the Pedagogy of Discomfort

These examples show us how students take part in constructing differences and the conditions of intelligibility. Radically, where frequently calls for listening are focused on the epistemic possibilities of knowing, or the conditions under which I can know the other's experience, the notion of listening informed by the pedagogy of discomfort is not concerned precisely with "getting it right." Rather, it regards the listener as "co-constructing" the truth of another's story: "the 'listener to trauma comes to be a participant and co-owner of the traumatic event . . .'" and "plays a tremendous role in the production of truth, and the relations of power are thus foregrounded" (Boler, 1999, p. 167). That is, testimony is a discursive practice in which testifiers and listeners co-construct the experience being relayed (Boler, 1999, pp. 166–168). Boler contends that experience must be understood not as "authoritative or inherently 'real' or 'true' but rather as a 'window into ideology'" (1999, p. 123). Within the educational context, then, this means that students examine how social and historical practices play a role in shaping the narrative being recounted—in our above examples of disability experience and gender identity—not to dismiss what is being said, certainly, but to understand the way that the discursive resources available for expression shape what is being said, how it is understood and, ultimately, the meaning it makes.

What the pedagogy of discomfort emphasizes, then, is how students must learn to examine the ways that they participate in such co-construction of narrative testimony and the ethical implications of this involvement. Says Boler, "Witnessing involves recognizing moral relations not simply as a 'perspectival' difference—'we all see things differently'—but rather, that how we see or choose not to see has ethical implications and may even cause others to suffer" (1999, p. 195). Because we play a part in others' suffering, because we are complicit in the social forces that perpetuate that oppression, we have a fundamental ethical obligation to evaluate and challenge our roles. Taking again the above examples of quality of life assessments of disability and student reactions to gender ambiguity, this would mean persons identifying as ablebodied or as gender-"normal," rather than employing their own imaginative engagement with the other's life, would focus their attention on their own critical resources for understanding that life and the ways that their political and emotional investments—their fear of disabled or gender-ambiguous bodies, their investment in norms of intelligence, beauty, behavior, etc.—inform their inability to see disability or gender otherwise and their patterned dismissal of persons' own assessment of valuable lifestyle and embodiment as unintelligible or misguided. But being exposed to these narratives and experiences of others is only a starting point. Entertaining the real possibility that the world could be or appear otherwise than how it appears to us and that we might have a role in obscuring or marginalizing that alternative perspective is where we want to get.

We can see, then, that through the tools of the pedagogy of discomfort students can become aware of how dominant ideas shape their meaning-making within listening. Teachers are, of course, central figures in this process because they likewise play an important role in both perpetuating and resisting the systemic patterns of exclusion and oppression that undergird schooling practices. Even as we must acknowledge the tremendous burdens on teachers—both to resist and uphold normative structures—we must still emphasize the need for reflection and reexamination of practice (Ware, 2002). Socially just listening practices would likewise involve teachers acknowledging and examining their own emotional investments, beliefs, and values—what Dori Laub (as cited in Boler, 1999, p. 169) calls their "listening defenses." Yet certainly acknowledging the need for this sort of critical reflection and reexamination of practice is easier said than done, particularly within an educational climate that increasingly limits teachers' pedagogical freedoms and impact on students' cultural analysis. Teachers, administrators, and even parents all experience the constraints of such a resistant climate. Further, in-service and pre-service teachers are frequently bombarded with diversity training programs and calls for increased "cultural awareness" of students' backgrounds and may experience a certain fatigue with such calls to evaluate their classroom practices. What *comfort* can the pedagogy of discomfort offer to teachers who face such realities but who nevertheless wish to advance this pedagogy's core practices within their classrooms and schools?

Linda Ware (2002) suggests that school reform can come through extended dialogue with teachers and a commitment to engaging with students' lived experiences. Foremost, however, it is important that teachers recognize that they are always situated within processes and institutions of social power. As Berlak (2005) points out, the cultural myths or secrets of racism, sexism, heterosexism, ableism, classism, and other forms of oppression are, however implicitly, ubiquitous in our classrooms and institutions, present as uninvited and unacknowledged classroom visitors (p. 142). Certainly, then, teachers' efforts to make these visible involve courage, creativity, as well as care for oneself and one's students. Often, students crave reassurance from teachers that "there is 'hope'" despite the overwhelming inequities of society (Boler, 2004). One common pedagogical tool that is often used by social justice educators to facilitate students' learning about cultural systems of oppression and inequality in a caring way is the practice of journaling. Berlak (2005) describes her use of journals in students' examination of their own emotional responses of anger, frustration, and sadness in being confronted with others' experiences of racism and classism. Journaling can enable students to express their personal reactions to the learning process, and to express more candid opinions that might differ from those of their classmates or their teacher. Further, journals can allow educators to gauge students' level of interaction with difficult material and where they are in need of support.

Teachers' resistance to and unmasking of dominant social frameworks does not need to take place on a grand scale. Indeed, because dominant perspectives are reinforced in schools through the active exclusion or omission as well as the negative inclusion of nondominant perspectives and experiences, teachers, administrators, and parents can all participate in resisting such marginalization of differences in small ways. For one, they can do so by including or by calling for the inclusion of nondominant narratives within the curriculum, the school, and their individual classrooms, and also by examining their own cognitive and emotional investments in maintaining the status quo. How are students' identities and cultural experiences being excluded in the classroom? How might they be included? In what ways are concepts being discussed? Is one way of life, one form of embodiment, being presented as normal and natural? What language is being used? Is that language loaded already with cultural and social messages, such as "blindness" in place of "ignorance" or assumptions of opposite-sex attraction and love? In thinking through their representational practices, teachers begin to examine and expose myths and assumptions simply by pinpointing linguistic convention, popular culture, even classroom activities. Certainly, while teachers' efforts to resist dominant school practices can be both politically and personally discomfiting, teachers' *lack* of resistance can be equally disturbing as they become increasingly aware of the realities of social inequities.

Finally, Boler (2004) cautions educators to acknowledge the ethical implications of the role they are undertaking as pedagogues of discomfort in challenging their students' familiar and comfortable worldviews (p. 131). Says Boler (1999), ". . . at a certain point, out of a pragmatic and ethical respect—as well as a concern for the resilience of the educator—one must recognize that the revolution (however envisioned) will not be accomplished by educators per se. The goal is greater clarity of our emotional investments and the ability to account historically for our values and their effects on others" (p. 199) Thus, even while we all, as teachers or as students, must examine our own positionality within systems of oppression, we must also acknowledge the collective and collaborative nature of systemic and lasting change.[3]

Notes

1. "Work Hard, Be Nice" is the longstanding motto of KIPP (Knowledge is Power Program) schools as part of their emphasis on character education. See http://www.kipp.org/our-approach/character. See also Matthews, J. (2009).

2. For a critique of this view, see Sophie Haroutunian-Gordon (2007, p. 150). According to Haroutunian-Gordon we may be wrong to assess this form of empathetic listening as properly a suspension of questioning or evaluation. Haroutunian-Gordon's critique is based in the argument that all listening involves a cognitive, questioning component, in which the listener raises questions about the speaker's utterances and his or her own beliefs.

3. This chapter was developed out of a paper presented at the 2012 *Philosophy of Education Society* Meeting. I am grateful to discussant Nick Burbules for his helpful comments, as well as my co-presenters and the audience participants for their questions and criticisms. I would like to thank Len Waks for his very helpful comments on an earlier draft of this paper, as well as his editorial guidance in publishing this chapter. I am also very grateful to my teachers and colleagues in Cultural Foundations of Education at Syracuse University for their insightful feedback and criticism.

Further Reading

Boler, M. (Ed.). (2005). *Democratic dialogue in education: Troubling speech, disturbing silence.* New York: Peter Lang.

Boler, M. (2004). Teaching for hope: The ethics of shattering worldviews. In D. Liston, & J. Garrison (Eds.), *Teaching, learning and loving.* New York: RoutledgeFalmer.

Ferri, B. A. (2006). Teaching to trouble. In S. Danforth, & S. Gabel (Eds.), *Vital questions facing disability studies in education vol. 2* (289–306). New York: Peter Lang.

Zembylas, M., & Boler, M. (2002). On the spirit of patriotism: Challenges of a "pedagogy of discomfort," *Teachers College Record.*

Zembylas, M. (2012). Pedagogies of strategic empathy: Navigating through emotional complexities of anti-racism in higher education. *Teaching in higher education,* 17(2), 113–125.

References

Baron, A. S., & Banaji, M. R. (2006). The development of implicit attitudes: Evidence of race evaluations from ages 6 and 10 and adulthood. *Psychological Science,* 17(1): 53–58.

Basile, N. [booya9d]. (2008, November 20). *American Carny Jennifer Miller.* [Video File]. Retrieved from http://www.youtube.com/watch?v=uoschCAdpjs

Berlak, A. C. (2005). Confrontation and Pedagogy: Cultural Secrets, Trauma, and Emotion in Antioppressive Pedagogies, in M. Boler (Ed.), *Democratic Dialogue in Education: Troubling Speech, Disturbing Silence.* New York: Peter Lang, pp. 123–144.

Boler, M. (1999). *Feeling power: Emotions and education.* New York, London: Routledge.

Bonilla-Silva, E. (2001). *White supremacy & racism in the post-civil rights era.* Boulder, CO: Lynne Reinner Publishers.

Bornstein, K. (2006). Gender Terror, Gender Rage, in S. Stryker and S. Whittle (Eds.), *The Transgender Studies Reader.* New York: Routledge, pp. 236–243.

Britzman, D. P. (1998). *Lost subjects, contested objects: Toward a psychoanalytic inquiry of learning.* Albany, NY: SUNY Press.

Burbules, N., & Rice, S. (1991). Dialogue across differences: Continuing the conversation. *Harvard Educational Review,* 61(4): 393–417.

Butler, J. (1990). *Gender Trouble: Feminism and the Subversion of Identity.* New York: Routledge.

Ellsworth, E. (1989). Why doesn't this feel empowering? Working through the repressive myths of critical pedagogy. *Harvard Educational Review,* 59(3): 297–325.

Case, K., & Hemmings, A. (2005). Distancing strategies: White women pre-service teachers and antiracist curriculum. *Urban Education* 40(6): 606–626.

Dowl, A. (2005). Beyond the bearded lady: Outgrowing the shame of female facial hair. *Bitch* Spring (28): 54–59.

Ferri, B. A. (2006). Teaching to trouble. In S. Danforth. & S. Gabel (Eds), *Vital Questions Facing Disability Studies in Education Vol. 2.* New York: Peter Lang, pp. 289–306.

Ferri, B. A. (2008). Changing the script: Race and disability in Lynn Manning's *Weights. International Journal of Inclusive Education* 12(5–6): 497–509;

Fausto-Sterling, A. (2000). The five sexes, revisited. *The Sciences* 40(4): 18–23.

Frye, M. (1983). *The politics of reality: Essays in feminist theory.* Freedom, CA: The Crossing Press.

Garland-Thomson, R. (2006). Integrating disability, transforming feminist theory. In L. J. Davis (Ed.) *The Disability Studies Reader Second Edition.* New York: Taylor & Francis, pp. 257–274.

Haroutunian-Gordon, S. (2003). Listening—in a democratic society. In K. Alston (Ed.), *Philosophy of Education 2003.* Normal, IL: Philosophy of Education Society, pp. 1–18.

Haroutunian-Gordon, S. (2007). Listening and questioning. *Learning Inquiry* 1(2): 143–152.

Hehir, T. (2002). Eliminating ableism in education. *Harvard Educational Review* 72 (1): 1–32.

Hytten, K., & Warren, J. (2003). Engaging Whiteness: How racial power gets reified in education. *International Journal of Qualitative Studies in Education* 16(1): 65–89.

Lewis, A. E. (2001). There is no "race" in the schoolyard: Color-blind ideology in an (almost) all-white school. *American Educational Research Journal,* 38(4): 781–811.

Linton, S. (1998). *Claiming disability: Knowledge and identity.* New York: New York University Press.

Lorber, J. (1994). *Paradoxes of gender.* New Haven: Yale University Press.

Matthews, J. (2009). *Work hard. Be nice: How two inspired teachers created the most promising schools in America.* New York, NY: Algonquin Books of Chapel Hill.

Mayo, C. (2005). The tolerance that dare not speak its name. In M. Boler (Ed.) *Democratic dialogue in education: Troubling speech, disturbing silence*. New York: Peter Lang, pp. 33–50.

McIntyre, A. (1997). *Making meaning of whiteness*. Albany: SUNY Press.

Medina, J. (2011). The relevance of credibility excess in a proportional view of epistemic injustice: Differential epistemic authority and the social imaginary. *Social Epistemology*, 25(1): 15–35.

Meyer, E. (2007). "But I'm not gay": What straight teachers need to know about queer theory. In N. Rodriguez, & W. Pinar (Eds.) *Queering Straight Teachers: Discourse and Identity in Education*. New York: Peter Lang, pp. 15–29.

Minow, M. (1990). *Making all the difference: Inclusion, exclusion, and American law*. Ithaca, NY: Cornell University Press.

Moya, P. M. L., & Markus, H. R. (2010). *Doing race: 21 essays for the 21ˢᵗ century*. New York, NY: W. W. Norton & Company;

Narayan, U. (1998). Working together across difference: Some considerations on emotions and political practice. *Hypatia*, 3(2): 31–47.

Scheman,N. (2001). Openness, vulnerability, and feminist engagement. *American Philosophical Association Newsletter on Feminism and Philosophy* 00(2).

Shapiro, J. P. (1993). *No pity: People with disabilities forging a new civil rights movement*. New York: Three Rivers Press.

Smith, B., & Sparkes, A. C. (2008). Narrative and its potential contribution to disability studies. *Disability & Society* 23(1): 17–28

Taylor, S. J. (2006). Foreword: Before it had a name: Exploring the historical roots of disability studies. In S. Danforth, & S. Gabel (Eds.) *Vital Questions Facing Disability Studies in Education Vol. 2*. New York: Peter Lang, pp. xii–xxiii.

Thompson, A. (2003). Listening and its asymmetries. *Curriculum Inquiry*, 33(1): 79–100.

Thompson, A. (2010). Listening at an angle, in G. Biesta (Ed.) *Philosophy of Education 2010*. Normal, Ill.: Philosophy of Education Society, pp. 1–10.

Verducci, S. (1998). Moral empathy: The necessity of intersubjectivity and dialogic confirmation. In S. Tozer (Ed.) *Philosophy of Education 1998*. Normal, IL: Philosophy of Education Society, pp. 335–342.

Verducci, S. (2000). A conceptual history of empathy and a question it raises for moral education. *Educational Theory* 50(1): 63–80.

Waks, L. J. (2010). Two types of interpersonal listening. *Teachers College Record* 112(11): 2743–2762.

Ware, L. (2002). A moral conversation on disability: Risking the personal in educational contexts. *Hypatia* 17(3): 143–172

Ware, L. (2008). Worlds remade: inclusion through engagement with disability art. *International Journal of Inclusive Education* 12(5–6): 563–583.

Zembylas, M. (2012). Pedagogies of strategic empathy: navigating through emotional complexities of anti-racism in higher education. *Teaching in Higher Education* 17(2): 113–125.

9

Listening in Human Rights Education

Learning from Life Stories of Survivors of Atrocities

Bronwen E. Low

McGill University

Emmanuelle Sonntag

Université du Québec à Montréal

I want to tell you a story. A true story. My story.

—"My two families" by Leontine Uwababyeyi

Introduction

The first-person accounts of survivors of genocide and other forms of violence have played a vital role in human rights education. For instance, projects such as the USC Shoah Foundation The Institute for Visual History and Education, founded by Steven Spielberg, have dedicated themselves to recording testimonies for access by educators and researchers. Despite their pedagogic importance, we also know that these stories can pose challenges to the processes of teaching and learning. They ask us to confront what Pitt and Britzman (2003) refer to as "difficult knowledge," which is "a concept meant to signify both representations of social traumas in curriculum and the individual's encounters with them" (755–776). While it is impossible to predict what students (and teachers) might find difficult in their pedagogical encounters, it is much more likely that learning will be affectively charged in response to representations of social and individual crisis. This raises important questions: When accounts of traumatic experience are envisioned as pedagogic, what is one hoping students will learn? How to ethically support students and teachers in engaging with the stories of people who have survived traumatic experience—while, importantly, respecting the interviewees themselves?

We have been exploring these questions as co-directors of the Education and Life Stories working group of a large oral history project entitled Life Stories of Montrealers Displaced by War, Genocide, and other Human Rights Violations (shortened here as Montreal Life Stories project). From 2007 to 2012, a team of university and community-based researchers conducted interviews with approximately 500 Montrealers with experiences of mass violence and displacement. Members of the survivor communities (Tutsi, Haitian, Cambodian, and Holocaust) were key partners in both the research and the diffusion of the project, fundamentally shaping the project's philosophy, activities, and outcomes. The Education group had the central task of disseminating the oral histories by developing curricula for secondary schools. One of group's principle accomplishments was developing a bilingual educational package called We are Here (*Nous sommes ici*) containing five Learning and Evaluation Situations (LES), the curricular units in the Quebec Education Program. The units are designed for "cycle two" secondary school, where the students are generally 14 to 16 years old.

Our goal while designing "We Are Here" was to have teachers and students engage with the life stories of human rights violations, in order to foster a more inclusive cultural memory that would develop "*le vivre-ensemble*," our capacity to live well together.

Given recent events in Quebec, including the 2008 Consultation Commission on Accommodation Practices Related to Cultural Differences struck in response to (media heightened) fears that immigrants to the province were making unreasonable demands, as well as the more recent proposal of a Quebec Charter of Values by the Parti Québécois political party (among others, prohibiting the wearing of visible symbols of religious affiliation by state employees), mean that the expansion of people's understandings of who "we" are is a significant social justice project. Featuring the stories of immigrants and refugees to the province of Quebec, the curriculum offers students a more complex understanding of the history and present of the province, as well as of human rights violations. First-person accounts bring world history and politics to life, helping us to understand the processes and human costs of violence and war, and expanding our awareness of our fellow residents and citizens. At the same time, we recognized that the "difficult knowledge" of human rights violations makes particular demands upon learners.

Given the centrality of listening to the theory and methodology of oral history (Norkunas, 2011), listening has fundamentally shaped how we think about teaching and learning from the life stories. We have been exploring the potential of a pedagogy listening as a means of supporting students and teachers in learning from the words, voices, meanings, and silences of people who have survived difficult or traumatic experiences. In this chapter, we explore the seven central tenets of this pedagogy of listening that we developed in relation to the life stories.

Yet, there is an irony in building a case for listening in schools. Students are commanded daily to "be quiet and listen to the teacher." Despite the long history in educational theory of critiquing this didactic model of listening, including in the work of Dewey (Waks, 2011) and Freire (2006), the student-who-listens-in-silence versus the teacher-who-speaks-loudly is still regularly invoked in practice as an ideal relation. The demand for silence is in part a pragmatic response to the inherent noisiness of schools, buildings often filled to capacity with hundreds (or thousands) of children or adolescents moving through them, playing, socializing, singing, talking, shouting, etc. At the same time, the listening imperative is also a key tool in the establishment of teacher authority and power. This demand for silence on the part of students can also hold true in the context of listening to difficult material such as the testimonies of Holocaust survivors, where respectful listening is often assumed to require silence. The educational history and present of this dynamic requires that, as part of the development of a pedagogy of listening, we must unsettle and rework commonplace understandings of what Waks describes (this volume) as passive informational listening in school.

Listening in Oral History

The Montreal Life Stories project promoted a model of "deep listening," in which interviewees were "listening for meanings, not just facts, and listening in such a way that prompts more profound reflection from the interviewee" (Sheftel & Zembrzycki, 2010, p. 199). Deep listening shares aspects of what Waks (this volume) describes as relational listening, including the value of quieting one's mind in order to better "listen for clues about the other's situation and hopes," although in this case the relationship is the very specific and relatively formal one between interviewer and interviewee. The commitment to relationality is closely tied to a key concept in the methodology of oral history, "shared authority" (Frisch, 1990), or what Greenspan (2010) describes in terms of learning "with" rather than "about." Traditional power relations between researchers and interviewees are moved beyond in favor of a dual authority in which the interviewees hold the authority in describing their experiences and the interviewers hold the authority of critical distance and professional training. Sharing authority in oral history takes dialogue seriously, and the perspective of the oral historian is bi-directional, envisioning both the interviewer and interviewee participating in a conversation. This means the act of listening transforms, in some way, the listening self. Norkunas (2011, p. 64) develops the idea of further, in the context of teaching oral history:

> Rather than occupying an objective position, a listener should expect to modify her or his self-awareness and identity as a result of engaging with the narrator and hearing the stories. When there are class and power differences between listener and narrator, a listener of conscience acknowledges them. Establishing an atmosphere of respect and equality of self in an interview means that neither the logic of the narrator nor that of the interviewer is privileged; instead the driving force of the interview lies in the interaction and tension between the two and the ways that each is revised, reconstructed, and elaborated upon as the conversation flows back and forth.

This vision of listening as negotiation reminds that listening can have significant consequences for the listener, and that listening is shaped and limited by the sociocultural reality of the listener. Self-aware listeners understand and acknowledge that their perspectives and understandings are situated and that this can pose challenges for listening across differences, especially those shaped by power inequities (see Norkunas, 2011, for listening exercises for oral history students which help them in the work of understanding). Similarly, Wong (2009, p. 240) describes the importance in the life story interview of interviewer and interviewee both having an awareness of their positioning in relation to the other as well as their presence and role in the co-creation of the interview. In our pedagogy of listening, we work to develop this self-awareness in the learner.

The life story literature places emphasis on the ways the story changes in the interaction between teller and listener, and the ways both parties themselves can be transformed. It provides us with an account of the co-construction of meaning involved in the dynamic relation between teller, tale, and listener. However, our task in the Education working group was to build curricula that drew upon interviews that were already recorded (although in one, we do have the students interview elders in their families). We therefore wondered how to translate this concept of self-reflexive, dialogic, and subjective listening in oral history to students' engagements in classrooms with pre-recorded life stories. We imagined them as active participants, revising and reconstructing in their own way. Since recorded testimonies of atrocity are most often used as pedagogic tools in museums and exhibits dedicated to human rights education, we also turned to the concept of curation.

Curation as Listening

Speaking of the future of museums, Manuel Borja-Villel, director of the *Reina Sofía* in Madrid, proposed that:

> A museum, first of all, should not act as the owner of the works it keeps or rents, but on the contrary should emphasise exchanges and sharing. And its policies can no longer be centred on the treasures, on finding the most rare works. In the end, for me, what matters is the invention of narratives and readings that will stimulate the public. Creating shared accounts. Telling many stories about art rather than the history of art. Making clear that this history is not static and individual, but choral (translation ours). (Guerrin, 2011, p. 4)

We are thinking of curation as a kind of listening, and listening as curation, staged in schools imagined as spaces for the production and collection of multiple narratives and readings that stimulate and engage. Curation, from the Latin *curare*, means "to take care of," (Lehrer, Milton, and Patterson, 2011). In our vision of the listening relation, students act as curators, charged with a responsibility to care for the life stories, producing and sharing their narratives and readings in response these, with the objective of stimulating and engaging the interest of others.

This concept of curation evokes Simon and Eppert's (2007) discussion of the "chain of testimony" that must be created in classroom "communities of memory" in which student listen to the life stories of survivors of the Holocaust and other atrocities. They argue that students must re-tell what they have heard in the testimonies, in order to represent history in a concrete form, for others. This re-telling would make clear the multivoiced, or what Borja-Villel calls "choral," nature of the stories' uptake. The student thus takes part in the project of history conceived of as actively making meaning from the past. In our materials, the students engage with and reflect upon the stories, and in the process make something new from what they have heard.

Towards a Pedagogy of Listening to Life Stories

In designing the curricular materials, we decided that the subject and life stories were better suited for older students, and so created the five Learning and Evaluation Situations (LES) for secondary cycle two where the students are generally 14 to 16 years old. Each LES is connected to a particular subject area and develops subject-specific as well as cross-curricular competencies. The units all ask students to engage with the life stories through a close and careful viewing of the videos, to respond to them in groups and individually through different medium, and to reflect on their own analytic and creative processes. In order to facilitate the use of the recordings, students mostly work with "digital stories" which are videos edited from the interviews by the subject and an editor. These tend to be under 10 minutes and bring together video, images, sound, and text.

All of the materials begin with an activity in which students listen to one or more of the digital stories created out of the project interviews. Our first Learning and Evaluation Situation (LES) is designed for use in English Language Arts and is entitled "What a Story!: Life Stories and Digital Storytelling." In it, the students listen to and discover the narrative structure of a digital story from a Holocaust survivor (or in French, a Tutsi whose family experienced the genocide in Rwanda), analyze it and then, in groups, create a new digital story based on a 30-minute excerpt from an interview with another survivor. They develop editing skills, and critically reflect upon the choices made in the process. The second LES, "Dialogue Time: Interviewing and Building a Collective Timeline" (Ethics and Religious Culture curriculum), has students listen to a documentary entitled "*I was there*," featuring segments from interviews with a Haitian woman, a Cambodian woman, a Chilean woman, and a woman who survived the Holocaust. After reflecting on the practice and ethics of interviewing, the students interview people from their own communities, and then create a collective time line based on the interviews. In the third LES designed for the History and Citizenship curriculum, "Mapping the Elsewhere Here," students listen to a series of digital stories from the project, map these stories onto visual cartographic representations of the city which they create, and then write and map some of their own narratives, exploring ties between identity and place. In the fourth LES, "Learning about the Tutsi Genocide in Rwanda through the Graphic Novel and Interview," students read excerpts from a graphic narrative about Rwanda by Rupert Bazambanza and watch and listen to a segment from the video interview with the artist. After doing some research, they create an additional page for the graphic narrative, where they present their position on the issue of military intervention and humanitarian assistance, a theme in the Contemporary World curriculum. In the fifth LES, "Between the Tracks: Creating an Audio Guide," designed for English Language Arts, the students listen to an audio guide whose objective is to commemorate in the streets of Montreal the genocide of the Tutsis in Rwanda. They practice listening exercises while reflecting on their abilities as listeners. They then create their own audio guide through a writing exercise. The audio guide is geo-tagged, situating the student production and their experiences within Montreal.

The theories discussed above inform our thinking about a pedagogy of listening inspired by oral history practice; some consciously shaped the writing of the curricular materials, while others are helpful as we revisit and reflect upon what we have created.

This pedagogy aims to:

Promote more democratic relations. Inspired by the concept of shared authority, we imagine the relation between student and teacher as a partnership as the class works together to co-construct knowledge and meaning from the digital stories. Such partnership also requires facing the challenge of listening to the beliefs of others which conflict with your own; Haroutounian-Gordon (2010, p. 2811) argues that when teachers allow "their listening to be interrupted by a challenging perspective, they open themselves to recognition of heretofore tacit beliefs, to new questions, and to new ideas about the resolution of those questions," an insight that we think can be extended to students.

Build a listening community. Within our LES, the students work together in listening and production groups, discussing and negotiating, in transaction, their understandings of the life stories and determining together the nature of their creative response. This community should support students through the process of grappling with stories and information that in some instances might scare or deeply sadden them.

Develop an ethics of listening. We understand that listening can be a powerful conduit to awareness of the experiences of others, and that this relationship is delicate in situations in which those others have had markedly different life experiences from the student. For instance, the introduction to the curricular guide includes a discussion of the ethics of doing oral history, including the concept of shared authority in the interview and in the classroom. For instance, after an initial listening exercise in "What a Story" in which students explore what they think

> "In the end, for me, what matters is the invention of narratives and readings that will stimulate the public. Creating shared accounts. . . . Telling many stories about art rather than the history of art. Making clear that this history is not static and individual, but choral."
>
> —Manuel Borja-Villel (Guerrin, 2011, p. 4)

are the central elements of a 30-minute interview segment with a Holocaust survivor, students are asked to discuss, among other issues: "The responsibilities that accompany listening to a difficult story" (LES, 2012, p. 26).

Support critical reflexive practice for students (and teacher) individually and as a collective. Students are regularly encouraged to self-reflect as they engage with the testimonies of others, exploring as they go how the stories might have changed them. Final integration activities at the end of the units ask the students to critically examine what they have learned. For instance, in "Dialogue Time," the students: "Write a one-page text or produce an artistic work about the experience of the interview as dialogue." And, at the end of "What a Story!" students are asked to discuss the implications of their choices as editors,

> to be critical of the created digital story. Consider the way that narratives can be modified, the meaning built into the digital story vs. the meaning of the interview, and questions of narrative form. (LES, 2012, p. 27)

As they seek critical distance from the story they have crafted, they are also thinking through the situated nature of their own perspectives and choices.

Explore the multitude of listenings. The collective nature of the assignments produce multiple responses (which Borja-Villel might call "choral") to the digital stories. For example, in "What a Story!" the student working groups create their own digital story versions of the same interview, making clear the many possible interpretations of a story, and the different emphases that can be made in the creation of the shorter text. In "Mapping the Elsewhere Here," each listening group determines what it sees as the key words or phrases to be placed on the map of Montreal, creating multiple cartographies of lived experience.

Foster a culture of close and attentive listening. The LES's cultivate the students' attention to their own listening processes. For instance, in "Between the Tracks," as the students create the audio guide, it is possible for them to "enter" the recording they have made; they can slow down the cadence, augment the sound, rewind or fast-forward. They cut, paste, annotate. They are auditors who intervene in what they are listening to, and interpret their listening for potential audiences.

Explore listening as curation. Students are given the opportunity to narrate and then exhibit their listening through various media, giving them shape and meaning in the form of digital stories, time lines, maps, audio-guides, and a page from a graphic novel. This shaping is the precursor to exhibiting their listening, as students share their work with each other and the wider community.

For example, in "Between the Tracks," students disseminate the audio guides they created, inspired by the one commemorating the Rwandan genocide, by connecting with the *Culture à l'écoute!* programme, which promotes the creation of audio guides in Quebec schools (see http://www.baladoweb.qc.ca).

Support students in making connections and taking a position on current events. In the LES, students are asked to make connections between what they hear and learn and their own lives. Rather than learning to think of human rights violations as existing in a separate reality, the curricula emphasise the legacy of trauma, the place of memory in everyday life, and the interconnectedness of human experience through the coexistence of different life trajectories and stories in Montreal. For instance, in "Mapping the Elsewhere Here," the students first map the life stories they have heard onto a graphic representation of Montreal, and then insert onto the map some of their own experiences. The resulting collective map showcases the ties of identity to place and as well as potential relationships, beginning with spatial ones, between the students and the Montreal Life Stories project interviewees.

> Crucial to the model of listening we propose here is that listening is both an individual and a shared process: what we hear while listening is highly personal, dependent on our social location and, at the same time, shaped by the listenings of others as well as our relation to the speaking other.

They are also supported in taking positions on contemporary issues and, in some units, moving to action. In "Learning about the Tutsi Genocide," students extensively research an element of the genocide in Rwanda in order to then "take a position on the issue of military intervention through the development of a supplementary page of the graphic narrative." Part of this process of taking a stand can involve various forms of action (without giving students a simplified notion of an adolescent's ability to intervene in violent conflicts at the international level). For instance, students are invited to:

> Promote the Rwandan commemorative audio walk that you listened to at the beginning of the LES, by creating a postcard campaign. The students could also create a comic strip to accompany the audio guide. (LES, 2012, p. 70)

Foster students' historical imagination. The pedagogy seeks to bring historical events to life through careful attention to the life stories of others. As Julian Treasure (2011: n.p.) remarks, "listening is one of the main ways in which we live the passing of time." The digital stories span the twentieth century and move into the twenty-first, animating historical events from across the globe through first-person perspectives and narrations.

Conclusion

Crucial to the model of listening we propose here is that listening is both an individual and a shared process: what we hear while listening is highly personal, dependent on our social location and, at the same time, shaped by the listenings of others as well as our relation to the speaking other. Our curricular units ask students to reflect carefully and exhibit what they are listening to, creating occasions for exploring individual and collective meaning-making and identities. We also argue that this close attention to the complex dynamics of listening can help refigure power hierarchies in school as well as communities. While critiques of traditional power relations in school are certainly not new, we hope that a renewed focus on listening in classrooms might help enact more democratic visions of education in which teachers and students are co-partners in a dialogic learning process, open and attentive to the perspectives and experiences of the other. This chapter is an initial articulation of what the elements of such a pedagogy might be, in relation to our curriculum but also for more general use and development in theory and practice by other researchers and teachers. We are currently working with teachers to study actual uses of the Learning and Evaluation Situations in order to better understand how the pedagogy might translate into practice.

Suggestions for Further Reading

Low, B., & Sonntag, E. (2013). Towards a pedagogy of listening: Teaching and learning from life stories of human rights violations. *Journal of Curriculum Studies* 45(6), 768–789.

Greenspan, H. (2010). *On listening to Holocaust survivors: Beyond testimony.* Second Edition. (St. Paul, MN: Paragon House)

Simon, R., & Eppert, C. (1997). Remembering obligation: Pedagogy and the witnessing of testimony of historical trauma. *Canadian Journal of Education*, 22(2): 175–191.

References

Guerrin, M. (2011, 19 novembre). L'Espagnol qui bouscule les musées [The Spaniard who's shaking museums]. *Le Monde.frSupplément Culture&idées* [Culture and ideas supplement], p. 1 & 4. Paris. Retrieved from http://www.lemonde.fr/culture/article/2011/11/17/l-espagnol-qui-bouscule-les-musees_1605628_3246.html

Freire, P. (2006). *Pedagogy of the oppressed*. London, England: Continuum.

Frisch, M. (1990). *A Shared Authority*. Albany, New York: State University of New York Press.

Greenspan, H. (2010). *On listening to Holocaust survivors: Beyond testimony*. 2nd ed. St. Paul, MN: Paragon House.

Harutounian-Gordon, S. (2010). Listening to a challenging perspective: The role of interruption. *Teachers College Record*, 112(11): 2793–2814.

Norkunas, M. (2011). Teaching to listen: Listening exercises and self-reflexive journals. *Oral History Review*, 38(1): 63–108.

Lehrer, E, Milton, C. E., & Patterson, M. E. (Eds). 2011. *Curating difficult knowledge: Violent pasts in public places*. Great Britain: Palgrave/Macmillan.

Pitt, A., & Britzman, D. (2003). Speculations on qualities of difficult knowledge in teaching and learning: An Experiment in psychoanalytic research. *International Journal of Qualitative Studies in Education*, 16(6): 755–776.

Sheftel, A., & Zembrzycki, S. (2010). Only Human: A Reflection on the Ethical and Methodological Challenges of Working with "Difficult" Stories. *The Oral History Review*, 37(2): 191–214.

Simon, R., & Eppert, C. (1997). Remembering obligation: Pedagogy and the witnessing of testimony of historical trauma. *Canadian Journal of Education*, 22(2): 175–191.

Uwababyeyi, Leontine. My two families. Retrieved May 1, 2013 at http://storytelling.concordia.ca/refugeeyouth/going-places-memoryscape-bus-tour-montreal/video/my-two-families-leontine-uwababyeyi

Waks, L. (2011). John Dewey on listening and friendship in school and society. *Educational Theory*, 61(2): 191–205.

Wong, A. (2009). Conversations for the real world: Shared authority, reflexivity, and process in the oral history interview. *Journal of Canadian Studies*, 43(1): 239–258.

10
_____

Listening in a Pedagogy of Trust

Katherine Schultz

Mills College

Introduction

Teaching is both a public and private activity. Across the world, teachers perform each day in front of a crowd of students; their moment-to-moment decisions—whether they are delivering a lecture, disciplining a student, or orchestrating a group conversation—are nearly always in public view and open to scrutiny. Moreover, teachers generally teach behind closed doors. Although their students may be intimately familiar with their stance and patterned behaviors, their actual practices are generally not known to their colleagues or even their supervisors. Teacher professional development thus introduces new variables; learning new pedagogies requires performing in front of peers and supervisors, and as such involves new risks and requires a high degree of trust.

In this chapter, I draw on my work with teachers in international settings to delineate a pedagogy of trust.[1] Arguing that trust—between and among teachers and students—is an essential component of teaching and learning, I suggest that the establishment of a climate of relational trust is an essential component of learning including learning to teach. The process of learning requires taking risks and entering the sometimes vulnerable state of not knowing. A pedagogy of trust guides educators to create conditions for building on principles of social justice elaborated in the introduction to this volume.

A critical starting place for the development of a pedagogy of trust is placing listening at the center of teaching and learning. Incorporating a listening stance into one's pedagogy implies entering a classroom with questions as well as answers and knowledge as well as a clear sense of the limitations of that knowledge. This stance toward teaching shifts classroom practice away from a didactic approach toward a pedagogy that respects and builds on the knowledge and experience each person brings to the classroom. I define listening as an active, relational, and interpretive process that is focused on making meaning and only possible in a climate of trust.

Professional development contexts are particularly useful sites to study the role of listening and trust in pedagogical practice. Like classroom practice, professional development is too often didactic and based on the premise that experts should deliver information to relatively passive teachers. Professional development can also be conceptualized as an active process, fundamentally based on listening and responding to local knowledge and needs, leading to a shift in interactional norms. When professional development takes place in international settings led by people who are outsiders and when teachers are asked to interact in ways that are unfamiliar or uncomfortable, the necessary level of trust increases. It increases still more when the setting is marked by recent trauma and conflict. A more nuanced understanding of how trust and listening are interconnected illuminates the challenges and possibilities of new approaches to professional development, especially in countries recently affected by war and disaster. It also has broader implications for teaching and learning more generally.

Teaching is fundamentally built upon relationships. While important work has been done on the value of collaboration among teachers in professional development work in the United States (Oja & Smulyan (1989); Lieberman (1996); Lieberman & Miller (1992, 1999) McLaughlin & Talbert (2001); Little (2002)), we know little about collaborative practices in international settings. The work I describe in this chapter is based on a set of practices developed with colleagues to support the professional growth of teachers and school change through professional development work in Haiti, Indonesia and Lebanon.

A focus of our work has been collaborative mentoring, a practice based on a belief in the importance of listening in teaching. In collaborative mentoring we introduced a set of practices that encourage teachers to learn from and with each other by beginning with the teacher's question and proceeding with feedback based on observations and the sharing of expertise rather than judgments and critique. Teachers are taught ways to engage in dialogue that builds on the knowledge and understandings both people bring to the classroom context. We began with the understanding that listening is tied closely to observation, questioning, and adopting a stance of uncertainty (Schultz, 2003). Rather than giving the teachers, administrators, and supervisors in each of these countries a set of arbitrary and culturally situated techniques embedded in assumptions of where expertise is located, our strategy has been to introduce them to methods for learning from each other that begin with listening and trust.

In what follows I analyze how listening, collaboration, and expertise have been central components of teacher learning in international contexts (Mutua & Swadener, 2004). Drawing on a range of data sources from three countries, including over thirty interviews in two of the settings (Indonesia and Lebanon), detailed field notes and videos of workshops, journals, and a variety of documents, I identify components of the emerging concept of a pedagogy of trust. I discovered the importance of relationship and trust as critical aspects of communication and mentoring when the learning is based on an exchange of knowledge that positions the mentor and teacher as both learners and listeners.

In each of the three countries, I was invited by an NGO (Non-Governmental Organization) to form a team of U.S. educators for work with local ministries of education.[2] Our intent in each setting was to introduce the teachers to processes for listening to and learning from each other in order to exchange ideas about improving their own teaching through the sharing their knowledge. In order to do this work we introduced the ideas through what we have come to call a pedagogy of trust.

Contexts of Trauma: Aceh Indonesia, Refugee Camps in Lebanon, Haiti

As part of a campus-wide response to the South Asian tsunami in 2004, I led a team of teacher educators from the University of Pennsylvania to Aceh Indonesia to partner with the International Rescue Committee's (IRC) Child Youth and Protection division to work with teachers, supervisors, teacher educators, and head teachers or principals to introduce strategies for improving their teaching and preparing new teachers who were hired as a result of this large scale disaster. This work continued over four summers.

During the first summer of our work in Indonesia, we introduced child-centered teaching methods to experienced teachers from across the Aceh Province working to rebuild an education system that had suffered the devastating effects of the tsunami and 30 years of civil war. As a consequence of the tsunami, thousands of people were killed and many more were left homeless. An estimated 4,000 new teachers were hired to replace those who perished in the tsunami. In the wake of the devastation, there was an opportunity to introduce the teachers to child-centered teaching methods that had previously been incorporated into the national curriculum with insufficient teacher preparation and professional development, as well as to strengthen the nascent teacher networks, the *gugus*, which had been introduced throughout the country. The disaster made it imperative that schools and teachers attend to the spectrum of needs of children who had survived what teachers referred to as the "trauma."

Over time our work became focused on "collaborative mentoring" practices that teachers, supervisors, and principals could incorporate into pre-service and in-service teacher professional development as well as school network meetings. Our plan was to teach child-centered, inquiry-based pedagogies as well as processes for educators to continue that work. We asked teachers, supervisors and head teachers to listen closely to one another to engage in collaborative mentoring through role plays and to work in collaborative planning and analysis groups, with the understanding that mentoring across roles in a hierarchical educational structure would require close listening and trust.

> "The notion of listening to teach assumes that the teachers and students will shape the classroom culture together. In addition, it presumes that there is a climate of trust that supports both students and teachers to take risks in what they say and how they listen."
> —Schultz, 2003

Teachers were accustomed to critique and correction; supervisors were used to making decisions about curriculum and instruction without teacher input. In order to change this dynamic and encourage teachers to learn from and with each other, we endeavored to establish a climate of trust where teachers and supervisors could try on these new roles.

Two years later, I had the opportunity to take these practices to Beirut, Lebanon, where I met with Palestinian teachers, supervisors, and head teachers who worked in Palestinian schools located in refugee camps across that country. As in Aceh, my colleagues and I did this work in collaboration with an NGO and a local agency (UNRWA), through a project we called "Listening Schools."[3]

In Lebanon we began by working with the entire staff of teachers and head teachers from four schools. Subsequently we met with a mix of teachers, supervisors, and head teachers from several schools and, in the final visit, with all of the supervisors and a group of 75 of principals who represented nearly all of the principals in the Palestinian schools in Lebanon. In Lebanon, most of the Palestinian refugees live in camps and attend UNRWA schools. The living conditions in the camps vary. Many are characterized by constant conflict, trauma, and unpredictability. All of the teachers spoke frequently about their daily struggles, the hardship imposed by the living conditions of the children and families in the schools, and their feelings of displacement that shaped their lives. In recent years, many of the schools have experienced high dropout rates as youth saw their opportunities to join the labor force diminished by the restrictions placed on the available jobs given their status as Palestinians. Many teachers reported feeling demoralized by their school climate. As in our work in Aceh, our emphasis with these educators was to introduce new ways of working together that respected and built on teachers' knowledge and expertise in order to improve the learning and lives of the children and families living in the harsh conditions of the refugee camps.

"Judgments about the intentionality of others play a central role in relational trust. As social interactions occur, participants attend not only to surface behavior, but they also seek to discern the underlying intentions that are likely to motivate the others' behavior and how these can be reconciled in the context of the mutual obligations understood among the parties."

—*Bryk & Schneider, 1996, p. 6*

In 2011, I was invited by a small NGO, Sionfonds, to work with the teachers and principals from three schools in Haiti, a country plagued by high levels of poverty and still suffering from the consequences of a devastating earthquake. Only 40 percent of the children in Haiti attend school, few go beyond a basic primary school education. We introduced these same ideas of collaborative mentoring to the teachers, while also emphasizing the importance of building community and trust to create schools where students, teachers, and community members are supported to engage in sustained learning.

In what follows I look across these three contexts to analyze central themes in order to develop the contours of a pedagogy of trust. I argue that building trust is an essential aspect of our work as outsiders invited to work with teachers in countries that have recently experienced war and devastation.

Teaching Listening: Establishing Trust in Haiti

We knew that it was important initially to build a sense of community in our international work, so that teachers would be less fearful about sharing their teaching ideas and practices with their peers and supervisors. Few of the teachers were accustomed to talking aloud about their teaching practices and some, especially those in Haiti, had received little preparation for their classroom responsibilities. We began our workshops with storytelling, initially asking teachers to tell and then write the stories of their names.[4] Through this activity, we emphasized that each teacher had stories to tell and knowledge to bring to our workshops and their classrooms. We wanted them to witness their own expertise so they would know that they could share knowledge with their colleagues.

Initially, the teachers told each other the stories with animation, faltering when we asked them to write them. Most of the teachers had not attended school beyond grade six or eight, and few wrote regularly in their daily lives. After some gentle encouragement, they all began to write. In a matter of minutes, each of the teachers had composed a story.

Once we were certain that the teachers were done, we went around the circle and asked each teacher to stand and read her or his story aloud to the group. The stories were varied and personal. Some made us laugh out loud. Others were poignant, revealing life-threatening situations connected to their names. A few examples illustrate the range of the stories. One teacher recounted:[5]

My name is Amos. It's a name from the Bible. And why did they choose that name for me? It was because I was the first born in my family. I was the only son of my father. And they gave me that name so that I could grow up with wisdom and understanding. And I'm very proud of that name because I feel that that name will stay [with] me.

A female teacher told this story to the attentive group:

My name is Carline. When my parents were going to have me, they wanted to choose a beautiful name for their daughter so they chose Carline. My mother told me the story that I was walking and then I went back to crawling. So they took me to the hospital and there were a lot of people who were discouraging. They said, your baby is not going to live. And my mother said it is only God who can give her life, I can't make her live. God cured me. So actually I went back to walking. And now every time my father looks at me, he says, look there's a kid I was going to lose. That's how it is.

After listening closely to each other's stories, in a few short moments, the group of teachers—from three schools scattered across the country—became a more cohesive group. As they told stories, they laughed together and gained a new level of understanding and comfort. They saw that if they stood and read their stories, their peers would pay attention to them, offering praise and encouragement. They saw the value of listening to each other's stories and being listened to, and of bringing such listening practices to their own classrooms where students might be fearful and intimidated to learn.

We used this activity to teach the importance of starting the school year by building community and establishing trust in classrooms. We talked explicitly about the ways that teachers could use storytelling and writing to get to know their students and provide them with a way to know one another. Through this process, we explained, they might create new and better conditions for learning. At the same time we wanted to engender an atmosphere of trust in our workshop so that the teachers would begin to be open to learning from one another.

Each time we have done this professional development work with teachers, we have begun the work by introducing the teachers to ways of building community and learning about one another. I cannot assert that teachers trusted each other or their leaders initially simply because they told stories from their lives. The sharing of stories and listening to the details that teachers themselves chose to reveal to one another, however, opened up new possibilities for teacher learning.

Introducing Trust into Teacher Practice: Collaborative Mentoring in Aceh

The final two summers we returned to Aceh, Indonesia, we traveled to several villages along the coast that were most affected by the tsunami. Our work centered on the introduction of practices to build knowledge and sustain educational improvement to classroom teachers, supervisors, and head teachers.

Our work in Aceh began as reconstruction work after a devastating natural disaster. Less than a year after the tsunami, the 30-year conflict that disrupted most parts of its society—including its schools—was resolved. Our work became closely connected to reconciliation and post-conflict institution-building activities. In our interviews and through our conversations, we learned that over 600 schools had been burned down in the first three months of martial law in Aceh in 2003. During this time, teachers often went to work with their uniforms in their bags to hide the fact that they were government workers. In some places, professional development was effectively stopped for several years. There was an atmosphere of distrust for teachers and public workers in the schools and throughout the region, given the tensions between the local and national government.

Through interviews and fragments of stories, we pieced together a partial understanding of the fragility of the teachers' work. This led us to begin our workshops with activities followed by explicit discussions about the importance of trust in working together as professionals. Teachers later commented that one of the most important aspects of the workshops was the freedom they felt to exchange ideas. Given the level of surveillance, especially during the long and often violent period of internal conflict, this opportunity to learn from one another and ask questions was a rare experience for the teachers.

During our third summer in Aceh, we decided to initiate a conversation about trust though an activity that demonstrated the concept. We also made a decision to shift our stance as leaders and talk more about our lives and work in order to model a different kind of openness. During the protracted conflict, teachers, parents, and children had frequently chosen to remain silent rather than jeopardize their lives and the lives of people around them. As a result, many teachers seemed to fear providing the wrong answers during the workshops. We knew that in order for them to learn from us and, perhaps more importantly, to learn from one another, they needed to begin by building relationships and community.

As an example, during one workshop we asked the teachers to form two lines. We gave them two simple tasks: first, to line themselves up according to their height without talking and second, to line up alphabetically according to their given name. In order to do each of these activities, the teachers had to really look at each other and later, ask each person his or her name. They seemed to enjoy this opening activity, even though it was completely new to them. Later, when we asked one of the translators what had stood out for her from the workshops, she replied, that it was the freedom the teachers felt to speak up. It was unusual for teachers to speak openly without first taking their cue from a head teacher or someone in a position of authority.

Our focus was on collaborative mentoring during the morning of one of these workshops. We introduced processes and phrases the teachers could use to give each other feedback for their work. We began by asking teachers to listen to each other's questions, followed by observations of teaching, and finally a mentoring conversation that built on the observation. We encouraged the teachers to use the phrases we introduced to open up and deepen the conversation. After lunch, we described an activity to help them to plan for future *gugus* or monthly professional development meetings during which we hoped they would teach each other the processes they had learned. We asked them to select a challenge to use as a focus for their meetings and then to plan a series of workshops around that issue.

First, we engaged them in a process to identify a challenge. They selected the topic of motivation. We took them through the planning process in which they elaborated what this problem meant, articulated their goals, the challenges, the materials and resources they would need, and finally they outlined the activities for a series of meetings. As they began to plan the next three months of their *gugus* meetings, it became clear that the teachers were highly engaged in this process. Practically everyone was involved in the conversation. Early on, one of the teachers said to me,"You're a professor why don't *you* tell us how we should motivate students." I repeated my stance that as teachers they have tremendous resources and should look to their group for expertise. I explained that, for instance, there might be someone who knew ways to motivate students to learn mathematics in Aceh and she could share that expertise with others, while another teacher might be able to explain how he motivated students in science. I also added a few general ideas such as the importance of making learning relevant to students, giving examples of how to build on students' interests and passions in mathematics, writing, and science. Explaining that we had teaching tools and processes rather than ready-made answers or pre-made teaching materials to offer them was tricky as it did not fit with their expectations. All the same, it was difficult not to give them a few ideas that could be easily construed as answers, to satisfy these expectations. Even this small step was a way of building trust while encouraging teachers to take small risks.

As they planned their workshops, the teachers decided that their first few meetings should be spent getting to know one another since they were from different schools and did not even know each other's names. They suggested the idea of eating dinner together at the first meeting and then playing a set of games like those we had introduced earlier that day. Next, they decided they wanted to learn more about each other's classrooms. They decided that they could do this through cross-visitations and mentoring. What was most exciting about this process was the level of engagement by the group. In addition, for the first time we had more certainty that the teachers would actually take the ideas back to their schools and *gugus* meetings and implement them. They seemed serious and committed to using their *gugus* meetings to learn from one another and to address pressing questions.

This decision to begin with activities and discussions about trust paid off. We noticed a different quality of interaction among the participants. This was demonstrated not only in how they listened to one another, their level of trust in answering open-ended questions, and their increased comfort with each other, but also because the teachers took up our ideas and then adapted them to their own contexts.

Introducing Trust into Teacher Practice: Collaborative Mentoring

Our work with the teachers was slow and required us to patiently introduce new interactional practices and ways of learning, sharing, and disseminating information. In an interview between one of the workshop leaders and a key Indonesian staff member, Ana explained just how difficult this work was for the teachers:

> **A:** It's hard, it's very hard because it's deep into the culture. It's not only about their own confidence, it is about this culture don't give them chance to share their ability. Your people will call you *sombong*. [Ana laughs.] If you teach somebody else, if you give suggestion to another teacher, give some observation to another teacher people will call you *sombong*.

> **R:** So another piece of it sounds like there just needs to be time for the *gugus* to develop and see if the trust develops and the ways of interacting can shift.[6] (Interview, 2007)

Ana explained that teachers were reluctant to display their knowledge and expertise for fear of appearing *sombong* or arrogant. They did not want to place themselves above others by appearing knowledgeable. By introducing the teachers to the stance of listening, we taught them more than we would have had we simply demonstrated new teaching strategies. As Ana indicates, we taught them to trust that they each had knowledge to share with one another. This was particularly complicated when we asked supervisors to participate as equals in the collaborative mentoring with teachers, which went counter to their typical roles and assumptions about expertise.

Ana also explained the significance of the collaborative mentoring process in which the teacher, rather than the supervisor initiated the questions. Typically the supervisor did all of the talking, essentially telling the teacher what he had done wrong, while insisting that he correct his teaching. As Ana explained:

> And they found that the school supervisors understand that it is two ways. It is not one way. I mean . . . it's not only one way; it is not the school supervisor who knows everything about the process in classroom. The teachers have to be asked, "What's happening?" "What do you want to happen?" . . . [I asked the teacher what was the most important thing that happened in this workshop and he said that it was when] the school supervisors come to the *gugus*. They start to first listen to the teacher, listen to the teacher about what do you think about your own teaching learning process. It's not coming from the supervisor first, but it is first coming from the teacher. (Interview, 2007)

Ana appeared to be genuinely surprised to witness that the supervisors were willing to listen to the teachers and respect their knowledge. She emphasized the importance of beginning with the teachers' own reflections.

We often doubted whether teachers found the tools useful. We asked them to do something difficult—believe that they had answers to give to others and that their peers could provide useful insights for them. We set up professional development sessions that ran counter to their expectations. We also asked them to replace demonstrations of "best practices" with listening and to believe in themselves and each other as sources of knowledge. The validity of this work was illustrated to us one day when the teachers persisted in the workshop despite challenging conditions, as illustrated in the following vignette.

On the third day of our work outside of a small village, we drove to a new school by crossing several new streams that had cut deep ruts into the road. The sky was bright and the flooding did not strike us as unusual. It had rained the previous night in the mountainous jungles and we were told that the illegal logging often caused rain water to flow rapidly into the villages. We arrived at the temporary school built on stilts. Teachers were waiting for us and we quickly moved the chairs into a circle against the narrow walls of the building so that we could start our work together. We spent the morning teaching and practicing collaborative mentoring. Even though the space was small, teachers clustered in groups, developed inquiry-based science lessons and mentored each other, mimicking our modeled lesson and using the collaborative practices we had introduced.

Midway through the morning, the head teacher politely interrupted our session and asked everyone to move their motorbikes so that the children could go home. When we visited schools, it was not unusual to see the children walking home and the teachers drinking coffee by mid-day. My first response was to feel exasperated that the children were going home so early, however, I said nothing. When we stopped for a coffee break a short while later, we learned the reason for the dismissal. The pathway between our building and the classrooms just a few meters away was filled with water that was rising quickly. Although the clear blue sky remained, the water continued to pour down from the mountains. A little more than an hour later when we stopped for lunch, we discovered that the water surrounding our building and filling the pathways was over two feet high. It was brown and filled with trash. Undaunted by the conditions, we asked the teachers to return at 1:30. As we watched them wade through the water, lifting up their skirts and rolling up their pant legs, we wondered if we were foolish to expect them to return. We stayed in the classroom hoping that the waters would recede. By the end of lunch, we realized we had to find a new location for the workshop. An open-air community platform near the river was the perfect location and so we followed the teachers and waded back to the road, carrying the computers and boxes of materials high over our heads.

What was most amazing about this day was that all of the teachers returned to the workshop in the afternoon and remained engaged until late in the day. When we concluded our work, a silence fell over us. The trust we had built was measured in this silence. We had been on an unanticipated journey together. They appreciated our willingness to travel so far and persist during flooded conditions to work with them. They acknowledged that this was our third year returning to Aceh and respected our commitment, implicitly indicating the value they saw in the collaborative mentoring practices from the morning. No one made an excuse about why they needed to stay home. We had ventured out together, taken risks, built trust, and together we learned.

When Listening is not Enough: The Fragility of Trust

The complex and shifting political dynamics in schools and communities shaped our work with the Palestinian teachers in Lebanon. Prior to and during our workshops, we visited schools in several of the refugee camps to get a sense of the teachers' work. Our visits included a camp where we were instructed to remain close to the entrance because the central area was volatile that day. The persistent conflicts, people explained, were caused by factionalism—competing groups with opposing beliefs and interests. We soon learned firsthand how politics was enacted in schools. Our visits gave us some knowledge of the school contexts and allowed us to build and deepen relationships with teachers and principals who attended the workshops. Our time was short, however, and it was difficult to learn enough, especially given the language and cultural divides.

As in Aceh, the focus of our workshops in Lebanon was collaborative mentoring. Through our work with the NGO, we were able to give the teachers art materials and a wide variety of children's books in Arabic and English. As a result, the collaborative mentoring was built around lessons that used these materials. We were made aware of the deep problems that shaped all of the teaching and learning activities in the schools and that contributed to the high dropout rates of the students. In response, we introduced a collaborative problem-solving process that involves careful listening based on an abbreviated version of the Descriptive Review process developed by Patricia Carini and educators affiliated with the Prospect Center for Education and Research (Carini, 2001; Himley & Carini, 2000).

We had the opportunity to work with 74 out of the 75 head teachers (principals) of the Palestinian schools in Lebanon. It quickly became clear that this group of principals was going to be much more difficult than our previous groups of teachers in Lebanon. In addition to their more resistant stance toward the ideas, especially those that privileged the knowledge of classroom teachers, the head teachers had strong opinions and spoke for long stretches of time without listening to each other. This was all compounded by the fact that we had to work with them in a single room that was too small.

We began the workshop by teaching a poetry lesson and asking the head teachers to write a poem about a specific time and place. We gave them several examples and hoped that this work together would dissipate the tense atmosphere in the room. Most of the principals began to write before we had finished the introductory activities. Their poems were filled with passion, addressing a range of topics including weddings, memories of surprising events, sickness, and stories of politics and loss. Sadness was threaded through the poems.

After lunch, we introduced the collaborative problem-solving activity that we suggested they might use in their own schools. We had found two more rooms, allowing us to break into three relatively small groups. We selected three principals we had worked with in prior workshops to present a problem of practice. I worked with Mohammed whose problem was framed by the question: "How can I lead the senior boys to attend all of their classes?" The structure of the activity is that the leader spends 10 minutes framing the question and describing the context of the question, followed by 10 minutes for questions and 10 minutes for recommendations.

Mohammed explained that the boys who frequently skipped classes were in the lowest track of the school (Economics) and did not attend the classes they perceived as unimportant for their graduation, including English and History. During those classes they lingered in the hallways and disrupted the other students and teachers. As people asked questions, it became apparent that Mohammed was a member of one political party (which we later learned was a "weak" political party) and the resistant boys were part of another political party (the "strong" political party in this camp). People at the school and in the community, who were members of the political party (or faction) associated with the students, apparently told them that it was acceptable not to go to classes. As a result, the principal felt that he had no recourse with the boys. He explained that the school was divided between people who were a part of the boys' political party and supported their behavior and people who were part of the principal's party, including all of the assistant principals, who wanted the behavior to change.

In the group itself, there were people from each of these two political factions. During the discussion, often when a person made a forceful statement, several people would contradict him with equal power and emotion. In facilitating the meeting, I felt as though I were staving off immanent physical fights as I worked to keep the discussion orderly. Some principals made a wide variety of suggestions to Mohammed including constructive ones such as giving the boys positive leadership opportunities and starting after-school clubs for them. One principal, backed by several others, said that Mohammed should leave his job because he had not acted decisively at the beginning of the year. He also asserted that Mohammed should come down hard on these boys and use strong punishment even if it meant closing the school down for a month. It was an intense and heated discussion during which Mohammed was silent for long stretches of time. At its conclusion, a number of people said that they appreciated Mohammed's honesty and the fact that he brought this problem to the group.

In this instance, it was difficult to insist on enough listening to ensure respect and trust in the group. The group played out its political dynamics rather than adhering strictly to the structure of the protocol we had introduced. At the conclusion of our time together, the director of education at UNRWA said that our workshops were the calmest he had ever seen in Lebanon. He explained that had often had to break up actual fistfights at these meetings among principals. I was unsure about how productive the conversation had been and how much the principals would actually take away from our work together. My ability to shape and guide the conversation was limited by my inability to understand the undercurrents of conversation in Arabic and my limited knowledge of the local political context. I was unable to build enough trust to allow the principals to truly listen to one another because of time constraints, the complexity of the politics that laced each conversation, and my lack of facility with the language including the nuances of the nonverbal communication (Schultz & Smulyan, 2007). Trust is not easily built across cultural divides. It takes time and skill. Yet without deep trust, listening across hierarchies of power was not possible.

Conclusion

Working across cultural, linguistic, and political boundaries in these three different countries, it was essential to begin with the practice of listening. This practice is a cornerstone of a pedagogy of trust. Listening allows teachers to come to know one another and recognize what and how they can learn from their peers. Yet, as illustrated in the final example, this process is slow and often difficult. It is critical to acquire local knowledge of politics, including how the distribution of power shapes interactions and decisions, along with language, in order to obtain a deeper understanding of the dynamics of how learning occurs among teachers. Conditions in the United States may differ along several dimensions from the schools described in this chapter. At the same time, most teachers work under conditions where they are heavily monitored and mistrusted. They are often hesitant to offer ideas or distinguish themselves from their colleagues. The notion of a pedagogy of trust suggests that teachers learn best from their peers in contexts where critique and judgment are suspended and they are given an opportunity to know one another well.

In addition to listening, a pedagogy of trust is characterized by several components including respect, opportunities to select the aspects of oneself to display to others in a public space, a shared belief in teachers' capacities, and a willingness to work across boundaries of difference. In a world where there are high stakes for both teachers and learners, a pedagogy of trust is essential.

In Haiti, Indonesia, and Lebanon, we worked to build trust with the teachers before we began our work together. In addition, we talked explicitly about the importance of trust in our work together. Importantly, we listened to the teachers and asked them to listen to each other. We trusted the teachers to know how translate their experiences and the teaching practices we introduced into their own contexts. Beginning with respect, deep listening, and trust, we worked across cultural and linguistic boundaries to forge new ways to work together and new processes for collaboration.

The results were striking. Teachers were willing to take new risks to try different ways of teaching, opening themselves up to learn from one another. They also engaged in difficult conversations about the challenges they faced in their classrooms. These interactions and discussions are rare in today's classrooms where teachers often close their doors to their supervisors and colleagues, out of fear that if they admit to any concerns or weaknesses, they will lose their job, rather than receive help in solving problems. This distrust is paralyzing. Our challenge is to change the discourse about teachers, teaching and learning, replacing distrust with a pedagogy of trust.

> "Listening to teach suggests receiving information through the heart and mind in order to understand, to learn, and to act. Teaching students to participate in pluralistic democratic communities means being present in the moment and responding and interpreting with both heart and mind."
> —Schultz, 2003

Only then will we see deep engaged teaching and successful learning in our classrooms.

Notes

1. A pedagogy of trust is an idea that I have developed from my work with pre-service, new, and experienced teachers in the U.S. and international contexts. Several people have written about the importance of trust in teaching such as Bryk, A., & Schneider, B. (2003).

2. It is important to acknowledge the teams of people who participated in this work and its development in Indonesia—in addition to our Indonesian colleagues, over the four years our team included Dean Brooks and Martin Canter (IRC), Rachel Throop, NancyLee Bergey, Angie Barr Feltman, Anita Chikkatur, Joy Lesnick, Jeanne Vissa, Chonika Coleman, Sharon Ravitch (University of Pennsylvania) and Lisa Smulyan (Swarthmore College). In Lebanon, in addition to our Lebanese colleagues, our team included Dean Brooks (NRC), Thea Abu El-Haj (Rutgers University), Judy Buchanan (National Writing Project) and Emily Robbins; and in Haiti, in addition to our Haitian colleagues, our team included Serena Clayton, Vanessa Bramlett, and Annie Blackstone (Sionfonds).

3. This work and title of the workshops is based on my book, *Listening* (Schultz, 2003).

4. This has become a common classroom activity and is based on the story, "My Name" written by Sandra Cisneros. Cisneros, S. (1991). *House on Mango Street*, New York: Vintage Books.

5. Serena Clayton translated their stories from Haitian Creole to English.

6. This interview was conducted by Rachel Throop who, as a graduate student, collected much of the data and was instrumental in the professional development work for three of the four summers we worked in Aceh, Indonesia.

Suggested Reading

Bryk, A., & Schneider, B. (2002). *Trust in schools: A core resource for improvement.* New York, NY: Russell Sage.

Carini, P. F. (2001). *Starting strong: A different look at children, schools and standards.* New York, NY: Teachers College Press.

Raider-Roth, M. (2006). *Trusting what you know: The high stakes of classroom relationships.* San Francisco, CA: Jossey-Bass.

Schultz. K. (2003). *Listening: A framework for teaching across differences.* New York, NY: Teachers College Press.

Schultz, K. (2009). *Rethinking classroom participation: Listening to silent voices.* New York, NY: Teachers College Press.

References

Bryk, A., & Schneider, B. (2002). *Trust in schools: A core resource for improvement.* New York, NY: Russell Sage.

Kohl, H. R. (1992). *I won't learn from you and other thoughts on creative maladjustment.* New York, NY: New Press.

Lieberman, A. (1996). Practices that support teacher development: Transforming conceptions of professional learning," in *Teacher learning: New policies, new practices,* eds. M. W. McLaughlin, & I. Oberman. (New York: Teachers College Press.

Lieberman, A., & Miller, L. (1992). *Teachers, their world and their work: Implications for school improvement.* New York: Teachers College Press.

Lieberman, A., & Miller, L. (1999). *Teachers: Transforming their world and their work.* New York: Teachers College Press.

Little, J. W. (2002). "Professional communication and collaboration," in *The keys to effective schools: Educational reform as continuous improvement.* W. Hawley (Ed.). Thousand Oaks, CA: Corwin Press.

McLaughlin, M. W., & Talbert, J. (2001). *Professional communities and the work of high school teaching.* Chicago, IL: University of Chicago Press.

Meier, D. (2002). *In schools we trust: Creating communities of learning in an era of testing and standardization.* Boston, MA: Beacon Press.

Oja S. N., & Smulyan, L. (1989). *Collaborative action research.* New York: Falmer Press.

Schultz, K. (2003). *Listening: A framework for teaching across differences.* New York, NY: Teachers College Press.

11

Promoting Listening by Augmenting Uncertainty

Stanton Wortham and Alexandra Michel

University of Pennsylvania

Introduction

Both education and socialization usually aim to reduce uncertainty by giving students or novices concepts, scripts, and self-understandings through which they can find their way about in a field. Educators give novices concepts and understandings through which they can subsequently listen—in such a way that they move toward more competent interpretation and action. Reducing uncertainty in this way is often useful, but in this chapter we describe an alternative: the counterintuitive pedagogical strategy of "augmenting uncertainty," in which students and novices are deliberately prevented from forming stable concepts, scripts, and self-understandings. The pedagogy of augmenting uncertainty aims to create listening of a different kind than that assumed in didactic pedagogy. Instead of listening through preexisting concepts, scripts, and self-understandings, our pedagogy encourages more *direct* engagement with the subject matter.

Drawing on our analyses of listening and related processes in both investment banks and schools, we argue that listening can involve an openness to resources that we have called "direct involvement" (Michel & Wortham, 2009). This is a normative concept, describing a productive form of engagement with others and the world. People listen most effectively when they remain open to new resources and patterns. This openness requires close attention to situations, without heavy reliance on scripts and other preexisting conceptualizations.[1]

This chapter describes how novices can, through the pedagogy of augmenting uncertainty, be taught to listen in this way. Both children and adults normally listen by applying preexisting schemas to what they see and hear, as described in classic cognitive theories (Piaget, 1967; Johnson-Laird, 1983). We do not deny that this occurs, nor that it can sometimes be useful, but we argue that it impedes the sort of direct involvement we advocate. In order to teach listening as direct involvement, educators must first break down the habit of listening in terms of prior understandings. This requires not only cognitive but also emotional and identity-related change for novices. Direct involvement is not a heuristic that can be easily adopted, but instead requires more fundamental reorientation and transformation of the learner. For this reason, we will argue, educators must attend to the whole person.

Once students have mastered direct involvement, they become more attuned to aspects of the situation—they listen more carefully to unique dimensions of what people are saying and doing and they act more effectively as components of larger systems instead of as isolated autonomous "thinkers" (Goodwin, 1995; Hutchins, 1995). The pedagogy of augmenting uncertainty accomplishes this by pushing students and novices away from stable concepts and scripts and toward direct involvement with concrete situations.

We describe this process of educating people to listen more directly by presenting data from a two-year study of novice investment bankers who were socialized using a pedagogy of augmenting uncertainty. The senior bankers created an environment in which novices could not succeed on their own, in which they had to move beyond their own expertise to draw on resources from others. This was initially traumatic for the novices, because they wanted to show that they were smart and could work independently. But they learned to move their preexisting ideas into the background and listen more directly to situations. We suggest that the pedagogy of augmenting uncertainty and the resulting stance of direct involvement could be applied to schooling as well.

Once students have mastered direct involvement, they become more attuned to aspects of the situation—they listen more carefully to unique dimensions of what people are saying and doing. . . .

Instead of simply giving students the concepts, scripts and self-understandings through which they subsequently organize their experience, it can also be productive to clear away their presuppositions and help them engage more directly with subject matter. Even though the data we draw on here come from banks and not schools, they suggest how school students might also be taught to listen more directly.

In this chapter we first describe what we mean by direct involvement Then we describe the practices through which one investment bank cultivated this orientation in its bankers.

We develop these into a broader pedagogy of augmenting uncertainty, which we argue can be productive in classrooms.

Direct Involvement

Working and learning are traditionally structured in individual-centered ways. This approach attends closely to people's existing knowledge and abilities and assumes that people work and learn effectively when the demands placed on them are close to their abilities. For example, organizations typically structure roles such that they are associated with clear goals, standards, and responsibilities. Role occupants are systematically selected and prepared accordingly, often by advancing them gradually to more demanding roles. Basic principles and techniques of learning—such as keeping the learner in a zone of proximal development or scaffolding (Vygotsky, 1997)—are all based on assessing what a person currently knows and stretching the person gradually beyond this current state of knowledge. As a result, learners accumulate concepts, scripts, and self-understandings that mediate their engagement with situations and subject matter. This can be productive in some cases, but it also has costs.

In this chapter we sketch the organization-centric practices at "Organization Bank" (OB), a successful U.S. investment bank. (The name and some identifying details have been changed to protect the identity of the bank.) These practices are explicitly opposed to typical individual-centered ones. According to OB's approach, the bankers' preexisting expertise was irrelevant. Bankers were assigned to projects purely based on availability, irrespective of roles and existing knowledge. To complete their tasks, they were forced to draw on the organization's resources, including their own skills, but also other people, templates, and technology. This chapter documents how the pedagogical strategy of "augmenting uncertainty" worked in this case to transform novice bankers into more successful practitioners who listened to others and attended to situations in a different way.

The goal of this pedagogical approach is what we call "direct involvement" (Michel & Wortham, 2009), which can be understood as a form of listening as well as other types of receptive action. Organization Bankers believed that their personal capacities were merely one among many potential resources that could contribute to their work. They did not focus on their own expertise (like existing concepts and scripts) as central explanations for action. They keenly listened to and used social resources more effectively because their preoccupation with abstractions and their own personal characteristics were cleared away. In other words, because they did not believe that their preexisting concepts and scripts would be key for understanding new situations and solving problems, they were more open to the nuances of new situations. They did not imagine that their personal characteristics were the best explanation for their actions and they did not focus on abstract schemas or properties of individuals. The bank forced them into this position. Individual bankers could not resort to abstractions because situational demands usually exceeded what the bankers knew and thus appeared too complex to be forced into preexisting categories and scripts. Senior bankers created more direct involvement—the clearing away of preexisting concepts and scripts and careful attention to situations—by forcing bankers into situations where they could not solve problems on their own because they did not have relevant knowledge and skills for the task at hand.

Junior Organization Bankers, as they learned this new approach, attended less and less to individual expertise and preexisting schemas. Instead, they learned to think, feel, and act with respect to concrete situational cues. After about six months with the bank, junior bankers explained that they were not as preoccupied with "ego problems." Because Organization Bankers did not perceive situations as being about *them*—that is, they did not feel that their own expertise and knowledge were at stake—they were less likely to feel anxious and less likely to direct their action in order to support preconceived notions about themselves. People who focus on using their preexisting concepts, scripts, and self-understandings to solve problems become attached to an image of themselves as experts and to their typical ways of understanding as valuable. This works well when those preexisting ideas are appropriate to a situation, but not when the environment changes and new ideas are required. As the Organization Bankers' own identities and preexisting scripts became less important to them, they more often attended to situational cues. Bankers monitored the details of situations so that they could find the relevant organizational resources to solve particular problems.

Organization Bankers came to attend more carefully to concrete, contextualized situations, and they developed solutions better tailored to the context. They did not construe their own expertise as a cause that influenced external situations. They saw identity and situation as united in action, as a configuration of resources that did not involve a fundamental split between the individual and the situation. They talked about the person-acting-in-a-situation, using notions like "task-orientation," not focusing on their own identities and expertise. Organization Bank thus illustrates an alternative way of using human resources. Instead of the more familiar pattern of encouraging participants to internalize organizational concepts and see themselves as the primary carriers of organizational expertise, Organization Bank encouraged bankers to clear away such abstract mediating concepts and focus directly on the concrete aspects of specific situations.

We refer to the psychological and relational pattern that the Organization Bankers exhibited as "direct involvement." This construct captures the psychological processes that allowed more seasoned Organization Bankers to behave as they did. Identity, cognition, emotion, and motivation worked together, all focused on situation-specific, task-related concerns. The Organization Bankers' notion of "task-orientation," which was the basis for our concept of direct involvement, captures the most important change: after six months Organization Bankers reoriented their attention from identity-related to task-related concerns. This change in attention involved the bankers attending to a broader set of resources for action and focusing on concrete tasks. Organization Bankers focused on situational cues and social resources, believing that successful action resulted from a social system that included, but was not limited to, the banker's own resources. Thus the bankers allowed social resources such as objects and task structures to participate more actively in the knowledge-generation process. Organization Bankers noticed the contributions that resources could make because they stopped being preoccupied with their preexisting knowledge and expertise.

What would direct involvement look like in school? Students would engage with subject matter in less scripted ways. They would not try to recreate what the teacher or the field already knows, but would instead remain open to new aspects of the subject matter. Sometimes, the interpretive discussions described by Haroutunian-Gordon and Meadows in this volume can produce direct involvement. Successful discussions do not involve students recreating preexisting knowledge about the text, but instead show students noticing new things in the text and using contributions from others to create interpretations that no individual could have generated alone. Direct involvement means students moving away from established canons of knowledge and approaches to subject matter, toward more creative engagement with material—not making up whatever they want, but developing evidence for new approaches and interpretations, attending to evidence in the text but using it in support of a new, emerging view across a group. In such a case students would focus not on their own knowledge, intelligence, and performance but on the collective task of developing

> *In schools, direct involvement means students moving away from established canons of knowledge and approaches to subject matter, toward more creative engagement with material. . . .*

greater understanding by combining insights form various participants. What matters is the new understanding, not the expertise of or the credit given to any individual.

Developing toward Direct Involvement

Organization Bank was forced to create this alternative method of working when it encountered a crisis that threatened its survival. Intending to grow its business rapidly, the bank had hired experienced traders. Because their mental models had been effective in the past, the traders employed these models without reflecting on their ongoing relevance. But the business environment became more complex and dynamic, while the traders continued their habitual strategies, and the bank had to fire more than 25 percent of its employees. This experience demonstrated the problem with expertise—experts over-rely on what they think they know and under-rely on resources like situational cues and other people. Instead of cultivating experts, the bank then designed its processes to focus bankers on collective resources. Of course, we do not mean to imply that that no one knew anything about finance at Organization Bank. People did have some expert knowledge. But Organization Bank kept people on their toes by exposing them to situations where their expertise was insufficient. For example, a merger expert who had become comfortable with most merger products might be moved to corporate finance or to the Frankfurt office—environments that are still intelligible, but novel enough for the banker to hesitate before applying preexisting notions. Thus the bank forced its people to listen attentively.

Organization Bank was able to reorient new bankers in this way—away from preoccupations with their own identities and expertise, toward direct involvement with concrete tasks—by making identity traits implausible and irrelevant. They became implausible as explanations for success because bankers could accomplish many tasks despite their lack of personal knowledge. They became irrelevant because the outcomes that a banker valued did not depend on the banker's preexisting knowledge, but instead on social resources. As bankers came to understand that they should monitor social resources instead of attending to abstract scripts and identities, identity and expertise moved into the background and they were able to participate more seamlessly in the larger organizational system that involved bankers and their tools as collective resources for solving problems.

According to the Organization Bankers, the crucial developmental insight was that they were consistently able to complete the projects that were assigned to them, regardless of their own knowledge and skill, because the bank's resources complemented their own resources. Whatever one banker did not know, he or she could get from this resource pool.

> You know, I eventually figured it out. This is not about me; it's not about how smart I am. This is about what you can do when you pull extraordinary resources together. I might not know whether the client should sell the business, spin it off, whatever. I might not even be able to do half of the analyses that I am responsible for. But I can still get it done and get it done well every single time because of the resources here.

Different bankers had the same insight because the bank's pedagogical processes facilitated this insight. The bank did so not by circulating norms, rules, and shared understandings and encouraging internalization—which is how culture normally operates—but by *blocking* norms and rules, by foregrounding uncertainty and not letting junior bankers develop stable scripts and identities. It did this, for instance, by placing bankers on deals that they knew nothing about, and forcing them to draw on other resources in order to do their jobs. Normally, a novice banker would build up expertise over time, through instruction, mentoring and practice. Then she or he would feel competent to do independent work. But at Organization bank they forced bankers to work on problem that they knew nothing about—for instance, forcing someone to work on a deal in an industry they were unfamiliar with, or on a problem like mergers where they had no prior experience. This seems pointless. How could a banker successfully solve a problem with very limited prior knowledge? But bankers learned to solve such problems by relying on help from others and tools available in the bank. In doing so, they became less attached to their own preexisting concepts—more attuned to the concrete opportunities in new situations and less likely to impose unproductive scripts on new situations.

Once they achieved this insight, Organization Bankers approached situations differently. For example, they paid careful attention in meetings to match the client's needs with the most suitable organizational resources.

> Before, I used to have this knot in my stomach in each and every meeting because I was just waiting for someone to ask me something that I was clueless about and worrying about what to say and about losing credibility. . . . Now these are the moments I live for . . . I ask tons of questions . . . then I literally say it flat out: I don't have the answer for you right now. But we'll get our heads together and make sure you get the best advice possible.

This quote shows that the junior Organization Bankers continued to experience high task uncertainty ("I don't have the answer") but that their attitude toward this uncertainty had changed. When first joining the bank they disguised their lack of knowledge to protect their identities as competent bankers and the impression that they had relevant preexisting knowledge, but they learned to use their uncertainty as a cue to guide data collection ("I ask tons of questions").

As the Organization Bankers' focus shifted from a preoccupation with their own expertise to an orientation toward the concrete task, their identity-related statements and actions changed, too. For example, after about six months Organization Bankers had more difficulty responding to ongoing questions about banker identity, such as "How would you describe yourself or your identity?" The otherwise eloquent Organization Bankers started stuttering, eventually saying something like "I just don't think about these things that much." The bankers also started to refer to themselves as "resources." According to most existing theories, an identity is an attribute of a person that it is stable across situations. In contrast, a resource cannot be defined apart from the particular situation to which it contributes. We found that the Organization Bankers came to conceive of themselves in a fundamentally different way—not as a biologically or psychologically bounded entity that has stable preexisting knowledge but as one aspect of a larger process. The situation-specific attributes of this process, not the situation-independent attributes of a banker expertise, determined what the banker did. The bankers thus enacted "self" more as a process of contributing—a kind of doing—instead of as a stable way of being. For example, the Organization Bankers over time became *less* likely to act as socially recognizable kinds of people. After about six months, the Organization Bankers were less likely to supply general identity scripts to situations and more likely to display "new" behaviors that were called forth by the concrete attributes of particular situations—a sensitivity to the concrete that they refined over time.

Augmenting Uncertainty

Uncertainty is one of the fundamental problems that organizations and their top managers face (Thompson, 1967). It is also of critical concern to other collectives, including the military (Wong, 2004), schools (Wortham, 1994) and a broad set of other socializing institutions (Levy, 2001). In the twenty-first century, uncertainty has reached an extreme level (Whetten & Cameron, 2005). These extreme conditions are likely to make uncertainty management an even higher priority for practitioners and a topic of increased interest to scholars.

Our research presents an alternative to existing models, almost all of which suggest uncertainty reduction, and we offer managers and educators a broader range of choices as they prepare people for an uncertain world. Put simply, we recommend uncertainty augmentation instead of uncertainty reduction.

We challenge the assumption that organizations and schools can manage uncertainty only by reducing it. This untested assumption is deeply embedded in both practical and academic work on organizational and psychological processes, as well as commonsense assumptions about how good decision making works. Our account of uncertainty augmentation suggests several counterintuitive conclusions. We argue that the uncertainty-reduction practices commonly used to enhance learning can in fact impede people's thinking. Despite both academic and everyday assumptions that would lead one to see uncertainty augmentation as a route to impaired individual decision making, we have shown that Organization Bank's uncertainty augmentation in fact helped bankers think. It can be better for a person not to know something than to know something too well.

If the schools' primary goal is to teach a stable set of knowledge, then uncertainty reduction makes sense. Provide students with established concepts and scripts, and incrementally build them into experts who recognize the typical patterns in a problem and can provide the appropriate solution. In the business world, however, it has become clear that this approach often does not work. Given a rapidly changing environment, employees must be adaptable. They must see new opportunities, not apply the same scripts to new situations. If schools are to prepare young people to be adaptable and creative, perhaps they should consider uncertainty augmentation as well. Instead of providing stable and incremental forms of understanding, educators should consider augmenting uncertainty— forcing students to rely on external resources, to notice new patterns because they confront situations they cannot manage with familiar concepts and scripts.

Given a rapidly changing environment, employees must be adaptable. They must see new opportunities, not apply the same scripts to new situations. If schools are to prepare young people to be adaptable and creative, perhaps they should consider uncertainty augmentation as well.

When one hears about chaos in organizations, one might imagine a breakdown of the fundamental elements of the organization. One envisions task-related communications disrupted, employees distracted and trying to make sense of what they do not understand, and factions mired in conflict trying to shape ambiguous situations to their own advantage. Communication and coordination, one could argue, only proceed in a productive way when they are designed purposefully and executed according to plan. In contrast, the chaos at Organization Bank both strengthened communication and helped coordinate problem solving. Precisely because there was a dearth of formal plans—few strategies, role expectations, purposeful training, and no matching of experts to tasks—bankers did not have the tools to do their jobs and were forced both to collaborate with one another and to notice new aspects of situations.

Professional service organizations like banks initially emerged to deal with situations that were too complex for traditional mechanistic organizations to handle. One cannot produce investment banking or legal advice with the same invariant procedures that one uses to produce a car on an assembly line. Professional service situations have unique elements that seem to require the judgment of an individual expert. Our account draws attention to a paradox, however. The more of an expert one becomes, the less likely one is to notice the uniqueness of situations. Individual experts are prone to acting just as mechanistically as are traditional organizations, relying on relatively invariant scripts and procedures. The Organization Bank case shows that uncertain environments require more reliance on systems of resources that extend beyond the individual. Organizations have the resources and internal complexity to match and manage environmental complexity, even when this complexity overwhelms the resources of an individual. Organization Bank coped efficiently with external complexity not through the planned procedures of mechanistic organizations, nor by using the judgment of individual experts, but instead through the ad hoc coordination of individuals each of whom lacked full, relevant expertise.

Organizations and schools typically orient people *away from* uncertainty and toward a limited number of abstract decision making or content standards. Organization Bank recognized that its business was highly uncertain, but it made the unusual choice to orient bankers *toward* this uncertainty—thus augmenting it—such that bankers would notice and use it better. Instead of orienting bankers to such abstractions as strategies, roles, and scripts, it withheld them. Bankers were not given plans or targets, and they were not referred to as having identities as one kind of expert or another. The bankers consequently made decisions with reference to the concrete details of specific situations. For example, Organization Bank's top management did not design strategies, but executed deals like other bankers. The bank did have strategies, but these were not typical top-down plans that dictated what bankers at lower levels should do. Rather, they were bottom-up and retrospective, emerging from the choices that bankers at lower levels had made in response to noticing market opportunity: "We looked back and noticed: 'Gee, we have a healthcare strategy.'" Instead of telling bankers what to do, the bank guided bankers by continuously making the consequences of their actions salient. For this purpose, bankers received an enormous amount of information on a daily basis, including reports about the revenues they generated, the cost of the resources they used, the time they were allocating to specific types of transactions and the deals they had lost to competitors. This information deluge contradicted deeply held tenets of cognitive theories, which recommend that organizations should reduce the information that confronts decision makers and give them interpretation guidelines. In contrast, Organization Bank trusted bankers to react productively to often-conflicting imperatives and believed that the person who knows the most concrete detail would make the best decision.

One illustration of Organization Bank's more organization-centric approach, mentioned above, is that it staffed bankers purely based on availability and not based on their individual expertise. When clients requested a particular banker to work on a deal, the banker who staffed projects usually said: "Our bankers are fungible." When one Organization Banker went on vacation or was overloaded, other bankers could seamlessly substitute on projects. These unexpected substitutions into unfamiliar projects were one important source of persistent uncertainty for bankers at all levels. This approach to staffing meant that bankers often had to deal with situations for which they had not yet formed concepts that they could apply, either because they were inexperienced or because the situations were inherently unpredictable. A banker at another bank remarked that this was "unthinkable" at his bank: "It just doesn't work that way. You can't replicate what your colleague knows at the drop of the hat." But Organization Bank made this strategy work, consistently outperforming other banks.

Organization Bank's socialization and routine work practices thus *augmented uncertainty* and thereby prevented participants from approaching situations with a set of abstract rules and concepts. Absent such general guidance, newcomers had to attend keenly to the concrete guidance available in particular situations, including task structures, data, technology and other people. In this more direct involvement, it was not clear to the participants what the relevant norms and concepts were. The pedagogical strategy, then, was to force people into situations where they did not fully understand and could not complete tasks on their own. Bankers then had to rely on other resources, both people and cognitive tools. Over time, this led novice bankers to change their approach to problem solving: they habitually came to attend closely to situations and potentially relevant resources, as opposed to relying on their own abstract scripts.

Organization Bank's uncertainty augmentation approach consistently placed bankers in situations that required them to draw on the bank's resources to accomplish their tasks. Organization Bankers then experienced themselves less as agents who accomplished tasks based primarily on their personal resources, and more as participants in a broader social system. Over time this created a more relational and contextualized sense of self for the new bankers, one in which they defined themselves based on the resources that they could bring to a situation (e.g., "I am here to understand how to connect you with our collective expertise on healthcare"). They consequently worried less about who they were as socially recognizable persons, as individuals identified with respect to their own capabilities (e.g., "I am an expert and I have learned how to handle this type of problem"), and more about what they could do with the help of a larger set of resources.

When people experience uncertainty as a more general, persistent inability to understand the environment, it does not make sense to learn stable concepts for future application. On the contrary, Organization Bankers came to distrust both existing concepts and the resources of an individual mind. They learned, instead, to *suspend* their existing concepts and draw on a diverse set of resources tailored to particular situations, including but not limited to their own concepts. We argue that persistent uncertainty in a setting such as Organization Bank can catalyze a previously unknown developmental trajectory, one that moves people toward a more collective, adaptable way of thinking, feeling, and acting in concert with others and the affordances of particular situations.

It might seem as if this approach could never work in school. Schools are built around the idea of individual expertise. We teach and test individuals as if their personal expertise and understanding is the goal, separated from others and relevant tools. How could students be forced to collaborate, to recognize their own limitations as a means of encouraging direct involvement? Given the typical structures of school, this would undoubtedly be difficult. But banks have also been traditionally organized around the expertise of individuals, and they have compensation and other practices built around the idea of individual expertise and accomplishments. Organization Bank managed to overcome these habits by augmenting uncertainty, because they saw the potential of direct involvement. Their bankers were more adaptable and anticipated new business opportunities more nimbly than competitors. Educating students to be creative and adaptable could have a similarly large payoff. The payoff of uncertainty augmentation is more substantial in the complex and dynamic environments that are increasingly common in our knowledge based economy—characterized by political instability, rapid changes in consumer tastes, technology, and regulation. Such environments require organizations and their participants to listen carefully to the uniqueness of situations and to continuously adapt, abilities that are fostered through uncertainty augmentation.

Clearing Away the Self

Persistent uncertainty can lead to a new developmental trajectory that we call "clearing away the self." Organization Bank designed this as an alternative approach to learning that counteracts cognitive rigidity in bankers. This form of learning does not involve the accumulation of concepts, as most cognitive accounts of learning assume. Nor does it involve becoming a socially recognizable person, as many sociocultural perspectives assume. Clearing away the self is a third alternative, one that describes how learners can act with respect to concrete situations, not based on preconceived abstractions—whether those abstractions are individual or collective.

Clearing away the self is an ongoing social process designed to reverse the stabilization of cognition and identity and to avoid the resulting cognitive rigidity. It has two components. First, it withdraws people's attention from an abstract identity. People usually monitor situations for aspects that may be relevant to their identity—looking for things that they know or believe could characterize the situation, looking for ways in which others' actions might have implications for their own standing, and so forth—because they believe that the self and the individual's knowledge is the most important cause of action. Such constant monitoring helps a person manage the self and use existing concepts to ensure successful action. Organization Bank's practices reversed this pattern of attention. They made it unmistakably clear that the self is not a privileged cause of action and that it therefore does not require constant attention (by forcing bankers to see that they could not solve problems on their own). The bank also made self-concepts less relevant because it prevented bankers from forming an identity that described who they were in this new context. Because bankers used a trait-based identity ("I am smart," or "I know all about the healthcare industry") less frequently to explain successes and failures, the chronic accessibility of self-relevant concepts and the resulting cognitive rigidity were reduced, and their grip over emotions, motivations, and behaviors was loosened. As a result, Organization Bankers were less likely to supply a predetermined psychological pattern to a situation. Their thoughts, feelings, and actions depended relatively less on their identities and relatively more on the unique aspects of different situations.

As the second component of clearing away the self, Organization Bank substituted a new explanation for the results of bankers' actions—namely the whole organizational resource system. As bankers realized that the larger organization was responsible for their successes, they shifted their attention even further away from self and toward the social situation. For the Organization Bankers, this shift also helped to undo the centrality of their self-constructs and opened the bankers to the idea of using organizational resources more often. Thus the process of clearing away the self, accomplished through the pedagogical strategy of augmenting uncertainty, led novice bankers to the more productive stance of direct involvement.

The pedagogical approach of augmenting uncertainty and clearing away the self was successful for Organization Bank, helping to create bankers who could listen and take other actions by being more directly involved with others and the world—without their action being mediated through stable, abstract schemas or self-understandings. But the approach did have costs. First, it was painful for the junior bankers because it involved a more profound type of change. New bankers began with an implicit sense that being a self means being a type of entity that has attributes, such as "I am competent." Most organizations simply require that people elaborate and add to their existing attributes. In contrast, clearing away the self required a qualitative shift in Organization Bankers' existential stance. They had to learn a different way of being and knowing that contradicted habitual practices in the larger society, habitual practices that they had followed their entire lives. They no longer could define themselves in terms of the stable attributes that previously had given meaning to their lives and helped them pursue goals. They had to give up the sense that life was largely predictable and that they could make sense of and master experience by developing expertise.

Second, augmenting uncertainty required that the bank have substantial control over novices' lives. It did in fact have such control, both through compensation and because novices wanted badly to succeed there. But other organizations like schools may not have such extensive control. Third, the bank's extraordinary resources allowed it to create an environment in which novices could draw on tools and people who provided the expertise needed to solve problems. Schools and other organizations do not always have such extensive resources, and in such places individuals may sometimes have to succeed on their own.

Given that a bank is not a school, could augmenting uncertainty work in schools? At first glance, it seems not. Schools are all about individuals developing their own knowledge, with the expectation that it can be applied across contexts. Thus they are typically designed to reduce uncertainty by asking teachers to teach what they know and students to accumulate relevant knowledge and skills. A few contemporary approaches to schooling, however, have begun to practice something that looks like uncertainty amplification. As mentioned above, interpretive discussion is one pedagogy that amplifies uncertainty and encourages students to build interpretations collectively (Haroutunian-Gordon, 1991, 2009; and this volume, Wortham, 1994 & 2006). In such classroom conversations the teacher does not offer definite answers but instead encourages students to explore "interpretive questions" that have more than one plausible answer. By maintaining both teachers' and students' uncertainty, such conversations can enrich students' understanding of subject matter and lead them to explore new ideas. In this and other pedagogies (like problem-based learning, for example), teachers augment rather than reduce uncertainty. Given the success of this approach for producing more adaptable and creative bankers, it may be that augmenting uncertainty and involving students with more open-ended systems of resources could lead them to listen and learn more effectively.

Note

1. This form of listening is similar to the kind of open listening described by Leonard Waks as "apophatic listening." See Waks (2010).

Suggested Readings

Michel, A., & Wortham, S. (2009). *Bullish on uncertainty: How organizational cultures transform participants*. New York, NY: Cambridge University Press.
Wortham, S. (2006). *Learning identity*. New York, NY: Cambridge University Press.

References

Goodwin, C. (1995). Seeing in depth. *Social Studies of Science, 25*, 237–74.
Haroutunian-Gordon, S. (1991). *Turning the soul: Teaching through conversation in the high school*. Chicago, IL: University of Chicago Press.
Haroutunian-Gordon, S. (2009). *Learning to teach through discussion: The art of turning the soul*. New Haven, CT: Yale University Press.
Hutchins, E. (1995). *Cognition in the wild*. Cambridge, MA: MIT Press.
Johnson-Laird, P. (1983). *Mental models*. Cambridge, MA: Harvard University Press.
Levy, R. I. (2001). Bateson and academia: Reflections on the fit of different kinds of visions with the business of departments of anthropology. (Paper presented at 7th biennial meeting of the Society for Psychological Anthropology, Decatur, GA, 2001).
Michel, A., & Wortham, S. (2009). *Bullish on uncertainty: How organizational cultures transform participants*. New York, NY: Cambridge University Press.
Piaget, J. (1967). *Six psychological studies*. New York, NY: Vintage.
Thompson, J. D. (1967), *Organizations in action*. New York, NY: McGraw-Hill.

Vygotsky, L. S. (1997). *The collected works of L.S. Vygotsky (Volume 4: The history of the development of higher mental functions)*. Trans. by M. Hall. New York, NY: Plenum. (Complete Russian edition published in 1987).

Waks, L. (2010). Two types of interpersonal listening. *Teachers College Record*, 112(11): 2743–2762.

Whetten, D. A., & Cameron, K. S. (2005). *Developing management skills* (6th ed.). Upper Saddle River, NJ: Pearson, Prentice Hall.

Wong, L. (2004). *Developing adaptive leaders: The crucible experience of Operation Iraqi Freedom*. http://www.carlisle.army.mil/ssi

Wortham, S. (1994). *Acting out participant examples in the classroom*. Philadelphia, PA: John Benjamins.

Wortham, S. (2006). *Learning identity*. New York, NY: Cambridge University Press.

12

Listening and Teaching in Online Contexts

Nicholas Burbules

University of Illinois, Urbana-Champaign

What is familiar is what we are used to, and what we are used to is most difficult to "know"—that is, to see as a problem; that is to see as strange.

—Nietzsche (1974, p. 301)

In this chapter I explore the role of listening in online teaching. By "online teaching" I mean technologically mediated teaching interactions among instructors and students, in both synchronous and asynchronous modes. These new approaches are playing a larger and larger role in teaching, especially in postsecondary settings. Normally such technologically mediated interactions are happening "at a distance," though increasingly they are being used in relation with, and as a complement to, live in-classroom interactions as well (as they are called, "blended" courses).

Innovations around online teaching and learning are having a transformative effect on higher education. Whether through MOOCs or other forms, universities are actively exploring how new technologies can improve instruction, expand access, and lower costs. The discussion has shifted from how online and blended courses constitute a cheaper second-best option that is "good enough" for those who cannot afford the "real thing" (that is, live on-campus teaching), to considering how these innovations can reform, invigorate, and actually improve teaching of all types—and how blended or hybrid combinations of face to face and online elements may constitute the best forms of all (Means, et al., 2009). I have been teaching such online and blended courses for about 15 years now, and like many others I find that lessons learned in my online teaching are changing and improving my regular in-classroom teaching: for example, moving from longer lectures to a series of "mini-lectures" that are more inquiry-oriented and interactive.

Moreover, reading and writing about this issue, and trying to articulate what is promising about these possibilities (as well as what is disturbing or potentially dangerous), has been an occasion for me to reconsider my own longstanding assumptions about teaching. I tend to think that the most transformative aspect of these new technologies is just this: that they are forcing a process of reexamining older assumptions about where, when, and how teaching and learning happen (Burbules, 2004 & 2006). In other words, the impact of new technologies is not just in their potential as a set of tools; but as a challenge to our concepts, definitions, institutional structures, and ways of thinking about education.

In this chapter I want to look at the issue of listening as an instance of this rethinking process: how listening practices are changed in the online context, and how certain ways that we ordinarily enact listening in teaching are challenged by the different affordances and limitations of that context. But then, thinking further, I want to bring these questions back to the topic of how these reflections on online teaching cause us to think differently about teaching and learning generally.

I am limiting this discussion mainly to the role of listening in online *teaching*.[1] Listening also plays a role in learning, on the side of students (listening to the teacher, listening to each other, etc.).

> The impact of new technologies is not just in their potential as a set of tools; but as a challenge to our concepts, definitions, institutional structures, and ways of thinking about education.

Those are important questions that I do not have the space to deal with here. But having said that, I do not want to overstate the distinction of the teacher and learner roles: in a listening relation the teacher becomes a learner as well, learning (or re-learning) something new ourselves about the subject matter being taught; learning something about the students with whom one is engaged; learning some things about one's self; and learning new things about the process of teaching, including the possibilities and the limits of online teaching.

Finally, "listening" in the online context also includes certain kinds of reading and interpretation—because much of the interaction between teacher and students, and among students, is mediated through text (though more and more students are posting their online comments as audio or video uploads). Because much of text-based online communication—instant messaging, brief observations and comments posted on Twitter, dialogues in discussion forums, and so on—often has the character of speaking, it is appropriate to think about the way we read these communications as a kind of "listening" too. We "read" things in other listening contexts as well: we read body language, gestures, tone of voice, facial expressions, and so on. Listening is never just about *spoken* words—and it is never just about words, either.

Next I will explore five specific areas where listening in online teaching contexts heightens our awareness of listening in other teaching situations.

First, listening in online teaching contexts has to go beyond listening to (or reading) what people are saying. In a regular classroom, there are all sorts of cues we are picking up that influence how we hear what is being said (as irony, for example): facial expression, tone of voice, body language, etc. We all have had the experience of irony or sarcasm or humor not transferring very well to the online context. (Oh, the emails I wish I hadn't sent!)

In these and other cases, our listening has to be active, looking past what was *said* to try to guess at what was *meant*. Online postings can sometimes be more elliptical than spoken comments; there is more of a culture online of brevity (as with many "tweets," with text-message abbreviations like LOL or IMHO, or with the use of emoticons that give a flavor of facial expression or tone—a wink, for example).

Listening is active also in requiring us to ask follow-up questions or probes (significantly, good listening sometimes requires *us* to speak). What is meant is not always apparent in what was said, and sometimes this also requires finding out things about who is saying it, and why. These are not add-ins to listening; they are *part* of good listening. A major challenge in online teaching, therefore, is representing the speaker clearly in one's mind, not just in a visual image but as a whole person. Video interactions can help with this but do not solve the problem entirely. Context, personal background and experience, what exists behind or between the lines of what is being said, all may need to be probed in order to allow us to listen effectively. This is doubly so in online teaching.

Sometimes, too, we need to be listening as teachers for the questions that may be out there among students that are *not* being asked. This sometimes involves hearing what others are saying from the standpoint of a novice; or, as we become experienced, drawing from our memories of the frequently asked questions that similar learners have had in other classes. We need to

> *Listening in online teaching contexts has to go beyond listening to (or reading) what people are saying.*

"hear" or anticipate those kinds of questions, in thinking through what we say and how to say it. What makes sense to us, or is clear to us, is often being heard or understood differently than we intend. Here again, listening and speaking are stages or aspects of the same process, not entirely separate activities.

In passing, let me note that in the work of Paulo Freire (and even further back, to Socrates' critique of the Sophists) lectures have gotten a bad name—"monological teaching," Freire calls them, the authoritarian teaching of the oppressor, whereas "dialogical teaching" is the egalitarian teaching of the liberator. I have long thought that this is an unhelpful dichotomy: that there are liberating, empowering sorts of lectures (and manipulative, authoritarian sorts of dialogues). But lectures in which you are actively anticipating and relating to the imagined questions of the audience can have a dialogical quality, can be more fully engaging and intellectually creative, than Freire's characterization gives justice to.

> We need to be listening as teachers for the questions that may be out there among students that are not being asked.

Listening to what is behind what is said matters perhaps especially to teaching philosophy. The argument or reasoning behind a comment, the understanding of an idea it reveals, the levels of meaning it might have, are factors in all sorts of classrooms, but particularly in the philosophy classroom. We are usually less interested in agreement with a single position, or seeking "right" answers, than with probing what the learners are thinking and how well they are formulating and defending their position. The same comment or question from two different students may portend very different underlying insights— for one it is a facile quip, for another a rich insight. (What would *you* say if a student asked, "If a lion could speak, would we understand him?")

Second, a related aspect of active listening is listening to silences. Huey-li Li (2002, 2004), Katherine Schultz (2009), Michalinos Zembylas (2004, 2007), and others have written eloquently about the quite different meanings that silences can have: uncertainty, boredom, thoughtful reflection, distraction, resistance, intimidation, lack of interest, alienation, exhaustion, confusion, and so on. When you aren't hearing anything, how can you tell what it means?

In online teaching contexts, silences can be, if you will, even more inscrutable than in face-to-face teaching. They can be unsettling when you are used to other cues about what is happening in the classroom. You say something and hear . . . silence. A teacher who is monitoring classroom dynamics can pretty easily identify the people who are not speaking up, and sometimes can infer or guess why they are not. It is harder to do that in an online class, especially a large class, because you have little direct evidence about why people are not participating. In a traditional class, some members may not speak up very often, but you can see that they are thoughtfully engaged. In an online class all you hear is dead air. The flow of postings in a synchronous chat session may come by so quickly that you are rushing to deal with the comments that are posted, not noticing the people or topics that are not present.

Silence is not always a bad thing. When you have an online class with multiple channels of communication (text/voice/video; synchronous/asynchronous; large group/small group/one-to-one, etc.), it is natural that some will participate more in some communicative modes than others; hence, who is present or silent at any one time (and why) may be harder to determine. Some may opt out or be absent in certain types of discussion because they feel more comfortable in other modes, and if so that is not necessarily a problem. But is that what their silence means?

Teaching of all sorts requires a certain tolerance for silence: when you ask a question, you should not jump in too quickly if there isn't an immediate response; the students may be thinking and need time to formulate their comments. This is not just a matter of "wait time"; it also depends on whether you want your class to be a place of contemplation, reflection, and creative thought. Such reflections may happen best in silence. Classroom discussions do not always need to be breathless non-stop gabfests; it is sometimes better when they are not. In asynchronous modes of online interaction, this opportunity to wait before posting is built into the technology—it's a benefit, not a limitation (especially, for example, for learners struggling to express themselves in a second language).

Third, even more than in most traditional classrooms, the teacher needs to be listening (which, again, may include reading) to student-student communications. Many student postings are directed not at the teacher but toward one another. Some teachers manage these kinds of discussion well in a traditional classroom, but there the teacher is the center of communicative attention much of the time and has certain customary privileges in managing or guiding the conversation (for example, calling on students, or trying to prevent certain individuals from dominating the conversation). By contrast, there is usually much more undirected student-student communication in online classes than in most regular classrooms. Students often create discussion pathways that the teacher does not control: for example, starting new threads in a conversation besides the topic or question the teacher started with). Here the teacher needs to broaden their focus on what they are listening for.

Listening to these student exchanges is a key part of teaching, in several respects: Are the students engaging the ideas and issues in the course material? Are they able to express themselves and construct arguments effectively? What questions do they ask, and what seems most important or relevant to them? What can we learn about the students and their interests and priorities from what they choose to talk about? Sometimes these student-student exchanges might appear to be "off-topic" (say, talking about their school situations or families, not about the readings or the teacher's comments), and it is true that sometimes rambling or indirect discussion needs to be brought back to the topic. But because a big part of online teaching involves fostering a collaborative community in the absence of regular classroom social dynamics, it is important to recognize that a certain amount of tolerance for this "off-topic" discourse is actually constructive to the course purposes because it builds affiliations among the participants. Other times, an issue that the teacher considers "off-topic" might actually indicate something that needs to be treated as "on-topic." For example, students might start talking about a movie they have seen; the substance of the movie may seem to have nothing to do with the discussion topic at hand—but then a student makes a connection, and because many others have seen the film this actually does become a basis for negotiating a new shared understanding of the material (as well as strengthening bonds within the student community). This is another way in which careful listening by teachers might teach them something. In this example, the teacher may decide to go see the film in order to use it as a way of framing other class topics as well.

Again, by listening to these student-student exchanges you can learn a good deal about the students: who they are, and what they care about. It provides opportunities to relate future teaching comments to experiences or events in their lives in order to make them more meaningful. So, in the end, perhaps such discussions aren't so "off-topic" after all.

Fourth, listening to people is a sign of respect. Carefully listening, and showing yourself to be listening, is often part of putting students at ease, and encouraging them to speak up more. People tend to think of speaking and listening as two sides of a communicative exchange, like the positive and negative poles of a magnet: one sending, one receiving. This is a very superficial view of communication. How we listen, how we receive, *encourages* others to speak; as noted previously, active listening can involve asking questions or probes that can help students express themselves better, can help them realize what it is they are trying to say, can help them say things that are more significant than they would have if we were just passively "receiving." In the flow of an ongoing interchange, speaking and listening are not entirely separate roles in the process. Asking questions and encouraging others to speak are sometimes also a part of good listening.

In an online environment where people cannot see each other, the teacher needs to show that he or she is listening through these and other means: through overt reactions that indicate that you are present and paying attention; that you are understanding what is being said; that you are thinking along with others and trying to anticipate what comes next. We indicate these kinds of responses in various ways in ordinary speech situations (through eye contact, nodding our head, and so on)—we need to develop non-face-to-face alternatives that achieve the same effect. Just as there can be "dead air" when someone isn't saying anything to us, there can also be "dead air" on the side of the listener: one cannot tell if the other is hearing, paying attention, agreeing or disagreeing, or if they even care. Communication often requires overt verbal or other kinds of feedback that show that others are listening. (Some videoconferencing systems allow the teacher or other class participants to post non-verbal signals in real time: smiling faces, silent "applause," or other graphic postings that indicate listening and support.)

Fifth, a key aspect of listening in teaching, not only but especially in online teaching, is listening to yourself. As you are speaking, whether in lecture mode, in conversation, or in writing, how is what you are saying likely to come across? Is the way it sounds necessarily the way you intend it? In the absence of visual cues or other evidence on the other side, how do you anticipate how your comments might be reinterpreted or misunderstood? Are you going on too long? (In my experience, students in an online setting have a shorter attention span and tolerance for monologues than they might in a regular classroom.) In the absence of certain indicators of their feedback, you have to be listening to yourself even more than usual from the standpoint of your audience.

This sort of self-monitoring must take place in every teaching context—and the ability to do this, while also speaking coherently, observing the class, planning what you will say next, and so on, is a skill that comes with experience. As a beginning teacher, it is often overwhelming just to try to say what you are trying to say, let alone engage in the kind of multi-perspectival self-listening I just described. Online teaching poses similar challenges: there is never just one thing going on (and dealing with the technologies themselves is not always a seamless or transparent process either). But this kind of listening to one's self needs to take place, because even more than in a regular classroom you are sending your comments out into a kind of void, and, as already discussed here, there are not the usual kinds of indicators that tell you how (or whether) you are coming across.

More and more teachers are using devices in regular classrooms, like "clickers," that allow them to ask students questions and immediately poll their responses to check whether they have understood the material covered, what their views are on certain issues, and so on; as noted, these capabilities are often built into course management software for online teaching. But this approach may be easier to implement with certain kinds of subject matters than others. For philosophers, for example, it is much harder to assess whether students are thinking things through with us as we intend for them to: it's not susceptible to yes/no questions or multiple-choice exercises. There are lengthier and more indirect ways to assess student thinking, but they won't give you immediate, direct feedback on a broad scale.

It can be difficult to listen to one's self through the imagined ears of learners who are not imbued with what one already knows. It is hard to know whether you have been clear in explaining something difficult; or, conversely, whether you are *over-explaining* it and depriving students of the chance to make some connections for themselves or to interpret something differently than you might. This, too, is especially important in philosophy: thinking through the problem or question often *is* the subject matter. There is only so much you can do to model those methods—and, as they say, giving your students a fish is not teaching them fish.

Listening to yourself in this way is also part of something I mentioned at the beginning: the process of *your* learning as part of your teaching, reflecting on and thinking about your subject matter and ideas in new and sometimes surprising ways. Many of us have had the experience of spontaneously saying something in the course of a class that suddenly makes a point clear *to us,* or that opens a new insight we had not considered before. It wasn't "in" our head and then we said it; the speaking/listening process puts ideas together in new and unexpected ways, but we had to be listening to ourselves to recognize it.

There is a danger in an online class, especially when you are sitting alone at a computer with a headset on, that you have little context for what you are saying and little immediate feedback from the students. Sometimes indeed it may seem that you are only talking to yourself. This is especially so in recording asynchronous lectures, such as podcasts for playback later, where you do not have a live audience at all. In all these circumstances, there may be very little feedback of the sort we are accustomed to in a regular classroom. This is why I am stressing the need sometimes to be *our own* listeners, to put ourselves in the position of the learner, even as we are in the midst of the process of teaching.

Clearly, these reflections on online teaching are also reflections about aspects of teaching generally. In this discussion I have continually moved back and forth between online teaching and teaching in ordinary classrooms, because what often happens is that an aspect of teaching we are familiar with and used to suddenly appears to us as strange in a technologically mediated context. It is like when a doorknob you have held and turned ten thousand times suddenly comes off in your hand: you see it as something different and strange because it doesn't work in the ways you are used to. Until then it had been just part of the invisible background of daily life and practice, but now you recognize (re-cognize) it as something to be questioned: why doesn't it work the way you are used to? It becomes a question, a problem. This is what the Nietzsche quote at the beginning points out to us.

In the same way, teaching online continually challenges us to re-cognize unquestioned aspects of our teaching practice that suddenly don't work, or that work differently than we are used to. And from these reexaminations of the familiar we often come back to the regular classroom with different understandings of what it means to teach. In this chapter I have explored a number of these:

> Part of teaching involves listening, and not just worrying about how to get others to listen to you.
>
> In technologically mediated contexts, reading can involve a kind of "listening" too.
>
> Part of teaching involves listening for the questions that students have, but which are not being asked.
>
> Lectures can be dialogical, and dialogues can be authoritarian and directive.
>
> Part of teaching is listening to silences, and recognizing the very different things that silences can signify.
>
> When the teacher is silent, listening to student-student interactions can reveal important understandings about who the students are and what they are interested in.
>
> Listening to "off topic" conversations can sometimes challenge the teacher's understanding of what is and isn't "on-topic."
>
> Active listening involves more than just sensitive receptivity; it often involves speaking, asking questions, and so on.
>
> Part of teaching involves listening to yourself, monitoring how what you are saying may be coming across (or not coming across), how what you are saying might be heard by others, and sometimes, even, hearing from yourself something that changes or clarifies or adds to what you intended to say—and thereby, in effect, learning from yourself.

None of these circumstances is unique to teaching and listening in online contexts, and certainly one might come to these realizations in ordinary teaching contexts or through other means. But because part of what online teaching does is to de-familiarize our ordinary practices, it can create an occasion for *re-cognizing* the assumptions and values behind our usual ways of doing things, and challenge us to find other approaches that work for this new context.

And that might be the most transformative thing about these new technologies for teaching.

Note

1. See, for example, Schultz, K. (2003). Katherine Schultz is part of an ongoing collaborative group dedicated to studies of listening, which has produced a large number of publications and conference papers going back at least ten years. The original core members of this group included Sophie Haroutunian-Gordon, Leonard Waks, A. G. Rud, James Garrison, Andrea English, Suzanne Rice, and Stanton Wortham. Additional members have moved in and out of the group over the years. Much of my thinking on listening owes a debt to the many discussions, readings, and collaborations we have shared. See, for example, Burbules, N. C., & Rice, S. (2010).

References

Burbules, N. C. (2004). Navigating the advantages and disadvantages of online peda-gogy. In C. Haythornthwaite, & M. M. Kazmer (Eds.), *Learning, culture, and community in online education: Research and practice* (3–17). New York: Peter Lang.

Burbules, N. C. (2006). Rethinking dialogue in networked spaces. *Cultural Studies ↔ Critical Methodologies*, 6, 107–122.

Burbules, N. C., & Rice, S. (2010). On pretending to listen. *Teachers College Record*, 112(11), Special issue, edited by Sophie Haroutunian-Gordon and Leonard Waks. 2874–2888.

Li, H. (2002). Silences and silencing silences. In S. Rice (Ed.), *Philosophy of Education 2001* (157–165). Champaign, IL: Philosophy of Education Society.

Li, H. (2004). Rethinking silencing silences. In M. Boler (Ed.), *Democratic dialogue in the classroom: Troubling speech, disturbing silence* (69–88). New York: Peter Lang.

Means, B., Toyama, Y., Murphy, R., Bakia, M., & Jones, K. (2009). *Evaluation of evidence-based practices in online learning: A meta-analysis and review of online learning studies*. Washington, DC: U.S. Department of Education.

Nietzsche, F. (1974). *The gay science*. Trans. by W. Kaufman. New York, NY: Vintage, 301.

Schultz, K. (2003). *Listening: A framework for teaching across differences.* New York, NY: Teachers College Press.

Schultz, K. (2009). *Rethinking classroom participation: Listening to silent voices.* New York: Teachers College Press.

Zembylas, M., & Michaelides, P. (2004). The sound of silence in pedagogy. *Educational Theory*, 54(2), 193–210.

Zembylas, M., & Vrasidas, C. (2007). Listening for silence in text-based, online encounters. *Distance Education*, 28(1), 5–24.

Contributors

David I. Backer is Visiting Assistant Professor of Social Foundations of Education at Cleveland State University. He received his doctorate in Philosophy and Education from Columbia University, Teachers College and his research focuses on social-political philosophy and educational communication.

Nicholas Burbules is the Gutgsell Professor in the Department of Educational Policy, Organization and Leadership at the University of Illinois, Urbana-Champaign. His primary research focuses on philosophy of education, teaching though dialogue, and technology and education.

Sophie Haroutunian-Gordon is Professor Emerita of Education and Social Policy at Northwestern University, where she directed the Master of Science in Education Program. She has published in philosophy of education and teacher education, and her books include *Turning the Soul: Teaching through Conversation in the High School* (University of Chicago Press, 1991), *Learning to Teach through Discussion: the Art of Turning the Soul* (Yale University Press, 2009), and *Interpretive Discussion: Engaging Students in Text-Based Conversations* (Harvard Education Press, 2014).

Winifred Hunsburger is a Lead Teacher at The Bishop Strachan School in Toronto, Canada. She received her doctorate from the Ontario Institute for Studies in Education, University of Toronto.

Megan J. Laverty is Associate Professor of Philosophy and Education at Teachers College, Columbia University. Her primary research interests are: the history of philosophy of education; moral philosophy with a focus on language and communication; philosophy of dialogue and dialogical pedagogy; and, philosophy with children and adolescents.

Bronwen E. Low is an Associate Professor and Graduate Program Director in the Department of Integrated Studies in Education in McGill University's Faculty of Education. Her current research includes community-media projects, the multilingual Montreal hip-hop scene, and the pedagogical implications of the life stories of human rights violations. Her most recent book is *Slam School: Learning through Conflict in the Hip-Hop and Spoken Word Classroom* (Stanford UP, 2011). She can be reached at Bronwen.low@mcgill.ca.

Elizabeth Meadows teaches undergraduate and graduate students in Elementary Education and in general education coursework at Roosevelt University. She earned her doctorate in Curriculum and Instruction from the University of Chicago with a focus on John Dewey, aesthetics, and progressive education. Her current research focuses on the intersections of listening, democracy, education, and the work of John Dewey.

Alexandra Michel received her PhD from Wharton, and now teaches at the Graduate School of Education, University of Pennsylvania. A recent book, co-authored with Stanton Wortham, is *Bullish on Uncertainty: How Organizational Cultures Change Participants* (Cambridge University Press, 2009).

Suzanne Rice is Professor in the Department of Educational Leadership and Policy Studies at the University of Kansas. Her interests include school lunch policies and the ethics of food, and the educational significance of human animal and other-than-human animal interactions.

Katherine Schultz is Dean and Professor at the Mills College School of Education. She received her PhD in Education at the University of Pennsylvania. Her books include *Listening: A Framework for Teaching across Differences* (New York: Teachers College Press, 2003) and *Rethinking Classroom Participation: Listening to Silent Voices* (Teachers College Press, 2009).

Emmanuelle Sonntag is an information scientist and sociologist. She is pursuing her PhD in Sociology on the topic of listening at Université du Québec à Montréal (UQAM). She tweets @lvrdg on listening, information literacy, information technologies, education, life stories, and radio.

Ashley Taylor is Visiting Assistant Professor of Educational Studies at Colgate University. She received her PhD in Cultural Foundations of Education from Syracuse University, where she specialized in Philosophy of Education and Disability Studies. Ashley's research focuses broadly on educational justice and differences of ability, including how ability/disability is conceptualized within frameworks of democratic citizenship education. She is also interested in the role of social justice pedagogies in learning across difference and the intersections of ability, race, and gender in conceptualizing educational equality.

Leonard J. Waks is Professor Emeritus of Educational Leadership at Temple University. His research focuses on MOOCs, the Internet, organizational complexity, and listening in education. He is president of the John Dewey Society and has recently published *Education 2.0: The Learningweb Revolution and the Transformation of the School* (Paradigm, 2013). He can be reached at ljwaks@ yahoo.com.

Stanton Wortham received his doctorate from the University of Chicago and currently serves as Judy and Howard Berkowitz Professor at Penn GSE. He has written on classroom discourse and the linguistic anthropology of education, interactional positioning in media discourse and autobiographical narrative, and Mexican immigrant communities in the New Latino Diaspora. More information can be found at http://scholar.gse.upenn.edu/stantonw.

Index

Aceh Province, Indonesia, 151, 155–57
activities, "learning by doing," 4
adult literacy, Freire, Paulo and, 26
appreciative listening, 7–8, 48, 55, 62–65
attitude, listening, 8–9, 30, 36
authority
   modulated, 106, 107
   teacher, 104

Backer, David, 5, 10
banking education, in the United States, 34
basic question (BQ), 80–82, 87
Bazambanza, Rupert, 142
Berlak, 131
Between the Tracks: Creating an Audio
   Guide, 143
Boler, Megan, 115, 117, 121, 124, 129, 130
Brazil, adult literacy efforts in, 26
Britzman, Deborah, 119
Brownback, Kathy, 104–5
bullying, perception of, 33

Cassidy, Kathy, 45–46
childcentered teaching methods, 151
children
   learning from, 16, 22
   philosophy and, 65–66
children's interest, as a learning tool,
   17–18, 73–74
Chilean Institute for Land Reform, 26

classic cognitive theories, 168
classroom practice, Reggio philosophy
   and, 20–22
classrooms, 3
codifications, 35
   in literacy instruction, 28
cognitive theories, classic, 168
collaborative mentoring, 150–51, 152,
   153, 158, 160
   in Aceh Province, Indonesia, 156–57
Common Core State Standards for
   English Language Arts & Literacy,
   79
communication
   in experiential education (EE), 46–47
   importance of silence in, 31–32
   and listening, 69
communication pattern, didactic, 4
community of philosophical inquiry
   (CPI), 57, 61, 62–63
concrete experiences, 40, 45, 50, 168,
   179
Conference Method, 10, 98
consciousness, critical, 32–33
Consultation Commission on Accommodation Practices Related, 138
contemplative listening, 7
conversation, dynamic, 124
CPI. See community of philosophical
   inquiry
"cram school," 1
critical consciousness, 32–33

critical listening, 8
critical pedagogy, 27–28, 29–30
  and listening, 36–37
Cuban, Larry, 3
culture circles, 26
curation, 141
curriculum, emergent, 17–18
Cushwa, Frank, 100

deep listening, 139
Dewey, John, 2, 8, 39, 40, 45, 72, 139
dialogic teaching, 86
dialogue
  importance of to teaching, 27–28
  listening and, 28–33, 85
  listening and silence in, 31–32
  Socratic, 102
  as a teaching tool, 35–36
"Dialogue Time: Interviewing and
  Building a Collective Timeline, 142
didactic pedagogy, 1, 3, 39
didactic teaching, 8
Dillon, James T., 101–2
direct involvement, 167–68, 169–74
disability experience, 125–27
discomfort, pedagogy of, 10, 113–21,
  127, 129–32
  claims of, 117–19
  gender and, 127–29
discussions
  importance of ambiguity in, 82
  interpretive, 69–83, 86–87
  listening for, 97, 102, 106–7
  pedagogy of, 99
  sample strategies for, 102–3
  teaching, 101–5
documentation, importance of, 19–20, 22
Dreeben, Robert, 3
dynamic conversation, 124

education
  experiential, 39
    definition of, 40
    listening and, 42–43
    models of, 40–45

problem-posing, 33
problems in, 71–74
Reggio Emilia philosophy and, 17–18
Reggio philosophy and, 22
role in oppression, 29
social justice and, 9–10
traditional, Freire thoughts on, 28–29
egg hatching project, the, Hundred
  Languages and, 18–19
emergent curriculum, 17–18
emotions, in education, 88
empathy, and listening, 122–25
Environmental Protection Agency, 35
Exeter Humanities Institute (EHI), 98,
  102
existential listening, 55, 65
Experience and Education (Dewey), 5, 40
experiential education (EE), 39
  communication and, 46–47
  continuity and narrative in, 45–46
  definition of, 40
  Joplin's model, 44–45
  listening and, 42–43
  models of, 40–45
    criticism of, 40–45
  experiential learning
  Joplin's model, 43
  Kolb and, 40–43
  types of listening and, 47–50
experimental learning, 6

Feeling Power: Emotions and Education
  (Boler), 116
Fiumara, Gemma Corradi, 54, 56
Foley, Margaret, 101, 102, 104
Freire, Paulo, 1, 10
  criticism of teaching methods, 28–30
  life of, 25–26
Freirean pedagogy, 35, 107–8

Gadamer, Hans-Georg, 86
genuine listening, 56
grammar, teaching of, 3, 4
Grayling, A. C., 54
Great Depression, 25, 100

Greer, Peter, 104

Haiti, 153
Harkness, Edward, 99
Harkness Conference Method, 5
Harkness pedagogy, 97
Harkness teaching, 98, 99, 100–101,
    108
  principles of, 105–6
Haroutunian-Gordon, Sophie, 5, 8,
    71–74, 80, 119
Harry Stottlemeier's Discovery (Lipman),
    56
hermeneutical listening, 55, 58–60
Hundred Languages, 16, 18–19, 21
Hunsburger, Winnie, 5, 10

"I was there," 142
ideology of ability, 125
incubator project, the, Hundred
    Languages and, 18–19
informative listening, 6
Institute for the Advancement of
    Philosophy for Children (IAPC), 56
International Rescue Committee's (IRC)
    Child Youth and Protection, 151
interpretation, importance of, 19–20, 22
Interpretive Discussion approach, 5
interpretive discussion process,
    standardized tests, 79
interpretive discussions, 69–83, 86–87
  and social justice, 70–71, 83
interpretive listening, 6–7
involvement, direct, 167–68, 169–74

Joplin, Laura, 40, 42–43, 43
Joplin-Cassidy approach/model, 46–47,
    50

Kansas River, 35
Kolb, David, 40–43
  theory of learning, 42

Latin America, 10
Laub, Dori, 131

learning
  experiential, types of listening and,
    47–50
  experimental, 6
  Kolb's theory of, 42
"Learning about the Tutsi Genocide in
    Rwanda, 142
Learning and Evaluation Situations
    (LES), 142–46
"learning by doing" activities, 4
Learning to Teach through Discussion
    (Haroutunian-Gordon), 71, 72, 74
life stories. *See also* oral history
listening and, 139, 140–46
Lipman, Matthew, 53, 56
listen, learning to, 79–81, 94
listening
  appreciative, 7–8, 48, 55, 62–65
  attitude, 8–9, 36
  contemplative, 7
  and critical pedagogy, 36–37
  as curation, 141
  deep, 139
  definition of, 6
  and dialogue, 28–33
  and direct involvement, 167–68
  for discussion, 97, 102, 106–7
  and empathy, 122–25
  existential, 55, 65
  genuine, 56
  hermeneutical, 55, 58–60
  informative, 6
  interpretive, 6–7
  in interpretive discussions, 69–83
  Kolb's model and, 42–43
  in online teaching, 183–92
  passive, 1, 2
  pedagogy of, 16, 74–82
  pedagogy of discomfort and, 119–21
  philosophical, 55, 60–62
  and philosophy, 58–60
  practical, 7
  as premise for learning, 16
  and the Reggio Emilia philosophy, 15,
    20–22

listening *(continued)*
  relational, 7, 30, 48, 106, 139
  silent apophatic, 7
  students, 54
  to teach, 153–55
    forms of, 5–6
  therapeutic, 7
  types of, 6–9, 47–50
listening attitude, 8–9
Listening Schools, 152
literacy circles, 28
Low, Bronwen, 10

Mackenzie, Catriona, 126
Malaguzzi, Loris, 16
Manuel Borja-Villel, Manuel, 141
"Mapping the Elsewhere Here," 142
Matthews, Gareth, 53
Meadows, Elizabeth, 5
mentoring, collaborative, 150–51, 152,
  153
modulated authority, 106, 107
Montclair State University (MSU), 56
Montreal Life Stories project, 138, 139
Moore, Becky, 104
Morrison, Toni, 86–87, 90

"narrative sickness," 1
National Commission on Popular
  Culture, 26
North Carolina Institute for the
  Advancement of Teaching, 71

observation, importance of, 19–20, 22
"On Defining Experiential Education"
  (Joplin), 43
online teaching, 183–92
oppression, 125
  in Brazil, 26–27
  impact on people, 26–27, 32, 70–71
  race and, 113–15
  social, 125
oral history. *See also* life stories
  listening in, 139, 139–41

Outward Bound program, 43

P4C. *See* Philosophy for Children
Paideia Project, St. John's College, 71
parents, and teacher collaboration,
  20–21
Parti Québécois, 138
passive listening, 1
pedagogical theory, Britzman's, 119
pedagogy
  critical, 27–28, 29–30, 35
  didactic, 1, 2, 39
  Freirean, 35
  Harkness, 97
pedagogy of discomfort, 5, 10, 113–21,
  127
  claims of, 117–19
  gender and, 127–29
  lessons from, 129–32
  listening and, 119–21
Pedagogy of the Oppressed (Freire), 5, 25,
  26
pedagogy of trust, 149–50, 151, 153,
  162–64
Perry, Lewis, 99–100
Phillips-Exeter Academy, 10, 97, 99,
  100
philosophical listening, 55, 60–62
philosophy, 53–54
  children and, 65–66
  pre-college, 54
philosophy education, children's right to,
  53, 56–66
Philosophy for Children (P4C), 54–60
Plato, 72–73, 85–86
practical listening, 7
pre-college philosophy, 54
problem-posing education, 33
professional development, 150
Prospect Center for Education and
  Research, 160
Pruitt, Bruce, 105

Quebec Charter of Values, 138

Reggio approach
  principles of
    emergent curriculum, 17–18
    Hundred Languages, the, 18–19
Reggio Emilia philosophy and, teacher,
  imagine of, 19–20
Reggio Emilia approach, teaching by
  listening, 5
Reggio Emilia philosophy, 15
Reggio Emilia schools, background to,
  15–16
Reggio philosophy
  classroom practice and, 20–22
  and education, 22
relational listening, 7, 30, 48, 106, 139
researchers, teachers as, 19–20
Rinaldi, Carlina, 16
Roman Catholic teachings, 10

Scheman, Naomi, 128–29
School and Society (Dewey), 2
Schultz, Katherine, 10
Scully, Jackie Leach, 126
self, the, 179–81
Sharp, Ann Margaret, 53
silence, in dialogue, 31–32
silent apophatic listening, 7
Sionfonds, 152
Smith, Lawrence, 101, 102
social justice/injustice, 9–10, 119–20,
  121
  and education, 9–10, 114
  and interpretive discussions, 70–71
social justice/injustive, and interpretive
  discussions, 83
social oppression, 125
Socrates, 86
Sonntag, Emmanuelle, 10
Sources of a Science of Education
  (Dewey), 5
Spielberg, Steven, 137
students' listening, 54, 75

Taylor, Ashley, 10

teacher authority, 104–5
teachers
  as co-investigators, 29
  as collaborators, 20, 155–57
  imagine of, 19–20
  learning to listen, 74–83, 82–83
  mentorship of, 81
  and the Reggio Emilia philosophy,
    17–18
  as researchers, 19–20
  trust among, 157–60, 162–64
teaching, 149
  and appreciative listening, 8
  "banking" method, the, 1
  dialogic, 86
  didactic, 8
  didactic pedagogy and, 39
  grammar of, 3, 4
  Harkness, 108
  by listening, 4–5
    forms of, 5–6
  online, 183–92
  online environment and, 183–92
  and relational listening, 8
  social justice and, 9–10
teaching, reasons for, 21
teaching discussion. See Harkness
  teaching
teaching methods, 2
  didactic, 1
  didactic methods, 2
  impact of testing on, 34–35
"test prep," 1
testing, standardized
  impact on teaching methods, 34–
    35
  problems in education and, 71
The Giving Tree (Haroutunian-Gordon),
  75, 76, 77, 80
therapeutic listening, 7
Thompson, Audrey, 121, 123–24
Thompson, M.
traditional education, Freire thoughts
  on, 28–29

traumatic events
  contexts of, 151–53
  listening and, 137–39
trust, pedagogy of, 10, 149–50, 151,
    153, 162–64
  among teachers, 157–60
  developing, 153–55
Tyack, David, 3

uncertainty, reduction of, 167–69
uncertainty augmentation, 174–78,
    179–81
United Nations Declaration of Rights, 10
United States
  education in, 34
  problems in education in the, 71–74

University of Recife, 26
UNRWA schools, 152
USC Shoah Foundation—The Institute
    for Visual History and Education,
    137

Verducci, Susan, 122, 124
Villa Cella, 15
Vygotskyian cognition, 102

Waks, Leonard, 122, 123
Ware, Linda, 131
We are Here, 138
What a Story!: Life Stories and Digital
    Storytelling, 142
World War II, 15